ObjectVision™
Programming for
Windows

ObjectVision™
Programming
for Windows
Donald Richard Read

Windcrest®/McGraw-Hill

New York San Francisco Washington, D.C. Auckland Bogotá
Caracas Lisbon London Madrid Mexico City Milan
Montreal New Delhi San Juan Singapore
Sydney Tokyo Toronto

FIRST EDITION
FIRST PRINTING

© 1993 by **Donald Richard Read**.
Published by Windcrest Books, an imprint of TAB Books.
TAB Books is a division of McGraw-Hill, Inc.
The name "Windcrest" is a registered trademark of TAB Books.

Library of Congress Cataloging-in-Publication Data
Read, Donald Richard.
   ObjectVision programming for Windows / by Donald Richard Read.
     p.   cm.
   Includes index.
   ISBN 0-8306-4194-7 (H)   ISBN 0-8306-4193-9 (P)
   1. Object-oriented programming (Computer science)
   2. ObjectVision. 3. Visual programming (Computer science)
   4. Windows (Computer programs)   I. Title.
   QA76.64.R43   1993
   005.4'3—dc20   93-9591
                                 CIP

Editorial team: Jennifer DiGiovanna, Acquisitions Fditor
               Kellie Hagan, Book Editor
Production team: Katherine G. Brown, Director
               Susan E. Hansford, Coding
               Wendy L. Small, Layout
               Brenda S. Wilhide, Layout
               Tara Ernst, Proofreading
               Jodi L. Tyler, Index
Design team: Jaclyn J. Boone, Designer
             Brian K. Allison, Associate Designer
Cover design: Sandra Blair Design, Harrisburg, Pa.
Cover illustration: Margaret Brandt, Harrisburg, Pa.   WU1

Contents

Acknowledgments

Because writing about computer technology is a strange and lonely craft, I am grateful to fellow laborers out there in cyberspace who manage to bring a human dimension to the relationships we develop at 9600 baud via modems and fax boards and the occasional analog telecoms that send little packets of "hello, how are you" scurrying along the twisted pairs.

The folks at TAB/McGraw-Hill, who occupy a cozy aerie on a mountaintop near the Mason-Dixon line in southern Pennsylvania, are an especially human lot. Without exception, the people in the acquisitions, editorial, and production departments have been cordial, friendly, and helpful—and you just can't get too much of that.

I am especially grateful for the fine work of Kellie Hagan, who has now edited several of my books. As an editor, she is a consummate professional who improves my writing so subtly that I am always convinced that the final product was what I had intended all along. And she is a jewel of a human being: considerate, responsive, and unfailingly cheerful.

Numerous other people deserve applause and a warm handshake: Melissa Robertson of IBM's Independent Vendors League; Nan Borreson of Borland International; Ron Cross of Mitnor Software, who supplied their fine PrntScrn screen capture software for OS/2; and Application Techniques, Inc., for their excellent PictureEze software for Windows.

Finally, warm thanks to Dr. Bernard Dolin, director of Elmsford Medical Center, for technical guidance and friendly encouragement.

1 The new world of visual programming

If you decide to build your own house, there are two routes you can take. You can do it the old-fashioned way: saw every board, drive every nail, and put every small component in place—even though many of the basic units you build (window and door frames, closets, even whole rooms such as bathrooms) will be identical to those that have been built for hundreds of thousands of other homes before yours (a classic example of reinventing the wheel).

But there's another option: You can order a *modular* home from a catalog of the many manufacturers of partially prefabricated units, and those bathrooms, window frames, etc. will be shipped to you already assembled. You simply lift them into place and attach them to the other components of your house.

A similar situation has evolved in computer programming, although the concept of modular units doesn't carry the stigma that prefabricated houses (often referred to scornfully as *prefabs*) carry with many people. If you're programming in Microsoft Windows, for example, and you want to create a new window, you have the option of rewriting all of the code from scratch, even though it has been written many times before and your goal is a window whose appearance and functionality—commonly called its "look and feel"—that's consistent with the appearance and functionality of windows in most other Microsoft Windows applications. (Uniformity in Windows

Object-oriented programming

programming is a much more positive attribute than it is in house construction, where repetition is a sign of corner-cutting, and uniformity can mean that you end up with little boxes that all look the same.)

However, you also have the option of saving mini-programs or subprograms you're likely to reuse in the form of program modules. This isn't a new concept, nor is it native to Windows programming; programmers have been using program modules since long before Microsoft Windows was a gleam in Billy Gates's eye. However, now that things have gotten GUI (an acronym for *graphical user interface*), you can represent those program modules with objects or icons on the screen, and construct programs by moving and placing these objects in relationship to each other. When you do that, you've gotten into *object-oriented* programming.

Programming objects have several advantages. For one thing, they can contain attributes (color, size, etc.) as well as procedural instructions (draw a line from 6,24 to 84,49). For another, they can be altered or evolved, i.e., you can use a program object to achieve a goal *similar* to the goal you achieved with the original object. Thus, you can make changes in the attributes and procedures originally associated with the object.

Visual programming

If a program permits you to work with objects—to program with objects that incorporate both procedural instructions and attributes or properties—and if it further permits you to arrange those objects in a visual array on your screen so that the arrangement comes to represent command syntax or a program instruction, then you're doing *visual programming*.

For example, in a program such as ObjectVision 2.1, which features object-oriented and visual programming, instead of rewriting all the code that gives you a new text field, you simply point to an object that represents a new field, click on it, and an object representing your new field will appear.

By freeing the program designer from the necessity of recreating every program object and function from a blank slate, object-oriented, visual-programming languages and applications such as ObjectVision 2.1 make programming accessible for many users who are frustrated and intimidated by the tedious procedure and tortured syntax of writing in a standard language such as BASIC or C. With ObjectVision 2.1, you can easily design your own applications or customize existing ones.

Just as the graphical user interface, or GUI—as employed by the Apple Macintosh interface, Microsoft Windows, and IBM's OS/2 2.0—represents a major step forward in ease of existing application use, so visual programming represents a major step forward in the ease of creating new applications and modifying existing ones. With ObjectVision 2.1, the Windows programming software for nonprogrammers, you'll find that the task of creating new Windows applications and interfaces is remarkably easy.

2 *Introduction to ObjectVision 2.1*

ObjectVision is a powerful program developed by Borland International to make it easy for nonprogrammers to create applications that take advantage of the easy-to-use Windows graphical interface.

To misquote a famous playwrite, "all the world's a database." Your closet is a database, divided into sets of objects: shoes, trousers, shirts, jackets, skirts, etc. Your garage is a database: paints and brushes, tools, yard implements. Your purse or wallet is a database—although the chances are you probably need to run an immediate Sort command.

In this Information Age, the problem is not how to get information; there's an overabundance of data and information. The problem, the challenge, and the opportunity is to provide easy access to all available information—to navigate through it and to extract, quickly and in readily usable form, what you need at any given moment.

ObjectVision is especially designed to help users meet that challenge, and can probably be best understood as an *information navigator*. Using the metaphor of a form, ObjectVision makes it possible for you to design a "front end" to let you create new databases, extract information from existing databases in several different formats, and arrange it all in a manner that's most useful and helpful to you, your business, your school, your organization, or your home.

ObjectVision works by moving you from one form to another, from one action to another, and from one software application to another. Borland International, the publishers of ObjectVision, call it their three-step or A-B-C process of creating new software applications. Part one, or step A, is the creation of the form, the immediate interface that greets the user and becomes the chief navigational aid in accessing information. Part two, or step B, is the creation of the decision tree or trees that move the user from the form to other parts of the program—which might include other forms or other software applications. Part three, or step C, is the creation of the links, where appropriate, between the ObjectVision form(s) and other applications— which might include databases such as Paradox or dBASE.

When there are multiple forms in an ObjectVision application, they are said to constitute a stack, and the main form of the application—or the top form of the stack—is called the goal. When you move back and forth between ObjectVision and another software application—such as Paradox or Quattro Pro for Windows—you do so via a link. And when you create an action in ObjectVision, that action is visually represented via a decision tree that might involve events or values.

Forms, stacks, event and value trees, and links are the basic elements of ObjectVision applications. You'll see examples of these components as you look through a few sample applications in this chapter.

ObjectVision sample applications

Perhaps the easiest way to understand the scope of ObjectVision and its ability to get you quickly and easily plugged into information you want to access is to take a quick look through the sample applications provided with the software. Let's browse.

To open the sample applications that come with your ObjectVision program, click twice on the ObjectVision Demos icon that should have been placed in the ObjectVision PRO group when you installed the program (see FIG. 2-1).

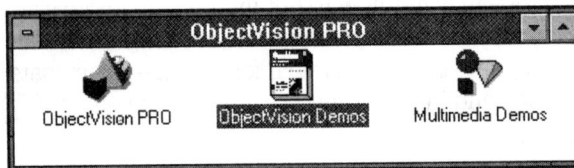

2-1
The ObjectVision PRO window, with the ObjectVision Demos icon highlighted.

The ObjectVision logo, obviously inspired by classic Roman architecture, appears briefly, and then gives way to the Demo Application menu, a full screen of buttons you can push to start up 23 different demonstrations (see FIG. 2-2).

For clarification's sake, ObjectVision PRO refers to the entire ObjectVision package, which includes not only the Demo and MultiMedia applications, but

File   Edit   Form   Field   View   Tools   Help

Demo Application Menu (Complete)

Real Estate Buyer Qualification	Contact Management	Expense Report	Hospital Admissions Form	Motel Reservation System	Time Billing System
Nutrition Expert System	Ernst & Young Survey	Checkbook Management System	Vehicle Maintenance System	Vacation Planner	Recipe Planner
Address Book	Game Show	Hangman Game	Home Inventory	Cost of Living Compare Two Cities	Job Estimating System
Order +db History	Wine Selection	Inventory Management for Parts Truck	Computer Diagnosis System	Auto Buyer Financing Guide	Exit

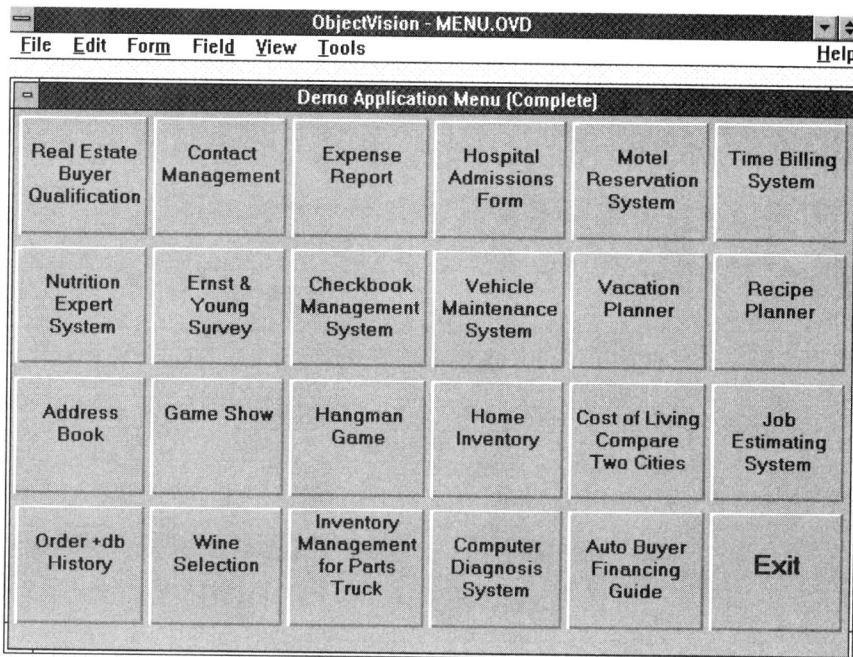

2-2
The Demo Application menu.

also Turbo C++ and Crystal Reports. I'm going to be addressing only ObjectVision in this book, however.

The range of applications you can create is apparent from the names on the buttons. Programs for business include Contact Management, Job Estimating, and Real Estate Buyer Qualification. Programs for the home include a Vacation Planner, Recipe Planner, and Home Inventory. And some of the programs for the kids are a Hangman Game and a Game Show.

Let's take a look at a few of these *apps* (hip computerese for applications—and small apps, such as those that come with OS/2 2.0, are called *applets*. Isn't that cute?) and see what their "front ends" look like and what sort of databases they access.

What could the Hangman Game have to do with databases? Point to the button, click the left mouse button, and take a look. When the program opens, you'll see the window shown in FIG. 2-3. Although most people have probably played this game, I'll take this opportunity to demonstrate the Help function. Click on the Help button, and the Hangman Help window will appear, as shown in FIG. 2-4.

This window tells you both how to play the game and how the application was created. So what does the game have to do with databases? Well, the game is based on a database file created in the format of the Borland database application Paradox. The *How it's Done* section tells you that there

2-3

The Hangman window.

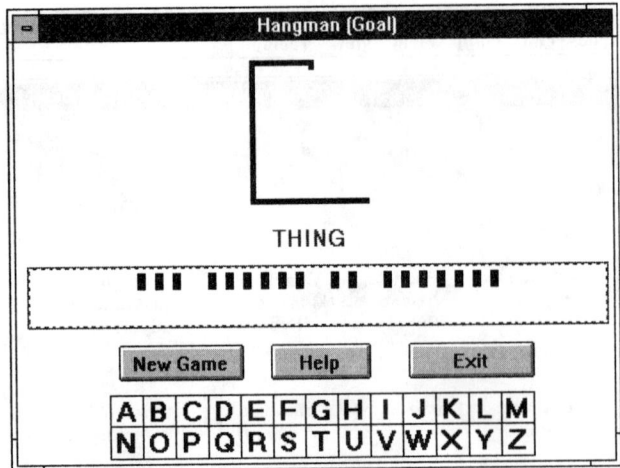

2-4

The Hangman Help window.

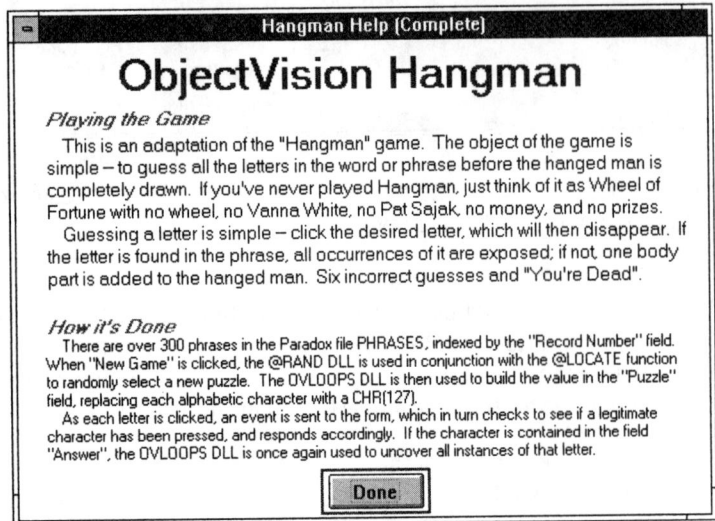

are over 300 phrases (including things, persons, places, quotes, etc.) in a Paradox file named PHRASES, and that the program selects randomly among those phrases. (Note: PHRASES is one field in a Paradox database named HANGMAN.) The *How it's Done* section also tells you more than you might be able to digest about how the application was put together.

Can you find that paradox HANGMAN data file? Use your Windows File Manager, and look in the C:\VISION\SAMPLE directory for HANGMAN.DB (see FIG. 2-5). If you're working in the OS/2 2.0 environment, the icon view of the SAMPLE directory and the HANGMAN.DB file should resemble FIG. 2-6. To see the contents of that database, load HANGMAN.DB into Paradox or Quattro Pro for Windows (see FIG. 2-7 and FIG. 2-8).

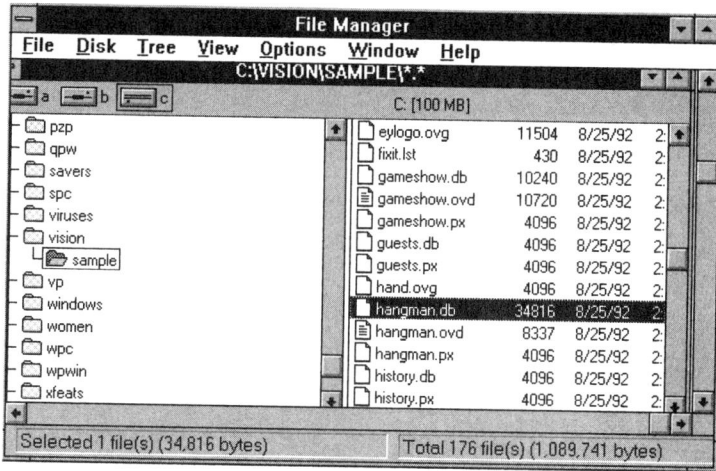

2-5
The HANGMAN.DB file highlighted in the File Manager.

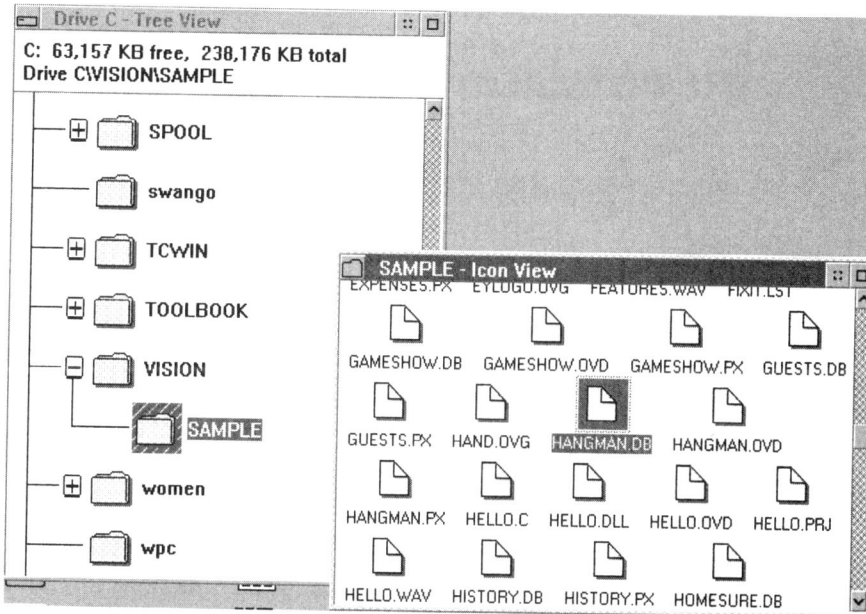

2-6
The C:\VISION\SAMPLE\ HANGMAN.DB icon in the OS/2 2.0 desktop.

So here's an ObjectVision application that's a game—but many games (including *Jeopardy* and *Trivial Pursuit*) are also based on databases, although you don't usually think of them that way. In FIG. 2-9, two correct letters (e and h) and two incorrect letters (b and r) have been selected, and two parts of the hanged man—his head and torso—have been added to the gallows. If you guess all the correct letters before the hanged man has all his parts, you win the game and get some positive reinforcement (see FIG. 2-10).

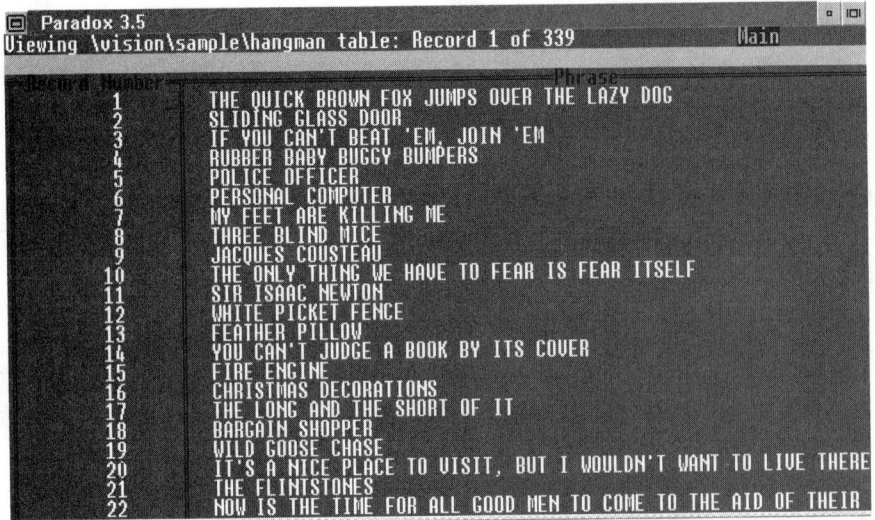

2-7

The Hangman database of phrases as it appears in Paradox 3.5.

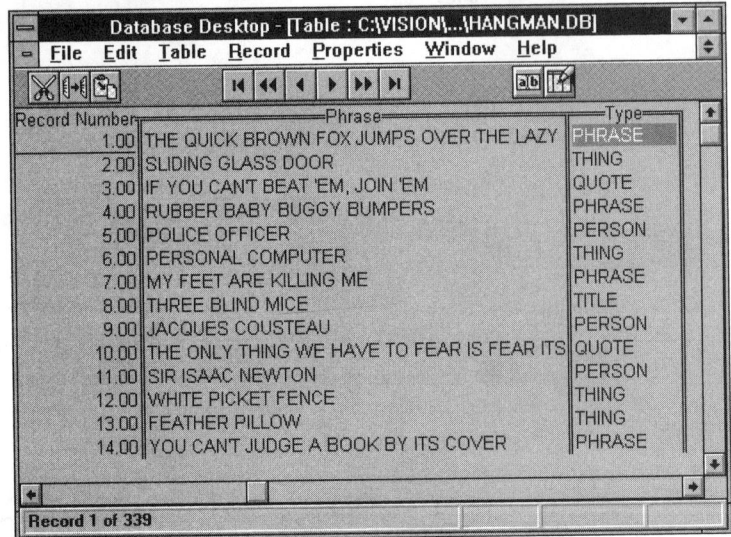

2-8

The Hangman database of phrases as it appears in the desktop database of Quattro Pro for Windows.

In order to tell you how you're doing, the program has to compare the letter you select and its position, with the corresponding letter and position in the database phrase. If your letter matches, it's substituted for all the blanks in the phrase where it should appear.

Click on the Tools menu at the top of your screen. It offers three options: Form, which activates the form tools and allows you to edit the form; Stack, which reveals the entire collection of forms that make up the Hangman application; and Links, which defines the links between Hangman and other applications (see FIG. 2-11). Click on Stack, and the collection of forms that

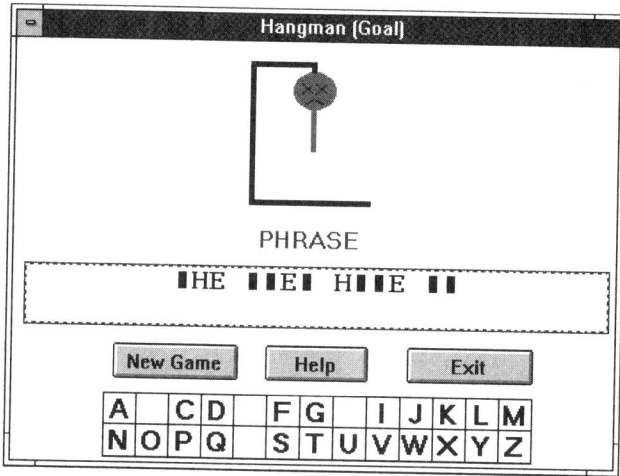

2-9
One game after two correct and two incorrect choices.

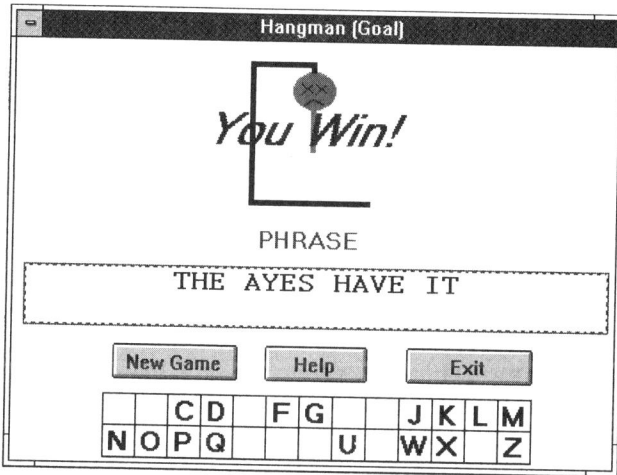

2-10
A winner in the Hangman game.

make up Hangman will be displayed in the Application stack window (see FIG. 2-12).

Close the Stack window by clicking twice on the close box and, returning to the Tools menu, select Links. The Data Links window, shown in FIG. 2-13, will tell you that there's a link, Phrase, to a database. To find out what the name of the Paradox database is, push the Modify button. A large, somewhat complicated-looking Paradox Link Creation window will fill your monitor screen (see FIG. 2-14).

From this window, you learn that the Paradox database or table is named Hangman (see the faint gray type in the Paradox Table box), and that the database has three fields: Record Number, Phrase, and Type. There's more information in this window, but we'll plumb those depths when we get down

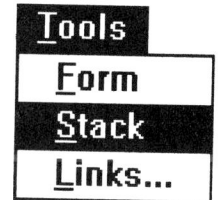

2-11 *The Tools menu, with Stack highlighted.*

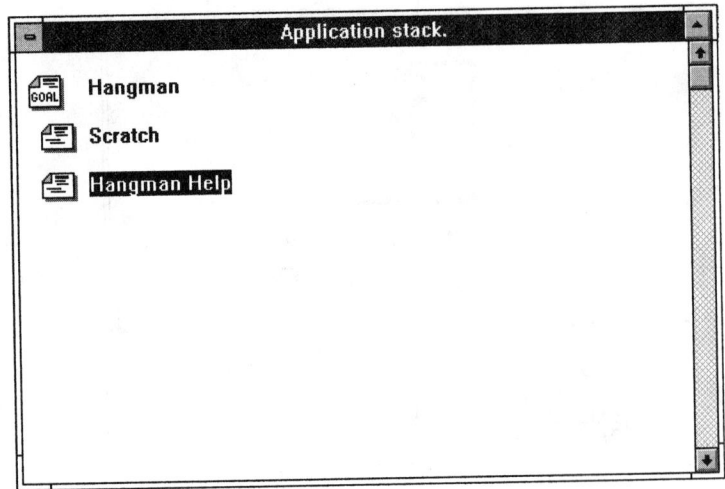

2-12
The application stack, with the Hangman forms.

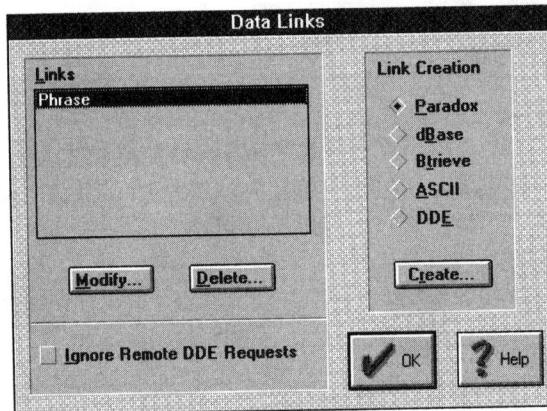

2-13
The Data Links window for Hangman, identifying a link to a Paradox field named Phrase.

to the nitty gritty in a chapter or two. Close this window and the Data Links window to return to the Hangman form.

As you'll shortly see, however, ObjectVision isn't all about databases. If you click on Exit in the Hangman window, you'll be returned to the Demo Application menu. Now select the Computer Diagnosis System button. A cute little computer system will appear in a window labeled PC. This all looks very simple; there are only three visible working parts on the screen: the computer system and two buttons, labeled Help and Exit. There is also an instruction to click on the part that is malfunctioning (see FIG. 2-15).

Click on the computer monitor. This action will take you to another window, which asks you a series of yes/no questions and offers possible explanations and corrective actions (see FIG. 2-16). Try it out: Answer Yes to the first question, Yes to the second question, and No to the third question. To this

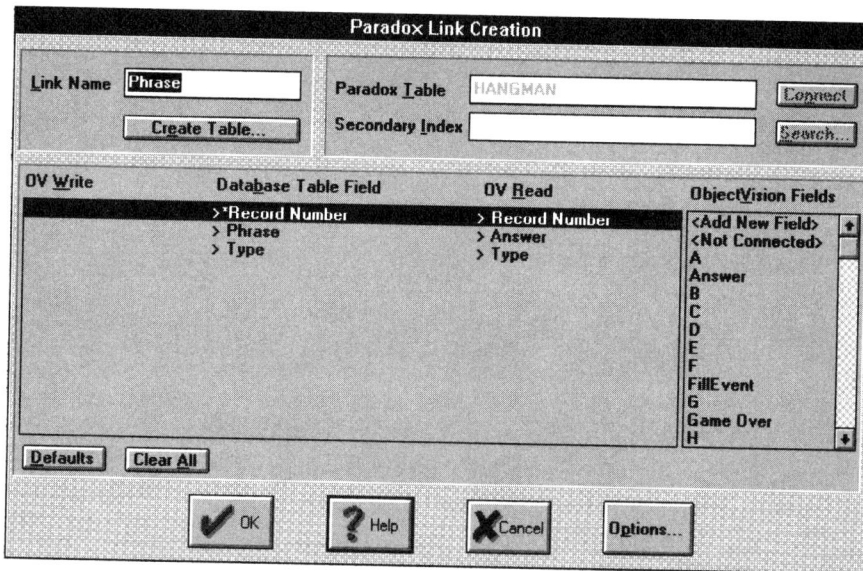

2-14
The Paradox Link Creation window.

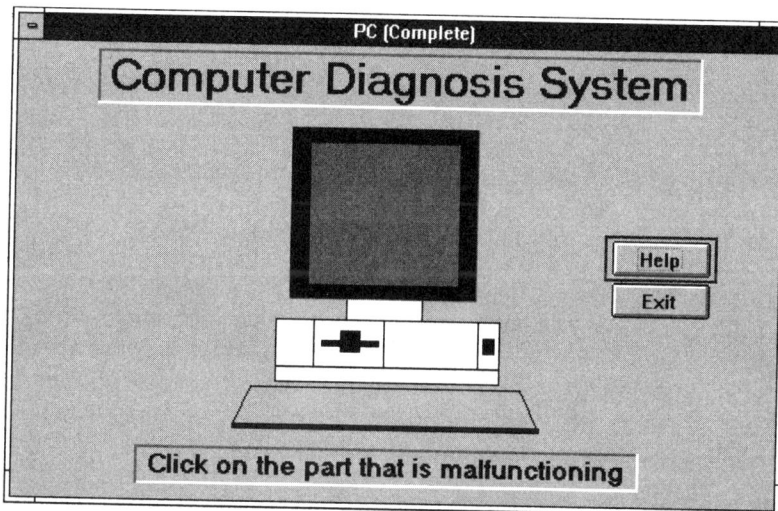

2-15
The main window or form for the Computer Diagnosis System.

point, you've gotten no response. Now answer Yes to the fourth question—is the display distorted? You'll now be offered some possible reasons for the monitor not working; the box lists four possible explanations (see FIG. 2-17).

There's no database behind this magic. What you're seeing is the operation of a fairly simple decision tree. Let's take a quick peek behind the scenes here; you're about to get your first look at the entrails of ObjectVision.

At the top of your screen, click on the Tools menu. When it drops down, you'll see three choices: Form, Stack, and Links. You'll get to know all three

2-16
The Monitor Diagnostic screen.

Monitor (Goal)

Answer questions in order

Is the monitor power light on? ◯Yes ◯No
Does the monitor display anything? ◯Yes ◯No
Is the display scrolling? ◯Yes ◯No
Is the display distorted? ◯Yes ◯No
If yes, is it distorted for one particular software program. (versus all the time)
◯Yes ◯No
Are the colors shades of one color? ◯Yes ◯No

Possible Reasons for Monitor not working

Actions to take for monitor

Close Form

2-17
The Possible Reasons box, telling you why your monitor might not be working.property.

Possible Reasons for Monitor not working
The display being distorted is usually caused by 1) the monitor being out of adjustment, 2) the video card is defective, 3) The monitor is defective, or 4) The software video driver is not correct for this monitor.

of those items intimately; for now, click on Form, which allows you to dissect (and alter, if you want) the fields that make up this window (see FIG. 2-18).

Let's see what mysterious inner workings lie behind that Possible Reasons window. Click on the window until it's surrounded by a dotted line and selection handles (see FIG. 2-19). Now position the mouse pointer somewhere within the field and click the right button. Clicking the right mouse button always gives you the property list for the currently selected object (see FIG. 2-20).

We'll explore this long list of properties later; at the moment, let's look at the value tree that's checked. Click on Value Tree; a new window will pop up, displaying a decision tree that will lead you to various possible solutions (see FIG. 2-21).

Tools
Form
Stack
Links...

2-18 *The Tools menu, with Form selected.*

2-19
The Possible Reasons field with selection indicators.

Possible Reasons for Monitor not working
The display being distorted is usually caused by 1) the monitor being out of adjustment, 2) the video card is defective, 3) The monitor is defective, or 4) The software video driver is not correct for this monitor.

Actions to take for monitor

This tree is pretty easy to follow. If the answer to the question "Is the monitor power light on?" is No, then the user is offered two possible explanations:

Your power source isn't turned on or is malfunctioning, or your on/off switch is off. If the answer is Yes, then there's no problem and the user is moved to the next question: "Does the monitor display anything?" Once again, an answer of No leads to a couple of suggestions and a Yes answer leads to the next question. You can use the vertical and horizontal scroll bars to see the whole decision tree.

2-20 *The property list for the Possible Reasons field.*

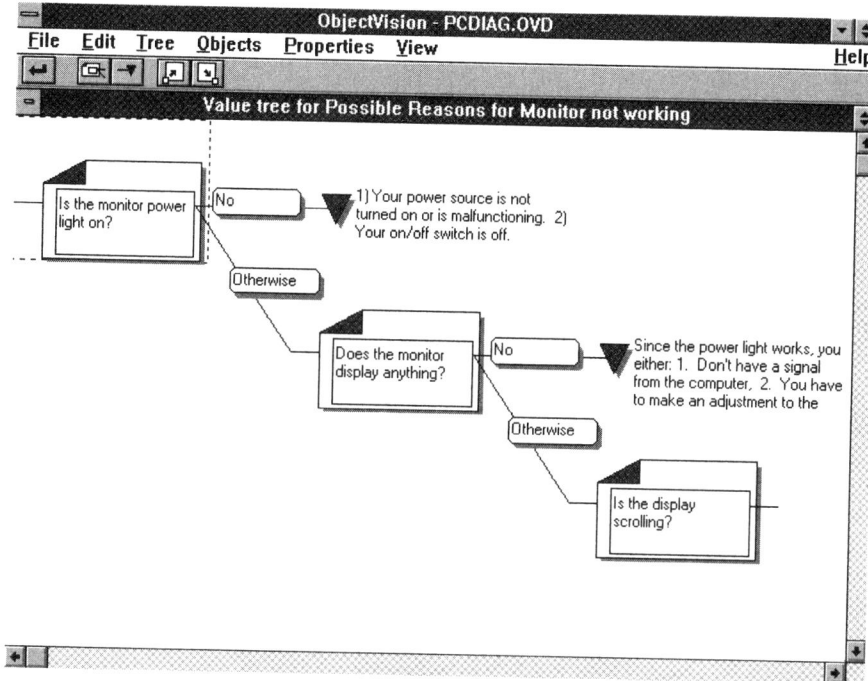

2-21 *The decision tree for diagnosing monitor malfunctions.*

There's a similar decision tree for the keyboard and for the CPU (central processing unit—the guts of your computer). Later you'll see just how easy it is to construct one of these trees. The immediate point, however, is that no database underlies this application; ObjectVision makes it possible for you to do many things in many ways.

Double-click on the Close button in the upper left-hand corner of the window to close the Value Tree window, then click on the Close Tool button to leave the edit mode (see FIG. 2-22). Press the Close Form button to leave the monitor form, then Exit to return to the Demo Application menu.

2-22 *The Close Tool button.*

Guess what? The Demo Application menu itself is an ObjectVision application—and quite a simple one, despite its great usefulness. There's only one form in the stack, there are no links to external databases required, and each button or menu block has the same simple event tree: When you click on that menu block, or text item, the program is directed to open the appropriate application file.

In the example shown in FIG. 2-23, the event tree for the menu block named Checkbook Management System has been opened. As you can doubtless surmise, the rough translation of this diagram is "When the user clicks on this text item, an @ function (more about them later) called @APPOPEN will direct the program to open an ObjectVision application whose filename is CKMENU.OVD."

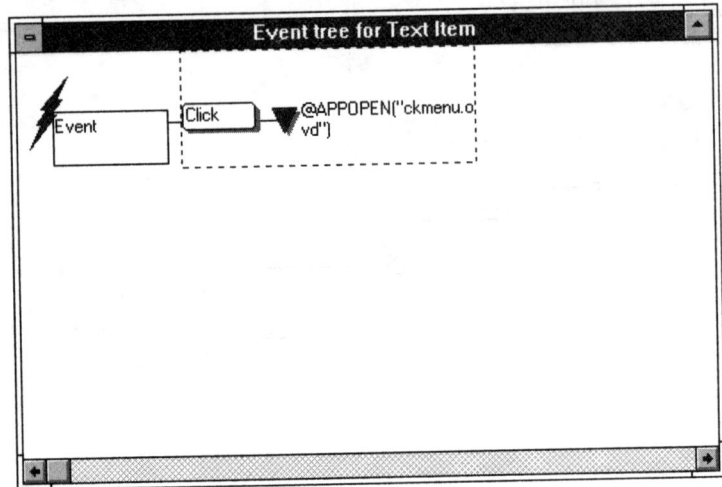

2-23
The event tree for the Checkbook Management System menu block.

The form metaphor

I've already pointed out that the form is the central metaphor of ObjectVision. In other words, Borland decided that the program would be easier to use, especially for the business user, if creating a new application's interface resembled an activity very close to the hearts and lives of business folks: the act of creating and filling out forms.

The danger of this metaphor, however, is that it can limit the range of possible uses and applications of ObjectVision, especially if, when you think of the word *form*, you think of things like purchase orders and inventory listings. The concept of a form in ObjectVision is much broader and less constrained. To get an idea of the variety of forms (and therefore of applications) that you can create in ObjectVision, just look at the opening forms of a few of the sample applications you can access from the Demo Application menu.

For example, open the Vacation Planner application from the Demo Application menu. In FIG. 2-24, you'll see the opening form—which doesn't look like a form in the usual sense. This program doesn't link with any database application; it simply consists of a series of forms in a stack, which you can view by opening the Tools menu and selecting Stack (see FIG. 2-25).

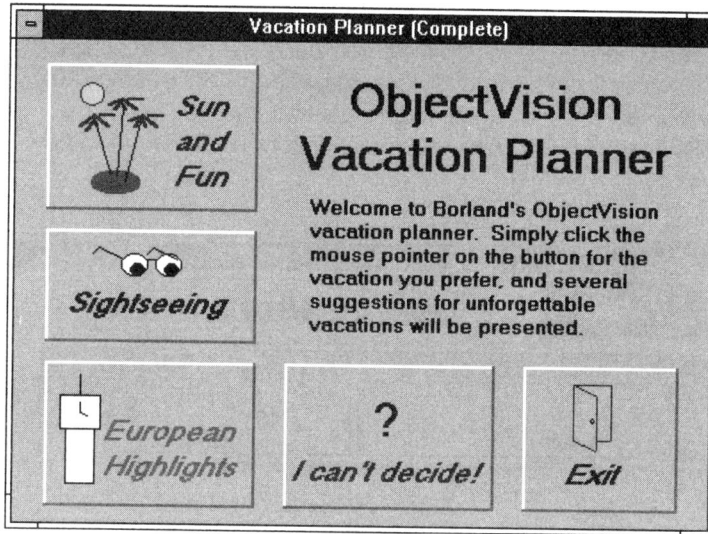

2-24
The opening form for the Vacation Planner.

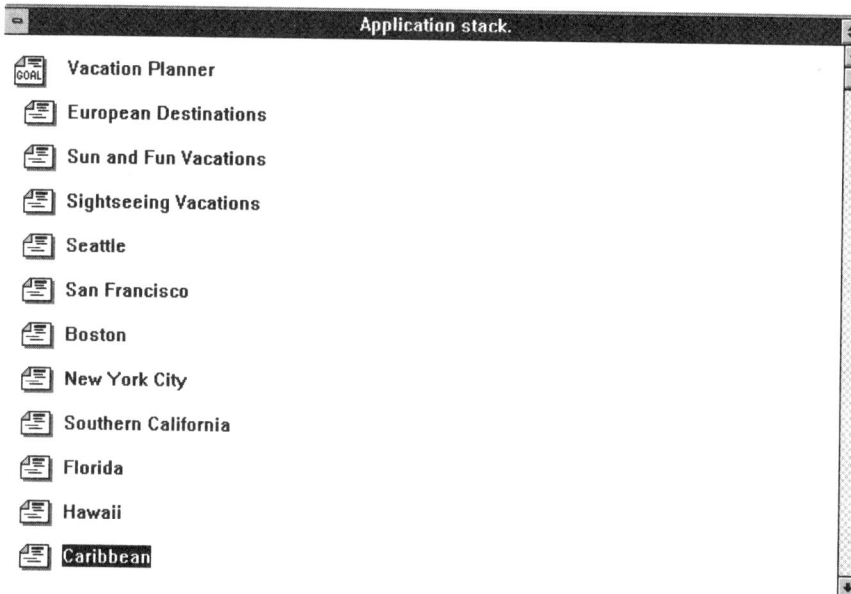

2-25
The "top" of the application stack for the Vacation Planner.

Instead of connecting you with a list of items in a database field, this application moves you through a series of forms as you might turn through pages in a book. (Indeed, the Asymetrix program ToolBook, another program for creating Windows applications, talks about "pages in a book," where ObjectVision talks about "forms in a stack." And, of course, the granddaddy of these visual authoring programs, Apple's Hypercard program for the Macintosh, uses the metaphor of 3×5 cards in a stack.) Close the application stack and exit from Vacation Planner.

Let's peek at another sample application: Select Game Show from the Demo Application menu. When it opens, you'll see another interface that looks nothing like a business form; instead, it's reminiscent of the TV game show *Jeopardy* (see FIG. 2-26). This application does depend upon a link with a database, but it's imaginative in design and not simply another form to be filled out.

2-26
The main form for the Game Show sample application.

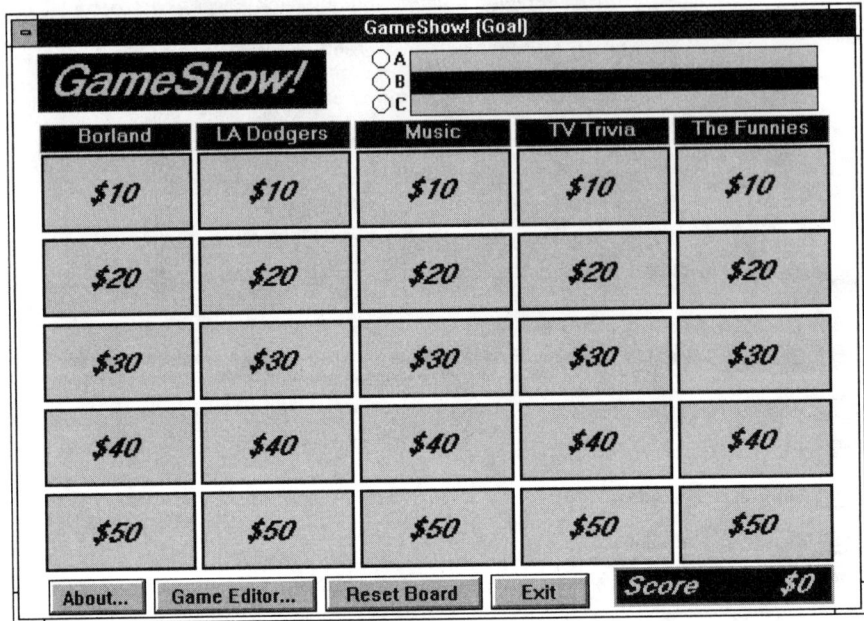

Exit Game Show, and click on Wine Selector. Now this scarcely resembles a form—but it is (see FIG. 2-27). Exit Wine Selector and the Demo Application menu.

The point is that ObjectVision has much more versatility and range than would appear when you talk of it solely in terms of database access and manipulation, or as a creator of business forms. You've now had a glimpse of what ObjectVision can do, and are almost ready to venture into how to do it.

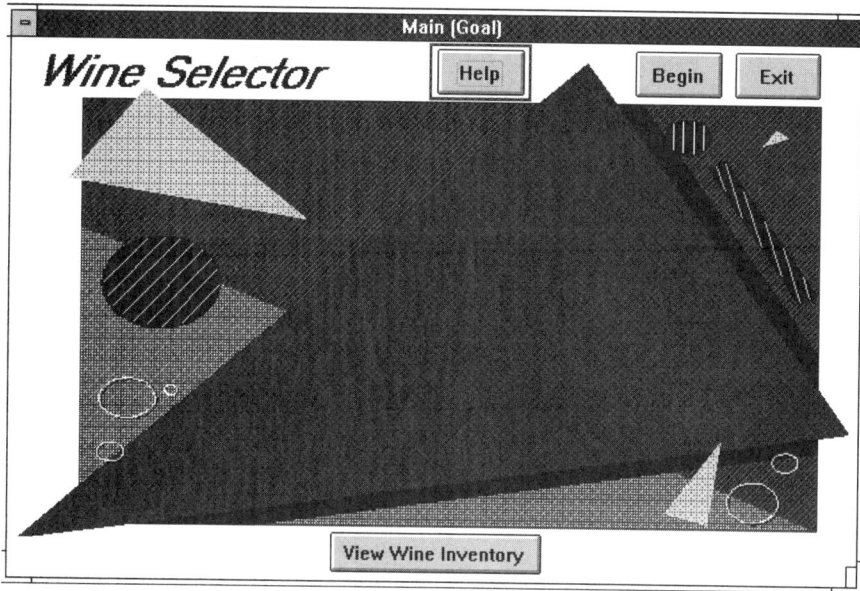

2-27
The main form for the Wine Selector application.

3 Basic navigation in ObjectVision

Before you launch a major operation, it's probably a good idea to take a preliminary, or orientation, cruise. This will give you a quick opportunity to start the engine, check the gearshift operation, locate the lights and windshield wipers, and kick the tires.

If you're an experienced Windows user, much of this will be old hat, because ObjectVision is a Windows-based application and uses the same arsenal of commands and procedures that most other Windows applications use. (If God had wanted us to learn a whole new set of commands with every program, She wouldn't have given us graphical user interfaces.)

Loading or starting ObjectVision

To start up ObjectVision, simply click on the program icon (see FIG. 3-1). Don't like the default icon? Well, you can select from a small array of program icons. Here's how: With the default program icon selected, as shown in FIG. 3-1, open the File Menu and select Properties (see FIG. 3-2).

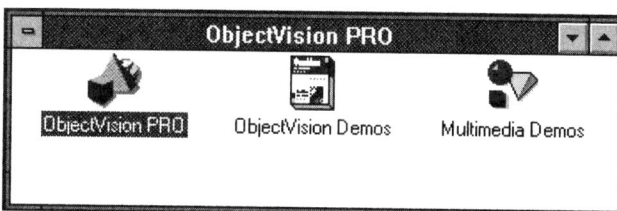

3-1
The ObjectVision program icon selected in the ObjectVision PRO group.

ObjectVision PRO

ObjectVision PRO   ObjectVision Demos   Multimedia Demos

File

New...
Open   Enter
Move...
Copy...
Delete   Del
Properties...
Run...
Exit WIN-OS/2...

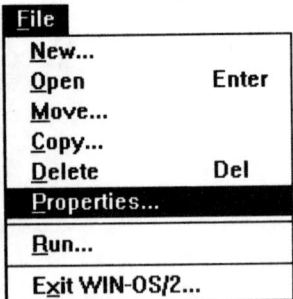

3-2 *The File menu with Properties selected.*

When the Program Item Properties menu pops up, click on the Change Icon button (see FIG. 3-3). This will bring up the Select Icon menu, which displays the program filename and the current icon (see FIG. 3-4).

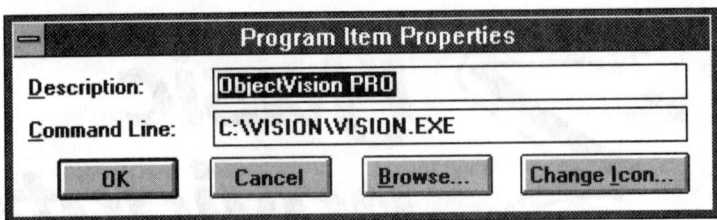

Program Item Properties

Description: ObjectVision PRO
Command Line: C:\VISION\VISION.EXE

    OK   Cancel   Browse...   Change Icon...

3-3 *The Program Item Properties menu.*

Select Icon

File Name: C:\VISION\VISION.EXE
Current Selection:

                    View Next

        OK   Cancel

3-4
The Select Icon menu with the default icon.

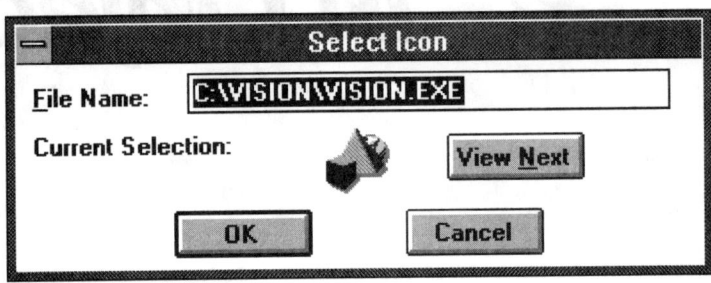

To see the other icon options, click repeatedly on the View Next button until you've seen all the choices (see FIG. 3-5). Note that the three icons in the top row are already in use for the ObjectVision demos and multimedia demos. For that reason, you might want to use the remaining four icon options for new applications you create.

3-5
The seven icon options.

The opening or runtime screen

To launch ObjectVision, click on the program icon (whichever one you decided on above). The initial screen will appear with the ObjectVision logo (see FIG. 3-6). The other two elements in this opening screen are the title—or application filename—bar and the menu bar.

3-6
The ObjectVision logo on the opening screen.

To open an existing ObjectVision application, click on File in the menu bar and select Open (see FIG. 3-7). The Open File window will be displayed on your monitor, showing the current directory (probably C:\VISION) and the list of all files with the extension .OVD, which is automatically assigned to ObjectVision applications (see FIG. 3-8). You'll be accessing some of the sample applications that came with your ObjectVision program to learn about the startup procedures, so switch to the C:\VISION\SAMPLE directory by clicking twice on the word *sample* in the Directories box. When you do, the list of all applications in the sample directory will appear in the Files box.

The menu file that accesses all these applications is called MENU.OVD (see FIG. 3-9). Scroll through the list of application files until you find MENU.OVD (or press the letter M until MENU.OVD is highlighted), then click on the OK

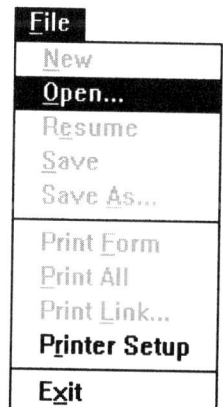

3-7 *The File menu with Open selected.*

3-8
*The Open File window showing
the C:\VISION directory.*

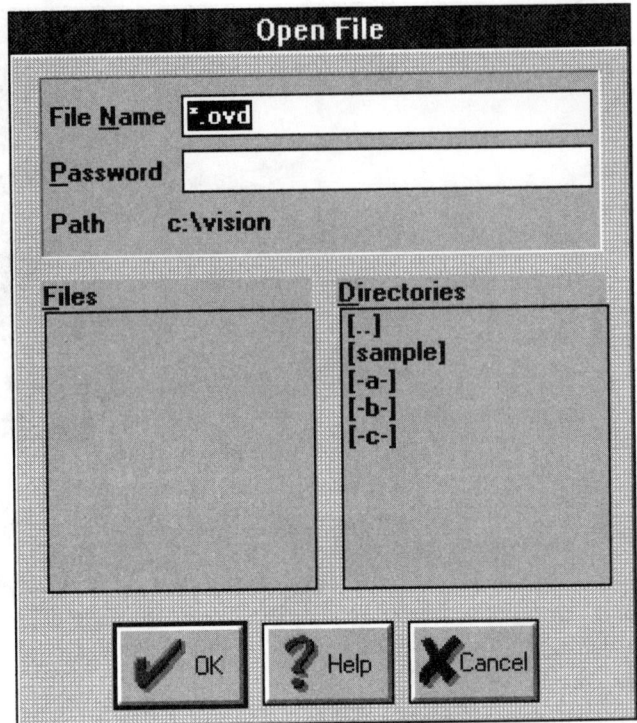

3-9
*The Open File window showing
the C:\VISION\SAMPLE
directory, with the file for the
Sample Applications menu
selected.*

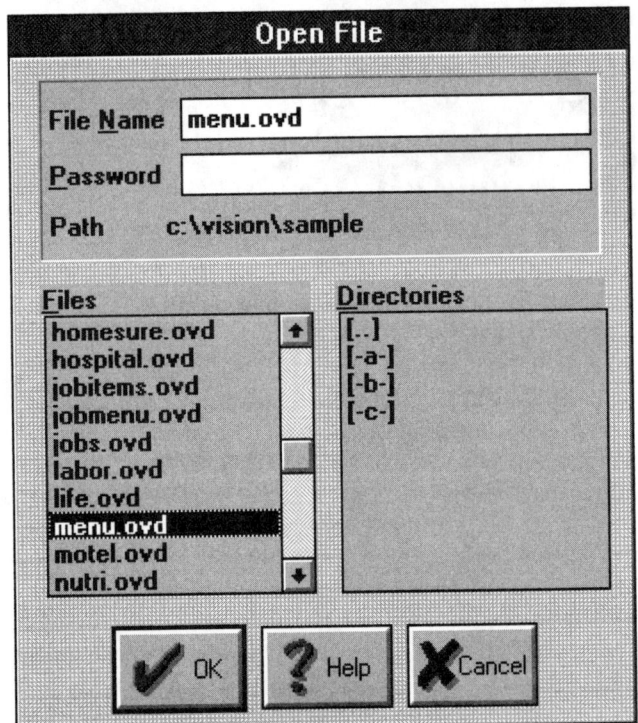

button. When you do, a new window, filled with the Demo Application menu, will fill your screen (see FIG. 3-10).

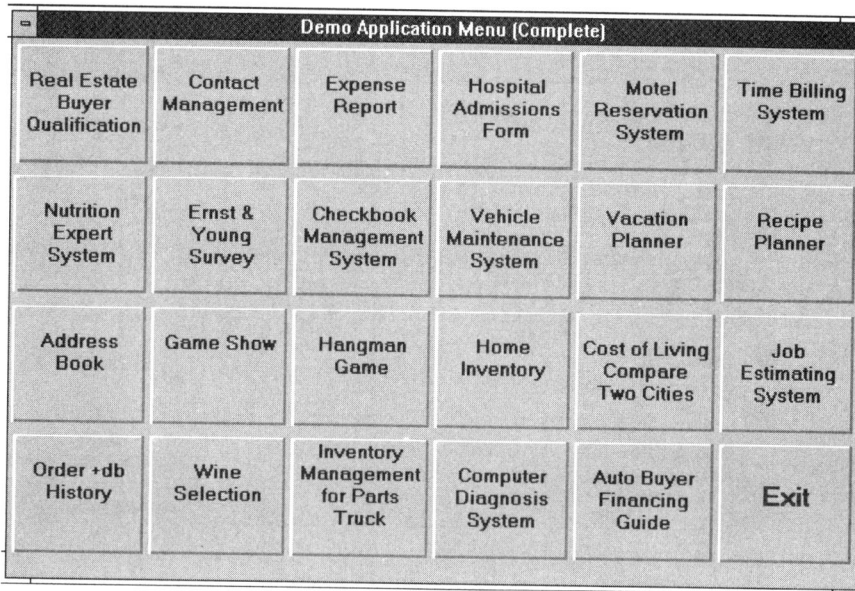

Demo Application Menu (Complete)					
Real Estate Buyer Qualification	Contact Management	Expense Report	Hospital Admissions Form	Motel Reservation System	Time Billing System
Nutrition Expert System	Ernst & Young Survey	Checkbook Management System	Vehicle Maintenance System	Vacation Planner	Recipe Planner
Address Book	Game Show	Hangman Game	Home Inventory	Cost of Living Compare Two Cities	Job Estimating System
Order +db History	Wine Selection	Inventory Management for Parts Truck	Computer Diagnosis System	Auto Buyer Financing Guide	Exit

3-10
The Demo Application menu.

Although this menu is itself an ObjectVision application, you'll use another application to illustrate the components and navigation procedures of ObjectVision. Every square in this menu is a button, so click on the one that says Address Book. Happily, the Address Book application will open in a new window, showing a very convincing representation of a page in a spiral-bound address book and a whole slew of buttons (see FIG. 3-11). This particular page of the address book features Philippe Kahn, president and chief executive officer of Borland International. It also sneaks in a little product hype; Mr. Kahn is a man of considerable accomplishments, so he can be excused for a bit of horn-blowing here. (He's also an amateur jazz musician, so the metaphor is especially apt.)

The window you're looking at contains the standard elements of an ObjectVision runtime screen or window: the application window, the title bar with the application filename (see FIG. 3-12), and the menu bar (see FIG. 3-13). A runtime screen is the screen in which you run an application, as opposed to a screen in which you would create or edit an application.

Now, we'll take a quick look at the menus on this runtime screen. Working from left to right, there are seven menus: File, Edit, Form, Field, View, Tools, and Help. Click on the Tools menu to open it, and you'll discover three options: Form tools, Stack, and Links (see FIG. 3-14). Clicking on Form puts the application into edit mode (see the title bar) and displays the object bar, a

The Tools menu

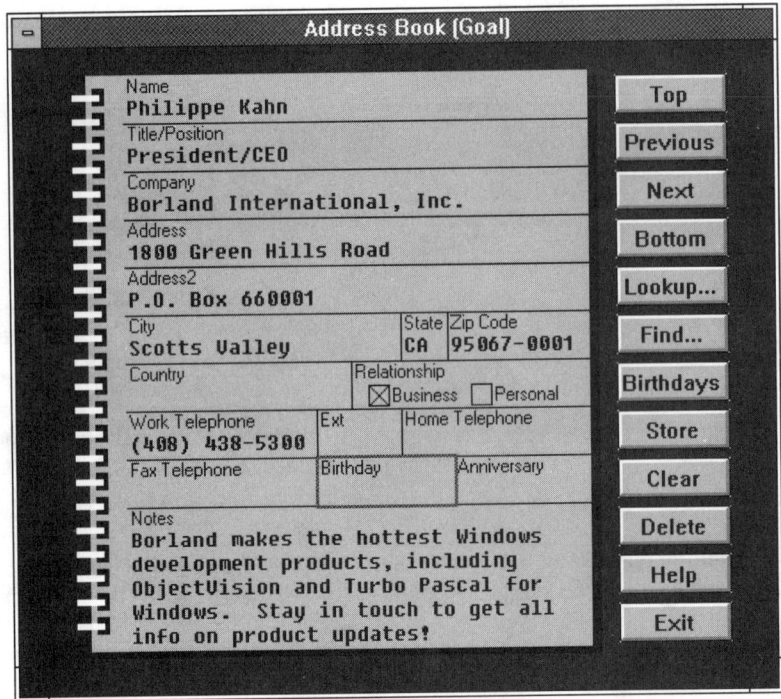

3-11

The Address Book demo application.

3-12

The title bar with the application filename.

ObjectVision - ADDRESS.OVD

3-13

The menu bar.

File   Edit   Form   Field   View   Tools   Help

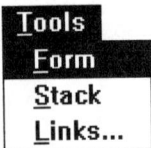

3-14 *The Tools menu, with Form selected.*

row of form tools (buttons or icons, as you prefer) that you use to place objects of various sorts on your ObjectVision form (see FIG. 3-15). The Object bar has eleven tools:

Close   Use this to exit the create mode and return to runtime mode (see FIG. 3-15a).

Field   Places new fields on a form (see FIG. 3-15b).

Button   Creates new buttons (see FIG. 3-15c).

3-15

The object bar, including the following tools: close (a), field (b), button (c), table (d), text (e), filled rectangle (f), rounded rectangle (g), line (h), graphics (i), stack (j), and links (k).

A   B   C   D   E   F   G   H   I   J   K

Table Places tables on a form (see FIG. 3-15d).

Text Adds text to a form (see FIG. 3-15e).

Filled rectangle For drawing (you guessed it!) filled rectangles on a form (see FIG. 3-15f).

Rounded rectangle Like above, but this one draws rounded rectangles (see FIG. 3-15g).

Line For drawing lines (see FIG. 3-15h).

Graphics For importing graphics to be used on your form (see FIG. 3-15i).

Stack Displays all the forms in an application (see FIG. 3-15j).

Links Displays the other applications and databases to which an ObjectVision application is linked (see FIG. 3-15k).

In edit mode, the menu bar changes; there are now seven menu headings. Reading from left to right, they are:

File The File menu has eight options (see FIG. 3-16). You can start a new file, open an existing file, save your work under an existing filename, or elect Save As to assign a new filename to your current job. Click on Print Form to get a printout of the form currently displayed, and Print All to print out all forms in the application. To alter your printer configuration or choice, choose Printer Setup. To leave edit mode and return to runtime mode, click on Close Tool. (You can also accomplish this by clicking on the Close Tool button.)

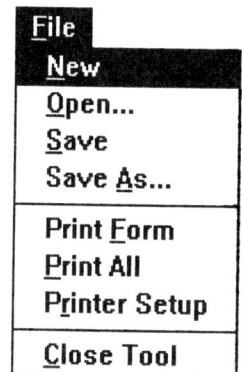

3-16 *The File menu.*

Edit The Edit menu offers you the familiar Windows editing options: Undo, Cut, Copy, and Paste. The only option that might be unfamiliar to you is Paste Link—which I'll explain later in the book (see FIG. 3-17).

Form Use the Form menu to start a new form, select one of the forms that belong to the current application, or find a field in any of the forms that make up the current application (see FIG. 3-18). If you select Find, the Field Name window will appear with a listing of all field names in all forms in this application (see FIG. 3-19). Select the Anniversary field from this listing, click on OK, and the desired field will be selected on the Address Book main form (see FIG. 3-20).

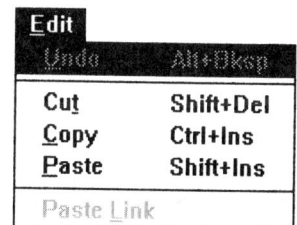

3-17 *The Edit menu.*

Objects The Objects menu is the alternative to the buttons in the object bar. Instead of clicking on the appropriate button, you select Field, Button, Table, etc. from this menu (see FIG. 3-21). You can also use this menu to examine the current default settings for each object.

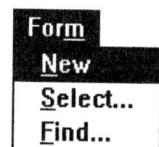

3-18 *The Form menu.*

Properties The Properties menu allows you to view the properties of an object, form, or stack (see FIG. 3-22). I'll discuss properties at a later point; one

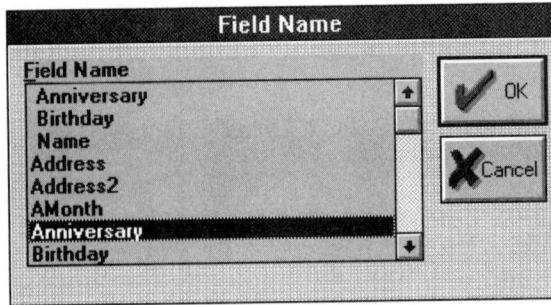

3-19
The Field Name window, with the Anniversary field selected.

3-20
The Anniversary field selected in the main Address Book form.

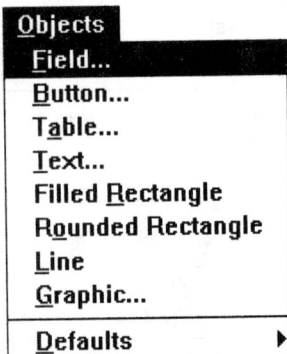

3-21 *The Objects menu.*

navigation tip, however, bears mention right now. If you select Object from the Properties menu, the program will display a submenu listing the properties of any object selected in the current form. You select an object by pointing to it and clicking the left mouse button. A selected object, such as a field, is surrounded by a dotted-line rectangle with selection handles at the corners. For example, if you select the Name field in the Address Book form, it will look like FIG. 3-23. If you now select Object from the Properties menu, a submenu will pop up, listing twelve properties (plus Help) that are assigned to the Name field (see FIG. 3-24). Properties that aren't assigned to this particular field—such as Fill Pattern and ScrollBar—are shown in faint type.

But there's another way to view the properties of any selected object. Point to the still-selected Name field and press the right mouse button. An independent property list, which applies only to the selected field, will pop up (see FIG. 3-25). Notice that there are no items in faint type; this menu is specific to this particular field.

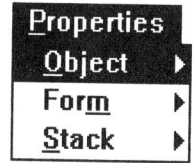

Properties
Object ▶
Form ▶
Stack ▶

3-22 *The Properties menu.*

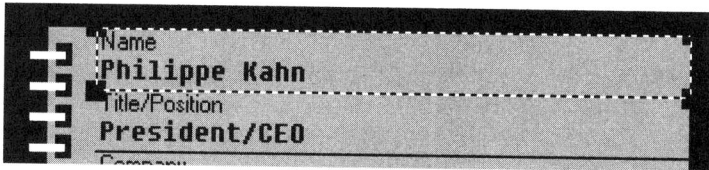

Name
Philippe Kahn
Title/Position
President/CEO
Company

3-23
The Name field selected in the Address Book form.

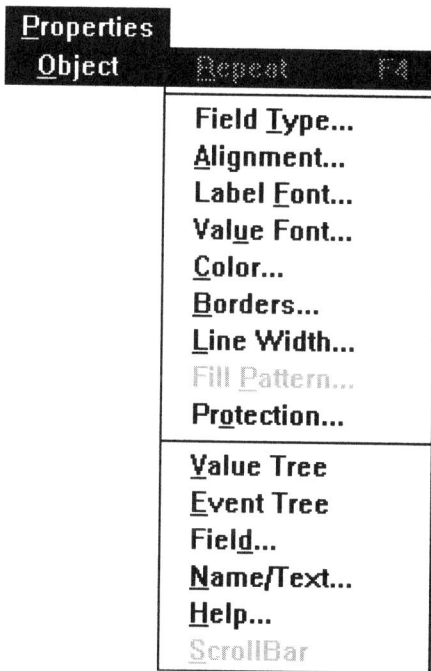

Properties
Object   Repeat   F4

Field **T**ype...
Alignment...
Label **F**ont...
Val**u**e Font...
Color...
Borders...
Line Width...
Fill Pattern...
Protection...

Value Tree
Event Tree
Fiel**d**...
Name/Text...
Help...
ScrollBar

3-24
The Object Properties submenu.

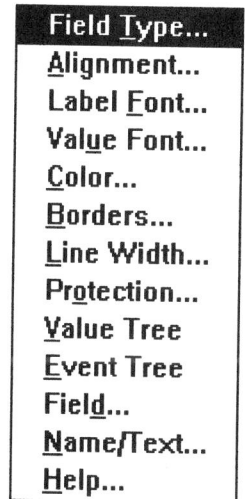

Field **T**ype...
Alignment...
Label **F**ont...
Val**u**e Font...
Color...
Borders...
Line Width...
Pr**o**tection...
Value Tree
Event Tree
Fiel**d**...
Name/Text...
Help...

3-25 *The property list for the Name field.*

View   The View menu lets you determine whether what you see on your monitor is the screen version of the application (with screen fonts, etc.), or the printer version, with the fonts showing as they are likely to be created by your selected printer (see FIG. 3-26). In FIG. 3-11, the Address Book application is shown with screen fonts. However, if you were to select Printer from the View menu, the font of the entries in the Address Book would be changed to approximate the current printer font. Figure 3-27 shows the Address Book application screen in Courier.

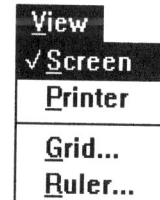

View
√ **S**creen
Printer
Grid...
Ruler...

3-26 *The View menu.*

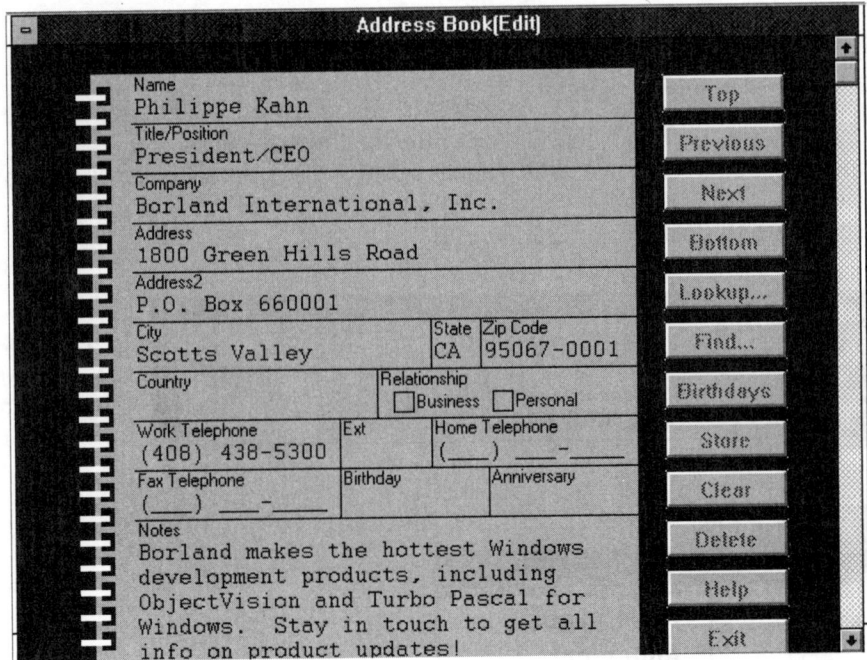

3-27
The Address Book form with Courier font after the printer has been selected.

3-28 *The Grid Style window.*

The Grid option in the View menu lets you select a grid density of Coarse, Medium, or Fine (see FIG. 3-28). In ObjectVision, objects are always placed according to a grid; you can't elect to work with a grid or without one, as you can with many drawing and presentation graphics programs. What you *can* elect is the grid pattern: Coarse is one character wide by one line deep, Medium is ½ character wide by ½ line deep, and Fine is ¼ character wide by ¼ line deep.

The Ruler option allows you to place a ruler at the top or left of the screen (or both), and lets you stipulate the ruler units in inches, centimeters, or characters (see FIG. 3-29).

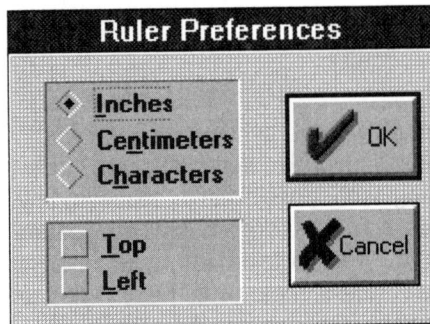

3-29
The Ruler Preferences window.

Tools This menu, shown in FIG. 3-30, allows you to view either the stack of forms that make up the application (see FIG. 3-31) or the links to other applications outside of ObjectVision—to Paradox databases, for example (see FIG. 3-32). Selecting Stack or Links from this menu is the same as selecting the stack tool or links tool in the object bar.

3-30 *The Tools menu.*

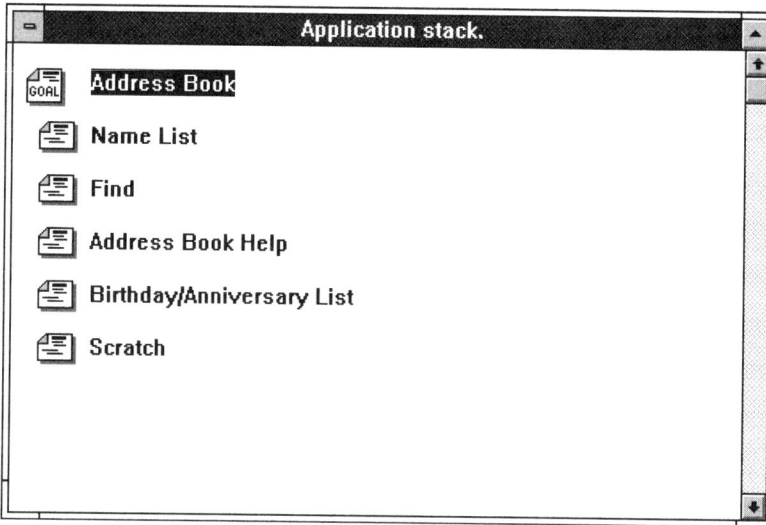

3-31 *The stack of forms that constitutes the Address Book application.*

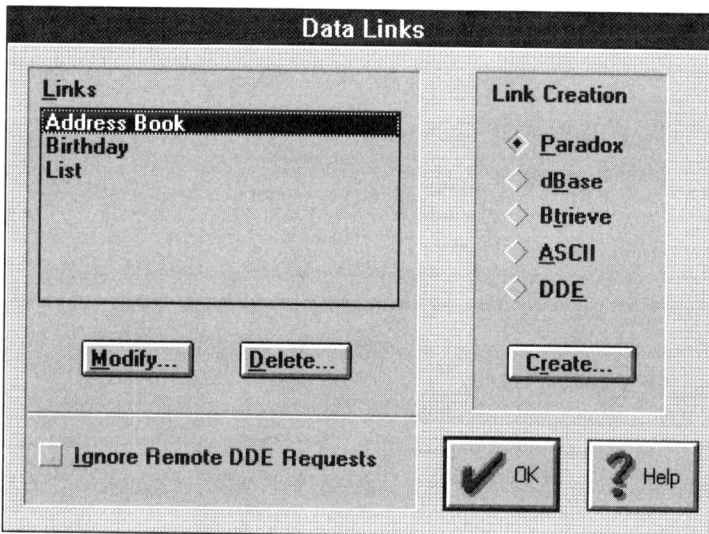

3-32 *The list of links to Paradox data files.*

ObjectVision identifies three kinds of Help that you can turn to for, well, help:

General help Select the Help menu at the far right side of the menu bar (see FIG. 3-33). This menu will lead you to either an index of ObjectVision help

Using the Help function

3-33 *The Help menu.*

(see FIG. 3-34), a list of commands (see FIG. 3-35), or a list of procedures (see FIG. 3-36). Figures 3-35 and 3-36 show the Help window for Form Tool commands and procedures.

Remember that these Help windows are hypertext windows—i.e., you can point to any word that appears in green, click the left mouse button, and you'll be transported into another level of definition, explanation, etc.

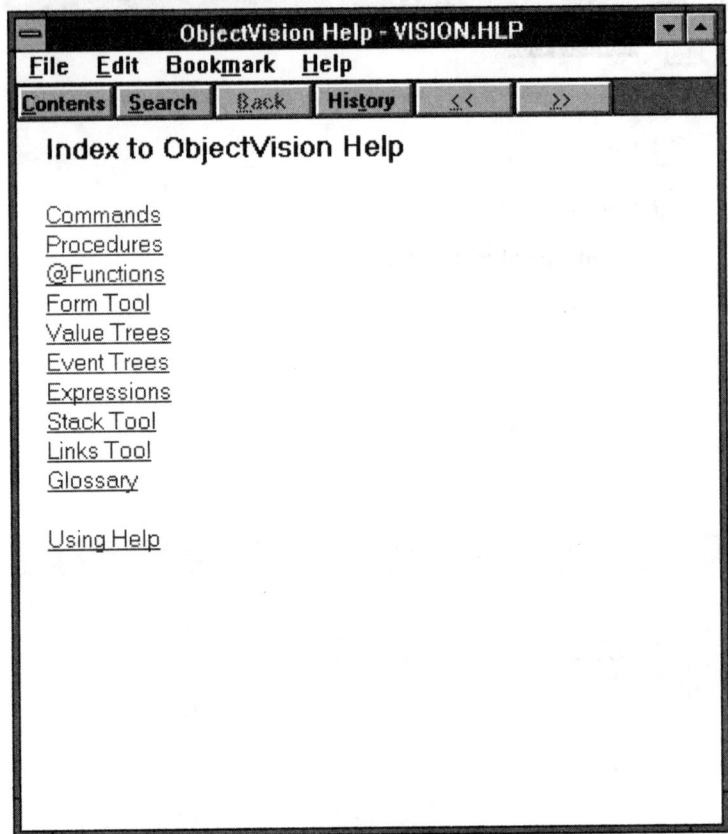

3-34
The Index for ObjectVision Help.

Context-sensitive help Press F1 to get help with the particular function you're trying to use or understand. In other words, you're getting help that's relative to the specific context in which you're working at the moment. To see how this works, open the Objects menu, use the down arrow to select Graphic, and then press F1. The Objects/Graphic Help window will appear, with details about adding graphics to a form (see FIG. 3-37).

Object-specific help This is the Help text you attach to objects (fields, buttons, etc.) that you place in a form. We'll explore this feature a bit farther down the road.

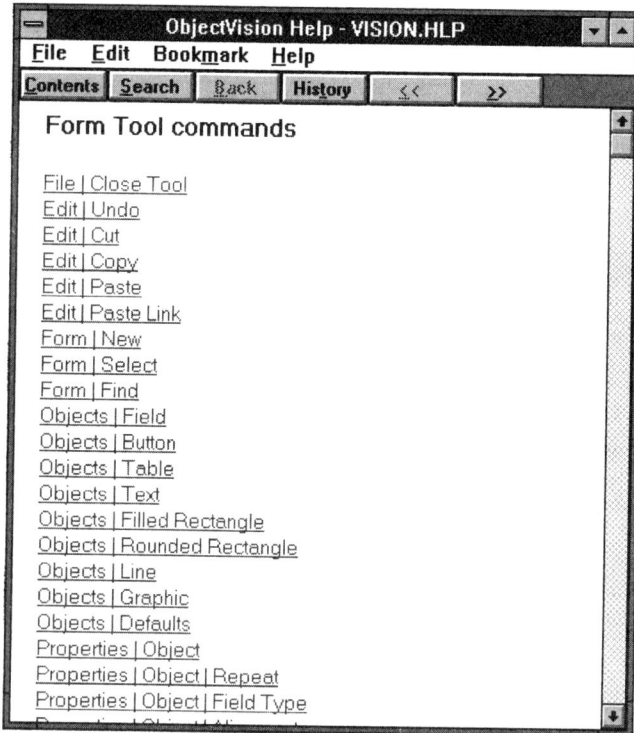

ObjectVision Help - VISION.HLP

File   Edit   Bookmark   Help

| Contents | Search | Back | History | << | >> |

Form Tool commands

File | Close Tool
Edit | Undo
Edit | Cut
Edit | Copy
Edit | Paste
Edit | Paste Link
Form | New
Form | Select
Form | Find
Objects | Field
Objects | Button
Objects | Table
Objects | Text
Objects | Filled Rectangle
Objects | Rounded Rectangle
Objects | Line
Objects | Graphic
Objects | Defaults
Properties | Object
Properties | Object | Repeat
Properties | Object | Field Type

3-35
The Form Tool Commands window.

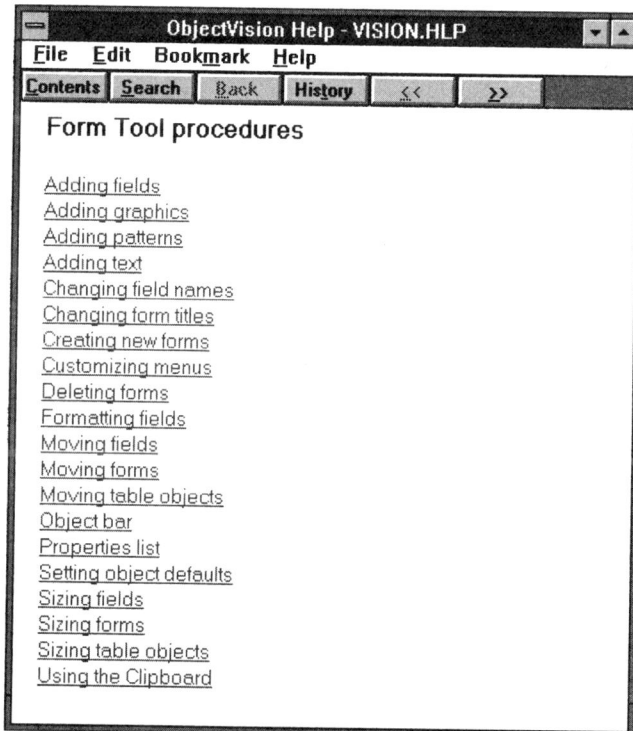

ObjectVision Help - VISION.HLP

File   Edit   Bookmark   Help

| Contents | Search | Back | History | << | >> |

Form Tool procedures

Adding fields
Adding graphics
Adding patterns
Adding text
Changing field names
Changing form titles
Creating new forms
Customizing menus
Deleting forms
Formatting fields
Moving fields
Moving forms
Moving table objects
Object bar
Properties list
Setting object defaults
Sizing fields
Sizing forms
Sizing table objects
Using the Clipboard

3-36
The Form Tool Procedures window.

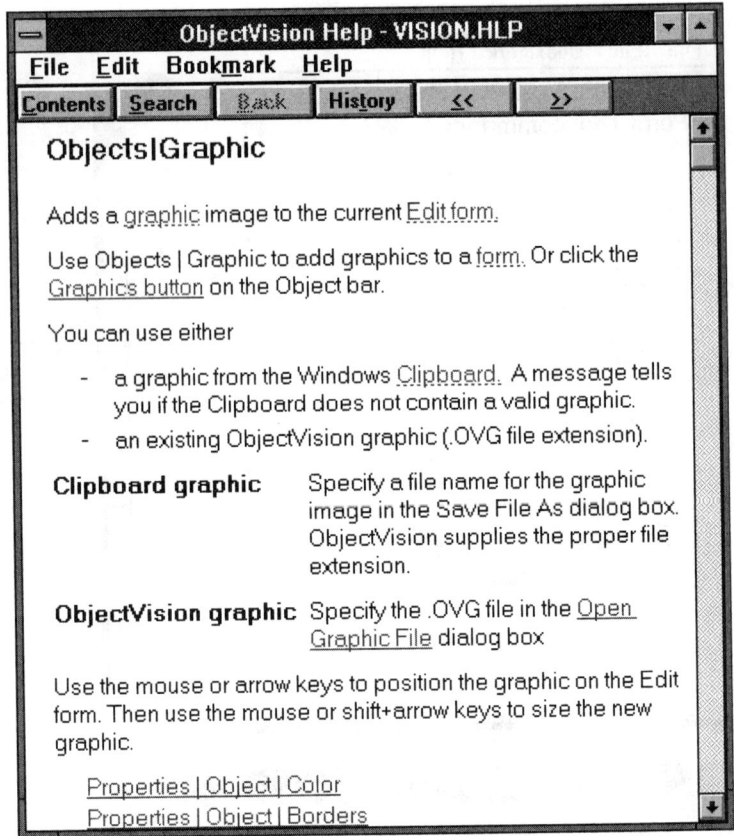

```
┌──────────────────────────────────────────────────────────┐
│ ─      ObjectVision Help - VISION.HLP          ▼ ▲         │
├──────────────────────────────────────────────────────────┤
│ File   Edit   Bookmark   Help                              │
├──────────────────────────────────────────────────────────┤
│ Contents │ Search │ Back │ History │ << │ >>              │
├──────────────────────────────────────────────────────────┤
```

Objects|Graphic

Adds a graphic image to the current Edit form.

Use Objects | Graphic to add graphics to a form. Or click the
Graphics button on the Object bar.

You can use either

- a graphic from the Windows Clipboard. A message tells
  you if the Clipboard does not contain a valid graphic.
- an existing ObjectVision graphic (.OVG file extension).

Clipboard graphic Specify a file name for the graphic
image in the Save File As dialog box.
ObjectVision supplies the proper file
extension.

ObjectVision graphic Specify the .OVG file in the Open
Graphic File dialog box

Use the mouse or arrow keys to position the graphic on the Edit
form. Then use the mouse or shift+arrow keys to size the new
graphic.

Properties | Object | Color
Properties | Object | Borders

3-37

The Objects/Graphic Help window.

The mouse & the keyboard

To conclude this preliminary section on navigating around ObjectVision screens, a word about the mouse and the keyboard. You might have noted some redundancies in certain operations; for example, you can access the properties of a selected field either by opening the Properties menu and selecting Object, or by pointing at the selected field and clicking the right mouse button. The latter method would seem to be easier, but one reason for the redundancy is that if you don't have a mouse you can access the menus from the keyboard.

To open any menu in the menu bar, hold down the Alt key and press the underlined letter in the menu heading. For example, in the Properties menu, the P is underlined. Once the menu is opened, you simply press the underlined letter (without the Alt key). Therefore, to view the properties of a selected object or field, press Alt–P and then O. This will open the same Properties menu list that you saw in FIG. 3-25. You can then select any item from the list by pressing its underlined letter. For example, you can view the name of the selected field by pressing N for Name/Text; the Field Name window will then appear with the field name displayed (see FIG. 3-38).

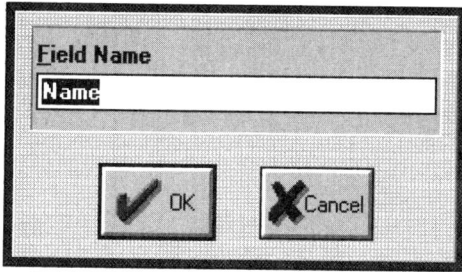

3-38
The Field Name window.

There are more tricks and shortcuts to maneuvering through ObjectVision that you'll learn as you go along. For now, however, you should be equipped to find your way around very handily.

4 Planning a new application

This book isn't intended to be an encyclopedic reference work that explains every possible function and use of every single feature and operation of ObjectVision. The documentation that came with your software takes care of that job. This book is designed primarily to be a tutorial, to take you step by step through the creation of a sample application with ObjectVision and, in the process, to introduce you to most of the commands and procedures. These commands and procedures, therefore, aren't in alphabetical order or explained in isolation, as you expect to find them in the software reference book, but demonstrated (by you!) as you actually use them to create a working application.

In order to make you feel that you're dealing with a real-world situation, I'm going to have you use ObjectVision to create an application that deals with a specific, concrete problem faced by the medical profession.

The application, or partial application, that you're going to create in this tutorial is called a physician's patient visit form. You've probably heard doctors complaining about the onerous burden of record-keeping that has been placed on them by various levels of government. In order for physicians to be adequately compensated for Medicare patients and patients covered by other insurance plans, they're now required to keep detailed and extensive records of each patient's visit.

In New York State, the Medical Society of the State of New York has issued detailed guidelines about the sort of record-keeping that physicians are now expected to do, and stated in a flyer it sent to its members, "Please feel free to reproduce the form for your own use."

Because they invited us, we're going to do just that. An approximate version of the Medical Society's form is shown in FIG. 4-1. (If you want to load this file into your own computer, you can find it in ASCII format on the disk that comes with this book—see the back of the book. The filename is DOCSFORM.K92.) For your convenience in referring back to the form, I've numbered each field.

```
                      Patient Visit Form

1. PATIENT:_____  2. CURRENT AGE:____
3. TODAY'S DATE:_____ 4. TIME:_____ 5. VITALS:_____
6. LAST DATE SEEN:_____ 7. PLACE OF SERVICE:_____
8. PATIENT'S CHIEF COMPLAINT/REASON FOR VISIT:_____
   _____
9. PATIENT'S HISTORY:_____
   _____
10. EXAMINATION:_____
    _____
```

4-1

The first page of a two-page daily record form for physicians.

```
11. MEDICAL DECISION MAKING (i.e., # of possible diagnoses, possible
treatment options, analysis of medical records and diagnostic tests,
risks of complications and/or morbidity or mortality):
   _____
12. PROGRESS OF PATIENT:_____
    _____
13. MEDICATIONS:_____
    _____
14. RECOMMENDATIONS/REFERRALS:_____
    _____
15. MEDICAL NECESSITY FOR ANCILLARY DIAGNOSTIC PROCEDURE(S):_____
    _____
16. DIAGNOSIS:_____  17. *TIME_____
    _____     *Please refer to guidelines
18. EXPECTED DATE TO RETURN FOR FOLLOW-UP:_____
```

Your goal in this tutorial is to automate the form, creating a Windows application that physicians or their assistants could use to create Medicare documentation with ease and increased productivity. So the "form" in this case really is a form and not merely a metaphor.

Let's brainstorm a bit about transforming the paper form shown in FIG. 4-1 into a screen form that resembles some of the ObjectVision applications you've seen so far. Do you want the screen form to look just like the paper form? Can you get all of the items on the paper form onto a single screen, or will a multiple-screen form be necessary? Which fields can be automated, i.e., filled in somehow by the computer? What sort of databases will you need to create or link to? Will there be any place or requirement for tables? Graphics? Calculations?

You're not equipped to answer all of these questions yet, but keep the following items regarding the nature of the patient visit form in mind:

- It's reasonable to assume that a doctor will already have his past patients on some kind of database, so when you fill in the patient's name and vital statistics you might be able to access that database for the information. If the patient is new, the data will of course have to be entered from the keyboard. That means there should be a way to tell the program whether the person is a new or existing patient, right at the beginning. If he is an existing patient, the application should be designed to enter name, age, last date seen, and medical history with little or no prompting.
- Today's date, time, and place of service should be automatically entered as soon as a new patient visit record is started.
- Some of the fields will have to be subdivided. For example, the Vitals field should include places to enter pulse rate, blood pressure, respiration rate, weight, etc. This field should also allow you to skip any data entry if the condition is normal. For example, the default value for the pulse rate might be normal unless the rate is abnormally high, in which case you would have to enter the actual value.
- Some of the fields—particularly those requiring text answers of indeterminate length (patient's complaint, examination, progress, etc.)—will have to be quite flexible in size. How do you do that?
- Information is likely, in many cases, to be dictated by the physician and entered by an assistant. In that case, the fields and instructions will have to be clear enough for laypersons to understand.
- Because the bureaucrats (no pejorative tone intended) to whom these forms are sent are likely to be most comfortable with forms that have a familiar "look and feel," you should probably, in this case, make the screen resemble the paper form as much as possible. And certainly the printout should look like familiar territory to those who are determining how the physician should be compensated.

Opening a new form

With some of these things in mind, let's plunge right in and get this patient visit form underway. From the ObjectVision opening screen, select Form from the Tools menu. When the Form Name window prompts you to anoint this new form, type (see FIG. 4-2):

Patient Visit

Click on OK, and your virgin patient visit form will make its inaugural appearance, letting you know that it's in edit mode (see FIG. 4-3).

Let's get the work space set up. You'll be working with visible rulers, so select Ruler from the View menu. When the Ruler Preferences box appears, click on the small boxes in front of Top and Left to make the horizontal and

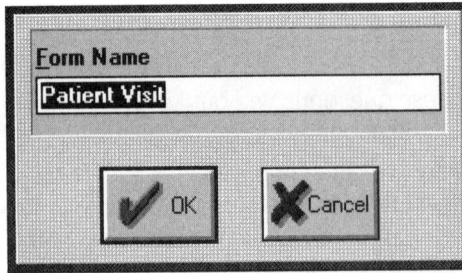

4-2
The Form Name window, with Patient Visit entered as the name of the new form.

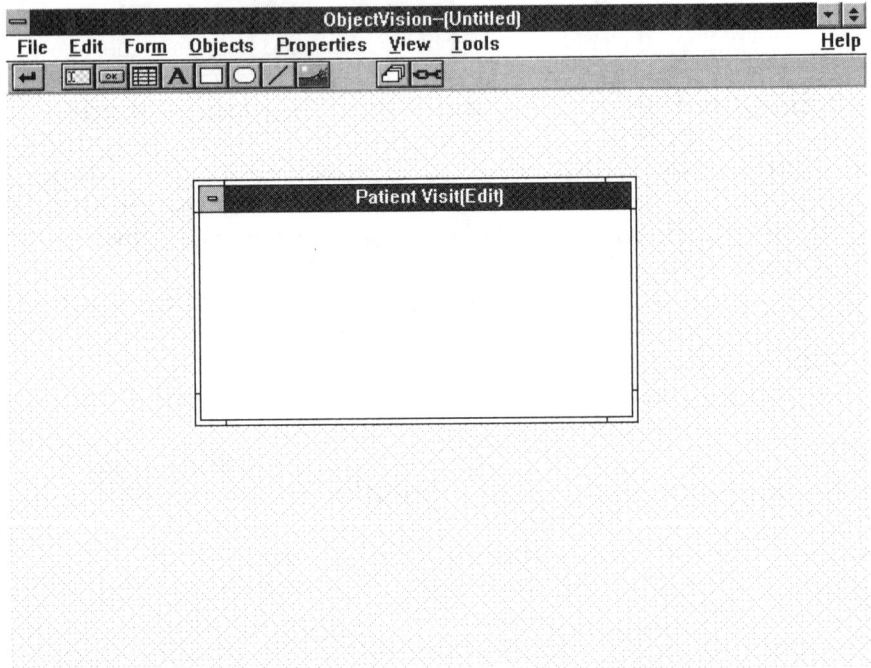

4-3
The first appearance of the new Patient Visit form.

vertical rulers visible (see FIG. 4-4). Click on OK, and the two rulers will appear in the new form (see FIG. 4-5).

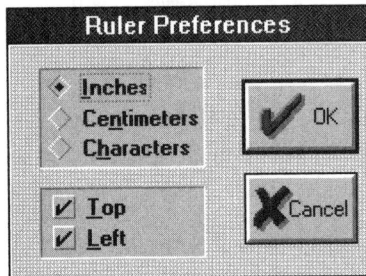

4-4
The Ruler Preferences window with Inches selected as the ruler unit, and Top and Left selected as the rulers to make visible.

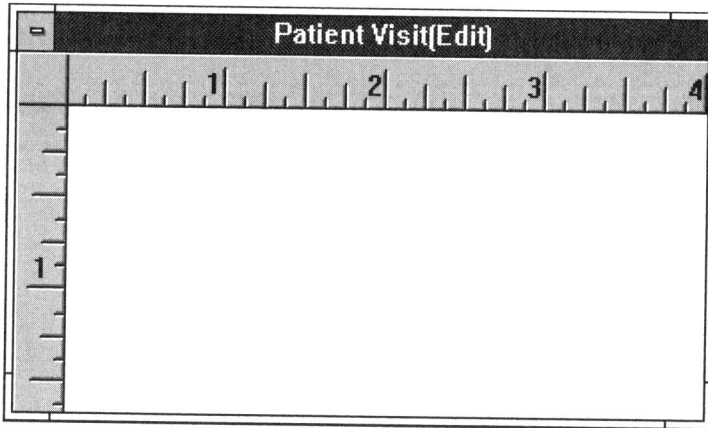

4-5
The new form with top and left rulers.

The new form should approximate an 8½×11 paper form, so you'll want to get the screen form as close to that as possible. Drag the new window to the upper left-hand corner of your monitor. Now resize the patient visit form so it fills your screen. To do that, move the pointer down to the bottom line of the window until it turns into a double-headed arrow (see FIG. 4-6).

Sizing the new form

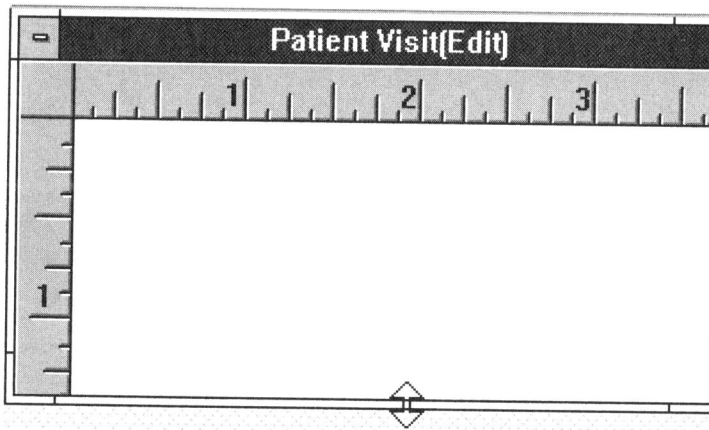

4-6
The double-headed arrow at the bottom border, ready for the resizing operation.

You can now drag the bottom border down to the bottom of your monitor by depressing the left mouse button and sliding the window until it reaches the bottom of the screen. In the same way, move the right border of the patient visit form all the way to the right. Your new form should now fill the screen, showing ruler dimensions of approximately 7½ by 4 inches. The 7½-inch width is fine; it allows for left and right margins of ½ inch. The vertical size of the form should ultimately be about 10 inches, but you'll take care of that later (see FIG. 4-7).

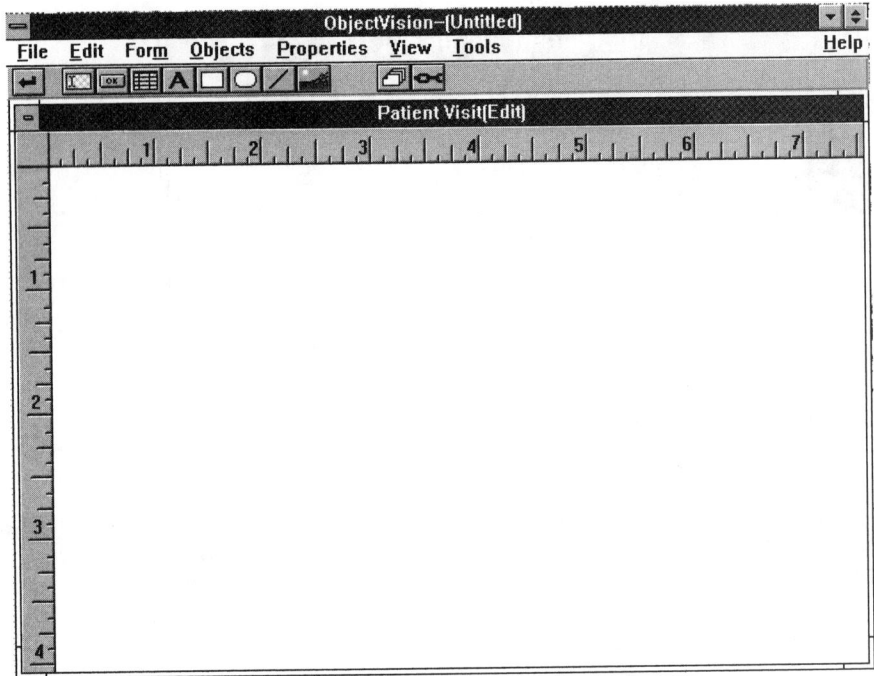

4-7
The patient visit form expanded to fill the screen.

To identify the physician's office, put a title at the top in a rounded rectangle. Call it the Elmsford Medical Center; that has a good all-American ring to it. The official colors of the clinic are blue and yellow, so place the name in yellow letters on a blue background inside the rectangle. That means you need to create two objects: a rounded, filled rectangle, and a text object that says Elmsford Medical Center.

Placing a rounded rectangle on the form

Click on the rounded rectangle button, and the pointer will become a small cross hair with a rounded rectangle. When you move the pointer, your position on the screen is indicated by a moving line in each of the rulers. Locate the pointer at the top of the screen at the two-inch point on the horizontal ruler, and click the left mouse button. The rectangle will be displayed on your form, with selection handles at the corners and shaded areas in the rulers to indicate its dimensions (see FIG. 4-8).

Sizing the rounded rectangle

To expand this rounded rectangle to the correct size, point to the lower right selection handle; your pointer will itself become a small black square like the selection handles. Press and hold the left mouse button, and drag the corner of the rectangle until it's about 4½ inches wide and about ¾ inch deep; then release the button. Your rectangle should now resemble the one shown in FIG. 4-9.

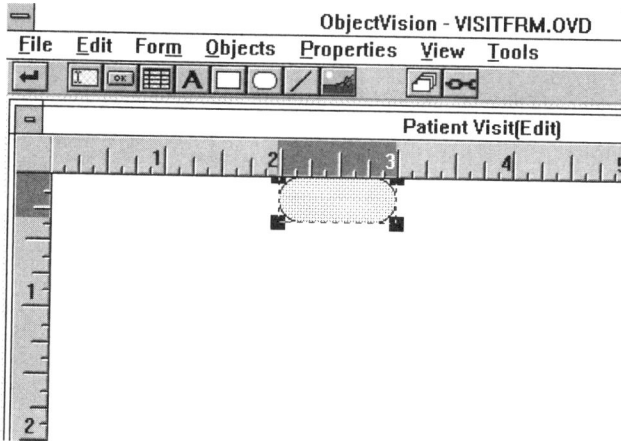

4-8
The first appearance of the rounded rectangle on your form.

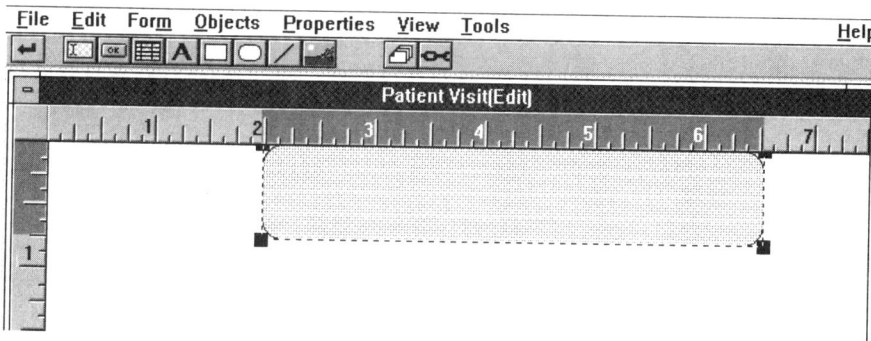

4-9
The expanded rectangle.

Now to change the color of the rectangle to blue. You'll need to access the rectangle property list (generated by the property inspector) by pointing to the rectangle and clicking the right mouse button. A small list of three properties (Color, Line Width, and Fill Pattern) will appear. These are all of the properties possessed by this rounded rectangle (see FIG. 4-10).

Select Color from this menu, and the Color window will pop up. At this point you can change the Background or the Border. Click on the selection list button below Background, and a color palette will appear (see FIG. 4-11). Click on royal blue (your palette might be different, especially if you're working with a monochrome monitor), then on OK, and your rounded rectangle will be returned in a new color (see FIG. 4-12).

Next, you'll add text to the rectangle. Click on the text object button and the Text Value window will pop up. Type (see FIG. 4-13):

```
Elmsford Medical Center
```

Changing the color of the rounded rectangle

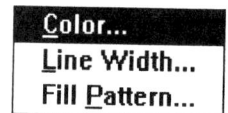

4-10 *The property list associated with the rounded rectangle.*

Adding a text object

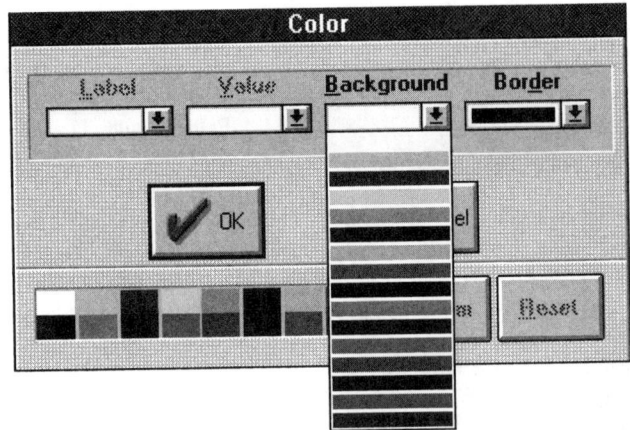

4-11
The color palette for the background of the rounded rectangle.

4-12
The rectangle in its new color.

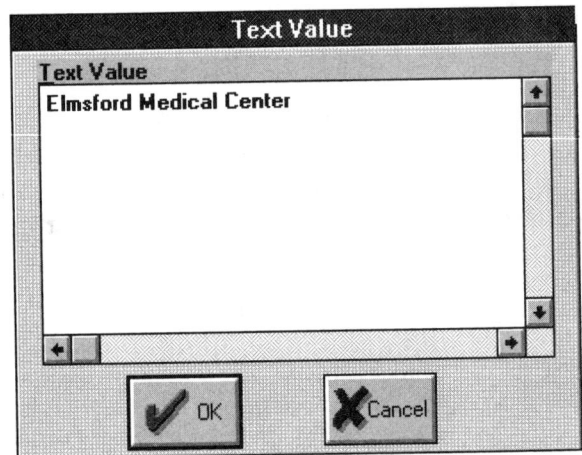

4-13
The Text Value window with the form-heading text.

Click on OK, and your pointer will be replaced by the text symbol; click in the upper left-hand corner of the rounded blue rectangle, and you've placed the text object (see FIG. 4-14).

Setting the properties of the text object

To assign properties to the text object in order to make it look the way you want, you'll use the property list again (point to the text object and click the right mouse button). In this case, you'll see that the text object has seven assignable properties: Alignment, Label Font, Color, Borders, Line Width,

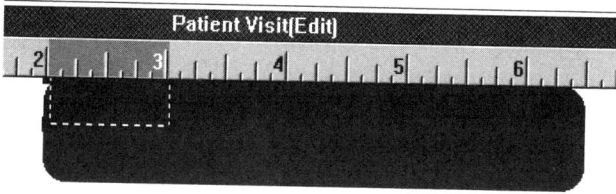

4-14
The new text object inside the rounded rectangle.

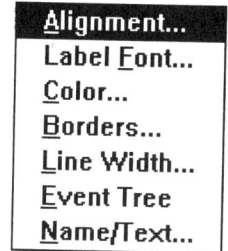

4-15 *The property list for the text object.*

Event Tree, and Name/Text (see FIG. 4-15). You'll want to deal with the first four properties.

Click on Alignment. When you see the Alignment window, click next to Center to get center justification (see FIG. 4-16). Next, click on OK to complete the action.

Aligning the text

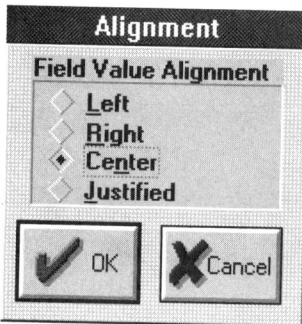

4-16
The Alignment window with center alignment selected.

Open the property list again by pointing to the text object and clicking the right mouse button. This time select Label Font. You'll be presented with a selection of several fonts in several sizes (see FIG. 4-17). Select Helvetica as

Setting the label font

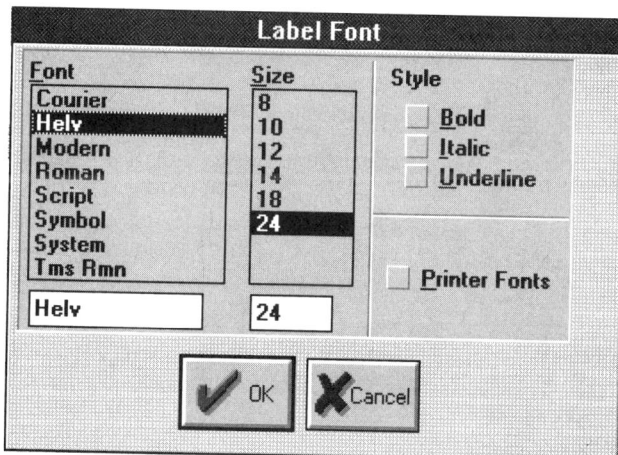

4-17
The Label Font window, with 24-point Helvetica selected.

the font and 24 as the size; then click on OK. When you're returned to the form, you'll no longer be able to see all of the name. Resize the text object by dragging the selection handles (see FIG. 4-18). Stretch the text object until it's the same size as the rounded rectangle, and center the text vertically in the rectangle (see FIG. 4-19).

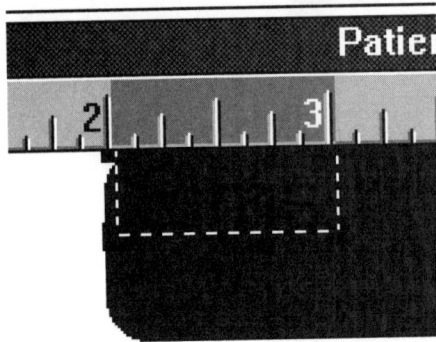

4-18
The text object with larger type.

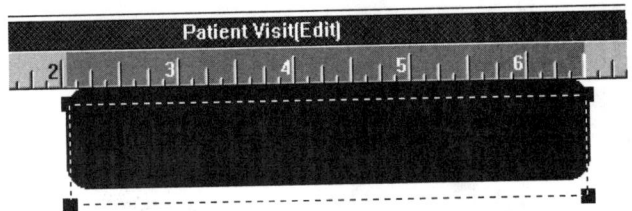

4-19
The text object resized and centered to fit the rectangle.

Changing the color of the text

To change the color of the text into Elmsford yellow, bring up the property list once again and click on Color. When the Color window is displayed, click on the selection button under Label and select a bright yellow (see FIG. 4-20). Press OK, and your shiny new logo will be almost complete.

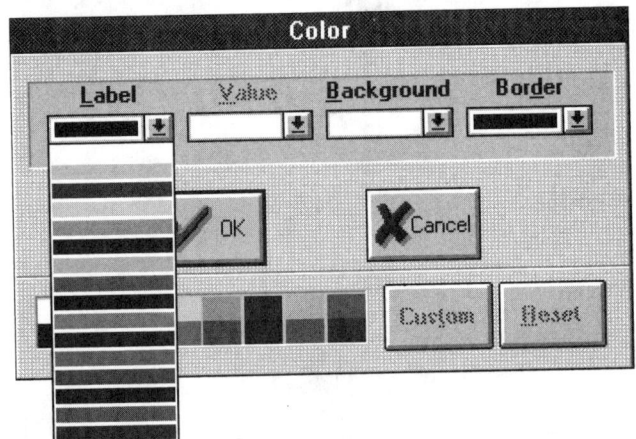

4-20
The Color window with the label palette displayed.

There's one more thing to do—the default for the text object puts a border around the text. To remove that border, bring up the property list one last time, select Borders, and when you see the Borders window click next to Outline to remove the check (see FIG. 4-21). Press OK, and the text border should be gone.

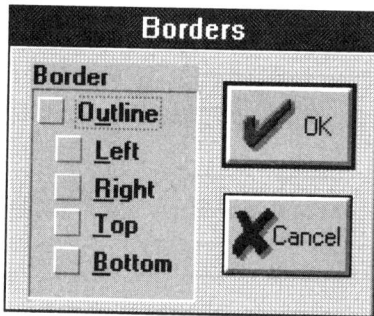

4-21
The Borders window with Outline turned off.

To view your finished logo, click on the Close tool, which will take you back into Runtime mode. Voilà! Your first ObjectVision application is launched (see FIG. 4-22).

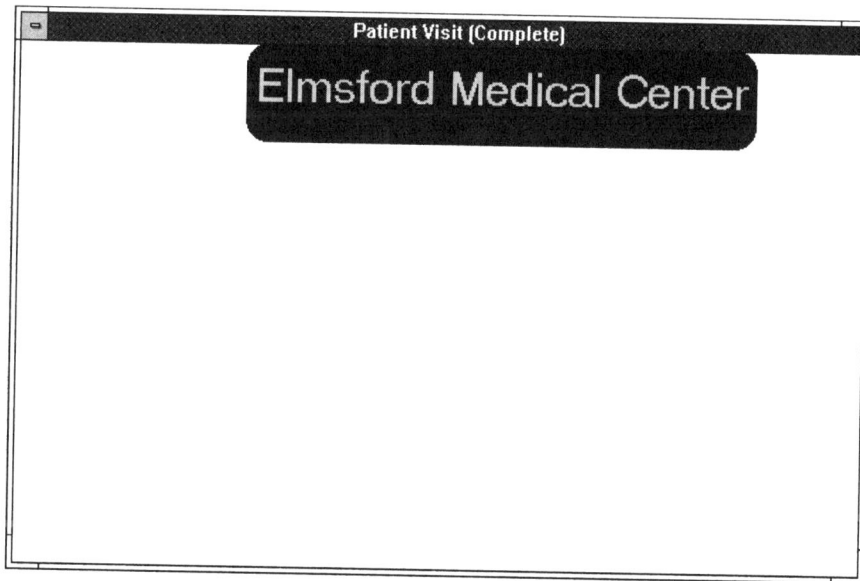

4-22
The new form in progress, in runtime mode.

Select Save As from the File menu to preserve your work, name this form VISITFRM (the program will provide the .OVD extension), and press OK. Take a breather. In the next chapter, you'll add fields to this form.

5 Working with fields

Now to begin to make this form a working application. Creating an ObjectVision application and making it work is a three-step operation. Borland International, in some of the company's training materials, describes it as an *ABC* process:

A is the application interface. This is the primary "form," with its fields, buttons, and other objects. *B* is the business rules that govern the creation of decision trees—both event trees and value trees—which provide the motive power or navigational directions that move the application from one field to another and one form to another. These decision trees provide the logic that makes the application work. *C* is the connection to data. In this third and final step, you create the links or connections between your interface, form, or stack of forms and external sources of data or information that your program needs.

An ObjectVision application might consist of only the interface and decision trees, or it might involve all three of the ABC steps. It won't work, however, with only the form. In this chapter you're going to begin to place objects on the form, but you won't be able to test your new program until decision trees and data links are in place.

Let's look ahead a bit. The patient visit form, in FIG. 4-1, shows that the first four fields are Patient, Current Age, Today's Date, and Time. In the Patient field, you're going to enter, of course, the patient's name. There's already a database of patient names, however, so if you're dealing with an existing patient you simply select the name from the database. The same database will provide the patient's age. If the patient is new, you'll have to fill out a patient information form—which means creating a second form for the application. The computer will provide the current date, and you enter the time of the visit.

Before you fill in any of the blanks on the patient visit form, therefore, you need a field (called a radio button field) to tell the program whether the patient is new or not. So the Patient field will become a radio button field, and you'll insert a new second field, called the Name field, for the patient's name.

First, then, the Patient field. At the opening ObjectVision screen, select Open from the File menu, highlight VISITFRM.OVD in the files list, and click on OK (see FIG. 5-1). Your blank form will appear, sporting the new Elmsford Medical Center logo at the top (see FIG. 5-2).

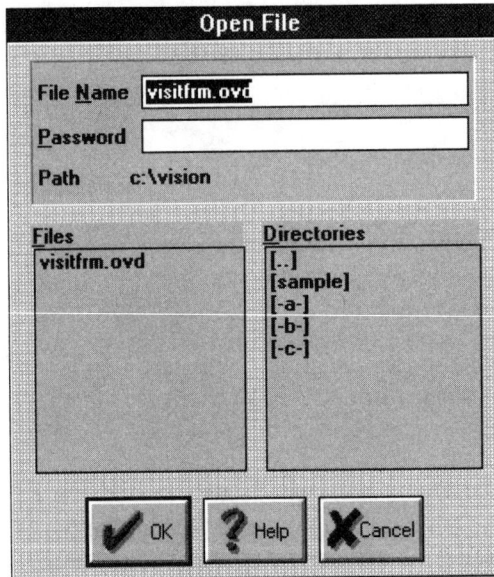

5-1
The Open File window, with VISITFRM.OVD selected.

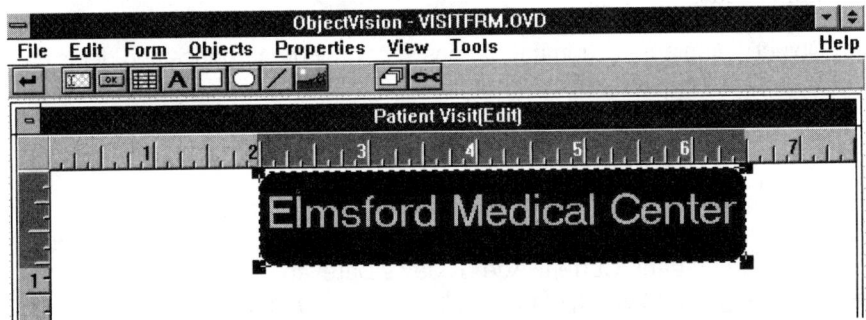

5-2
The Elmsford Medical Center logo at the top of the new form.

To shift into edit mode, select Form from the Tools menu. You're now ready to place the first field, or field object, on the form.

Click on the Field tool, the second button from the left on the button bar, and the Field Name window will open (see FIG. 5-3). Type Patient as the name of the first field, and click on OK. Your mouse pointer will become a miniature version of the Field tool with a crosshair; position the crosshair at the left margin of your workspace and the one-inch point on the vertical ruler (if your rulers aren't visible, turn them on from the View menu). Click the left mouse button, and the Patient field will appear in selection handles (see FIG. 5-4). Stretch it to two inches by dragging one of the right-hand selection handles to the two-inch mark.

Field tool

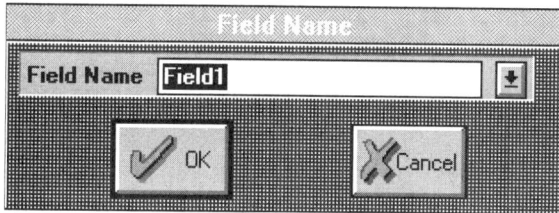

5-3
The field tool and Field Name window.

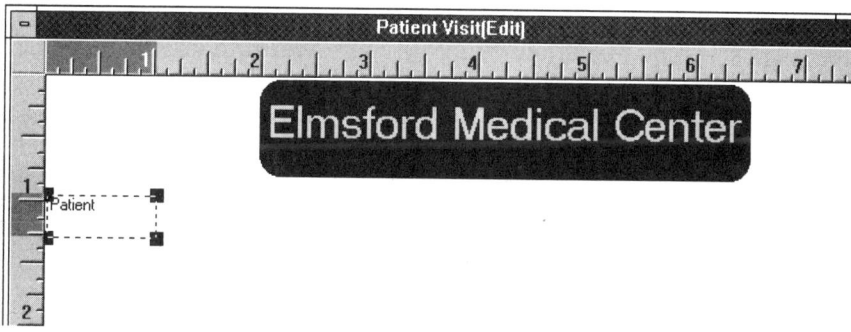

5-4
The first, or Patient, field.

To add the second field, click on the Field tool again and this time type Name for the field name. Place the crosshair at the upper right-hand corner of the Patient field and click the left mouse button. When the Name field appears, stretch it to the 4.5" mark on the upper ruler (see FIG. 5-5).

In the same way, add three more fields, each one inch wide, to the first line: Current Age, Today's Date, and Time. When you're finished, your screen should look something like FIG. 5-6.

Now you could actually insert data—or what ObjectVision calls values—into these fields. But first let's tell those fields what kind of fields you want them to be. Point to the Patient field, click the right mouse button (called the

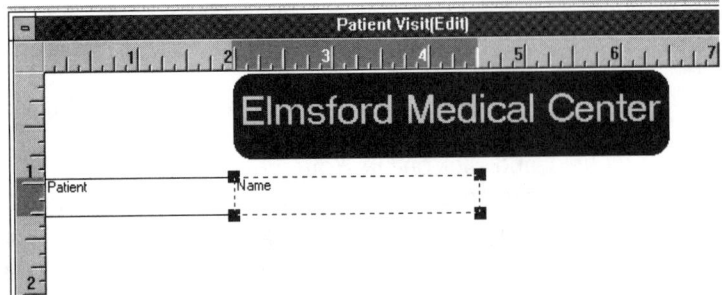

5-5
The Name field in a position adjacent to the Patient field.

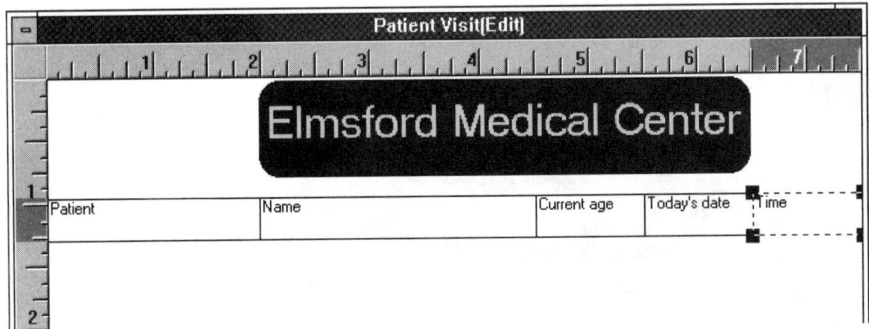

5-6
The form with five fields added.

Field **T**ype...
Alignment...
Label **F**ont...
Val**u**e Font...
Color...
Borders...
Line Width...
Protection...
Value Tree
Event Tree
Fiel**d**...
Name/**T**ext...
Help...

5-7 *The property list for the first field, with Field Type selected.*

property inspector), and a property list, similar to one you've seen before, will pop up (see FIG. 5-7). To define the field type, point to the Field Type option and click the left mouse button. When the Field Type window appears, you'll see 14 different kinds of fields listed (see FIG. 5-8). You'll also see that there's an option that allows you to choose whether to display the field name or not.

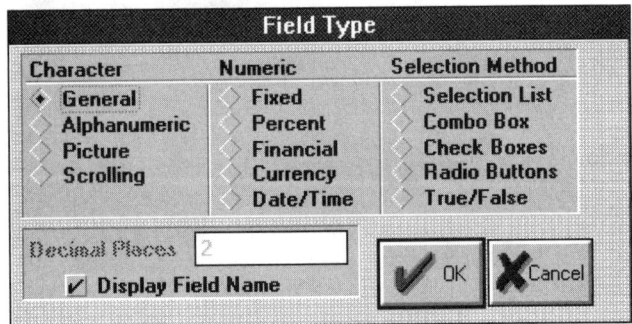

5-8
The Field Type window.

In order to keep you from drowning in more information than you can use right now, I won't discuss all the field types. If you're curious, however, refer to the Help function for an explanation of the various types (see FIGS. 5-9A and 5-9B).

Properties|Object|Field Type

ObjectVision provides the following field types to control display formats:

CHARACTER:

General	Default display suitable for both numeric and text values. After a value is entered into a General field, ObjectVision converts it.
Alphanumeric	Accepts any keyboard character. Unlike the General field type, it does not try to convert the value.
Picture	Displays text values that must match a specific pattern when entered. For more information, see Match and reserved characters.
Scrolling	Displays large text values that can be scrolled vertically.

NUMERIC:

Fixed	Displays numeric values with a fixed number of decimal places.
Percent	Displays numeric values as a percentage.
Financial	Displays numeric values with commas separating thousands and parentheses for negative values.
Currency	Displays numeric values with commas, parentheses, and currency symbol.
Date/Time	Displays DateTimeNumbers in a variety of date and time formats.

5-9A
The explanation of character and numeric field types provided by the Help function.

SELECTION METHOD:

Selection List	Displays a list of values. Select one of the values (there is no type-in box).
Combo Box	Contains a list of values, but displays only the selected one. To see the rest, click the down arrow to the right of the box. Click another value to select it, or type a value in the box.
Check Boxes	Displays a list of values with a check box beside them. To select a value, click its box.
Radio Buttons	Displays a list of values only one of which can be selected at one time.
True/False	Displays logical values that are either True (checked) or False (unchecked).

5-9B
The explanation of selection-method field types provided by the Help function.

The **Display Field Name** check box can be unchecked to prevent display of the field's name.

Additional information

Properties | Object | Repeat

I said earlier that the Patient field should be a radio button field. This is a common term in Windows programs, probably inspired by the buttons on a car radio that let you select the station. In a radio button field, you get a list of values, or choices, with little circles or "radio buttons" next to them. You can select only one.

Select Radio Buttons from the Field Type window, click on OK, and the Expected List window will pop up. This is the list of values that you'll expect to choose from in this field. In this case, the choices on the list should be New, for new patients, or Prior, for previously existing patients.

Click in the New Value box, type New, and click on the Insert button. Then type Prior and click on the Insert button again. Your Expected List window should now show two values—New and Prior—in its Values box

Defining a radio button field

(see FIG. 5-10). Click on OK, and your field will be returned with buttons next to the two choices (see FIG. 5-11).

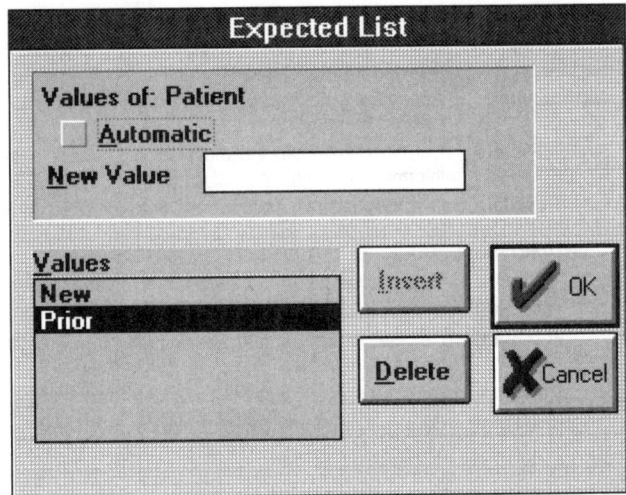

5-10
The Expected List window, with New and Prior entered as the list of values for the radio button field.

5-11
The Patient field with two new radio buttons.

Changing the value font & size in a field

Want to make those buttons and their text a bit bigger? Go back to that field property list by pointing to the field and clicking the right mouse button. This time, select Value Font from the list. When the Value Font window is displayed, select Helv (Helvetica) 10 as the font and size (see FIG. 5-12).

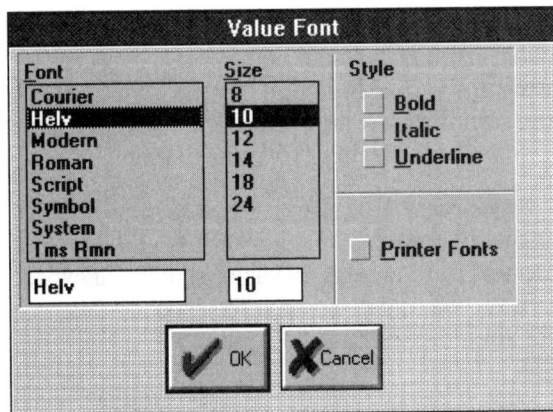

5-12
The Value Font window with Helvetica 10 selected as the font and size.

Click on OK. The field will be returned with the buttons and text in a larger size (see FIG. 5-13). (If your field was returned without the radio buttons, it probably means that the font size you specified was too large for the space you had allotted to the field, and you have to do some resizing. When your field space is large enough, the buttons and text will appear.)

5-13
The Patient field with buttons and text in a larger size.

The Name field is going to be a combo box field—that is, your user will have the choice of either entering a new value (in this case, a patient name) in the field or selecting an existing patient from the list. Point and click the right mouse button to bring up the property list for the Patient field. When it pops up, click on Field Type and select Combo Box from the Field Type window. Click on OK, and when you return to the patient visit form it will look as if nothing has happened. But it has; you'll see.

Setting up a Combo Box field

Examine the properties of the Current Age field; you'll see that the field type is General. This is the default value that's set if you don't select something else. For now, that's fine. Click on OK or press Enter.

Now you're going to make today's date a Date/Time field, which means that it will have a very specific format that you select. Bring up the property list for the Today's Date field, select Field Type, click next to Date/Time, and then click on OK. You should now be looking at the Date Type window (see FIG. 5-14). Select the top format on the list—8/1/90—and click on OK. Repeat the procedure for the Time field, selecting the 3:15 PM format for entering the time (see FIG. 5-15). When you click on OK, you are once again back to your patient visit form, and nothing obvious has happened.

Creating a Date/Time field

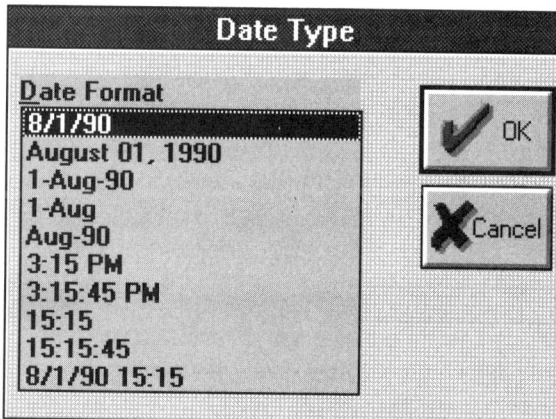

5-14
The Date Type window with a date format selected.

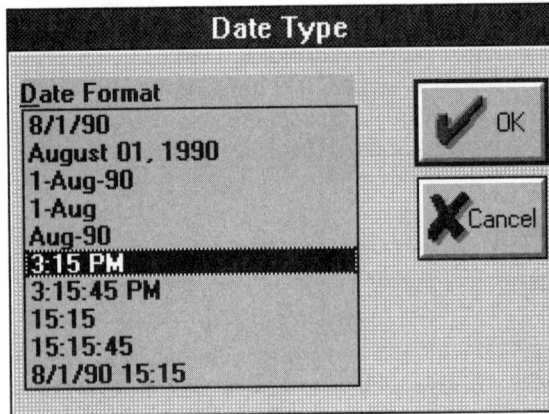

5-15
The Date Type window with a time format selected.

Removing field borders from multiple fields

Let's do one more thing. All of the fields you've created so far are surrounded by borders. Those borders don't really do anything, practically or aesthetically, so let's get rid of them. As a matter of fact, you can get rid of them all at once—and this is an operation to remember.

Because you just did some work on the Time field, that field is probably already selected. If if isn't, click on it to select it. Then, while holding down the Shift key, click on the Patient field on the opposite side of the form. That maneuver should select all the fields you've entered, because when you select one field, depress the Shift key, and click on a second field, you select all contiguous fields (all fields touching each other), as shown in FIG. 5-16.

5-16
The patient visit form with all fields selected.

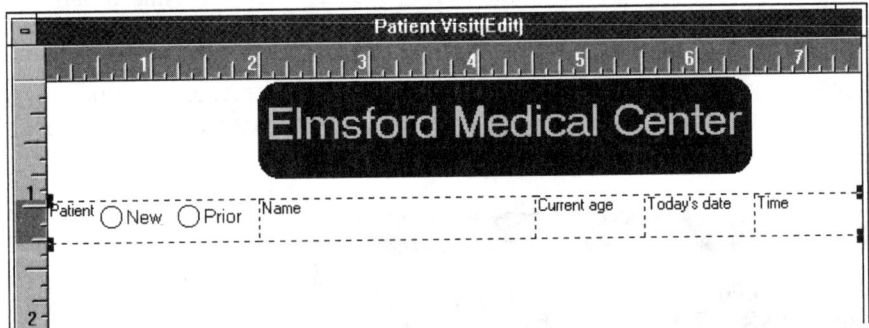

Now point anywhere in that selected group of fields and click the right mouse button. You'll bring up a property list that applies to the whole collection—so it's a somewhat abbreviated form of the property lists you've been looking at (see FIG. 5-17).

One of the items on that list is Borders; select that option, and a Borders window will show up (see FIG. 5-18). Outline is checked, which is the default option. To remove the outline from your fields, simply uncheck Outline and click on OK.

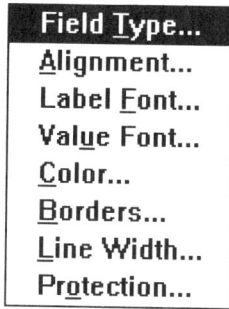

Field Type...
Alignment...
Label Font...
Value Font...
Color...
Borders...
Line Width...
Protection...

5-17 *The property list for the collected fields.*

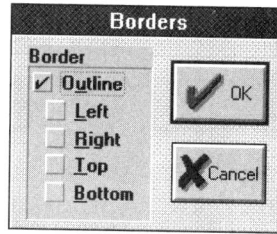

5-18 *The Borders window, with Outline checked.*

Now press the Close tool—the one at the far left of the button bar—to return to runtime mode, and you'll see your form with all borders removed (see FIG. 5-19). The first field is outlined; the program is waiting for you to make an entry there.

This isn't a working form yet; it still needs decision trees and links. But you've made a big beginning by placing fields on the form.

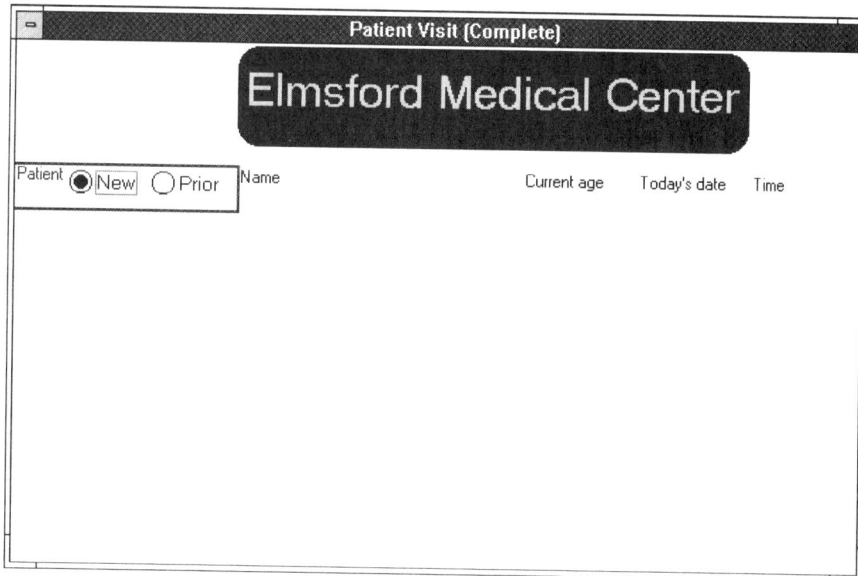

5-19
The patient visit form in runtime mode with field borders removed.

6 *Secondary forms & buttons*

As you began to build the patient visit form in chapter 5, you probably noticed that you needed more than a single form. Much of the information for the patient visit form comes from a database that's created via a second form—the patient information form.

You're going to do three things in this chapter. First, you'll create that secondary form, the patient information form. Second, after placing some fields on that new form, you'll take a look at some new field types. Finally, you'll place some buttons on the new form; they'll come in handy down the road.

In case you don't have the application open at the moment, launch ObjectVision and open your application in progress, VISITFRM.OVD. The main, or goal, form in its current state of development should look like FIG. 6-1. Open the form tool by selecting Form from the Tools menu (see FIG. 6-2).

Creating a secondary form

This is going to be a new form, so when the object bar appears select New from the Form menu (see FIG. 6-3). The Form Name window will pop up; type Patient Information as the name for the new secondary form, or subform (see FIG. 6-4). Click on OK to confirm, and your new blank form will be placed into the center of your screen (see FIG. 6-5). Enlarge the new form so that it's about the same height, but not quite as wide as the patient visit form (see FIG. 6-6). Try sizing it to about five inches wide and four inches high.

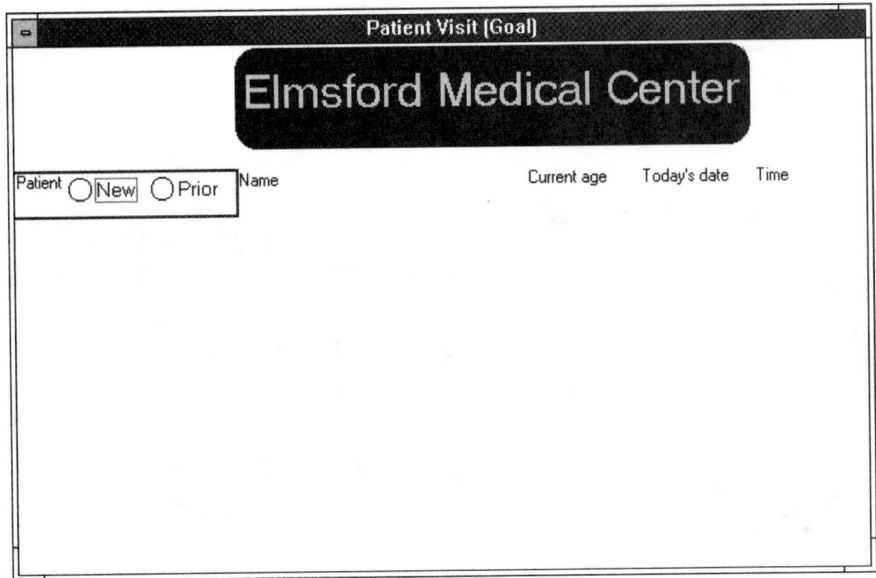

6-1
The patient visit form in an early stage.

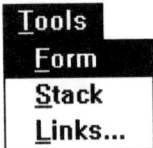

6-2 *The Tools menu with Form selected.*

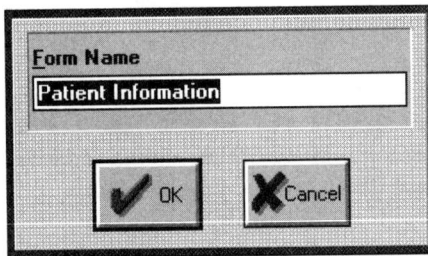

6-3 *The Form menu with New selected.*

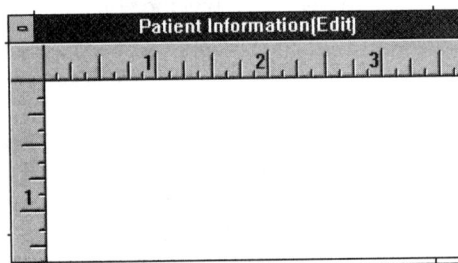

6-4
The Form Name window with Patient Information entered as the name for the new subform.

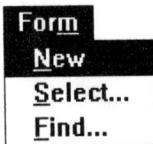

6-5
The new patient information form.

Now you'll have to place a number of fields on this new form. Your form should have a text object, Patient Information, at the top, and the following list of fields: Name, Street Address, City, State, Zip Code, Home Phone, Office Phone, Date of Birth, Insurance Carrier, and Employer. To see the arrangement of the fields on the form, refer to FIG. 6-7. You can do these on your own as a practice exercise, using the field-placing skills you acquired in chapter 5.

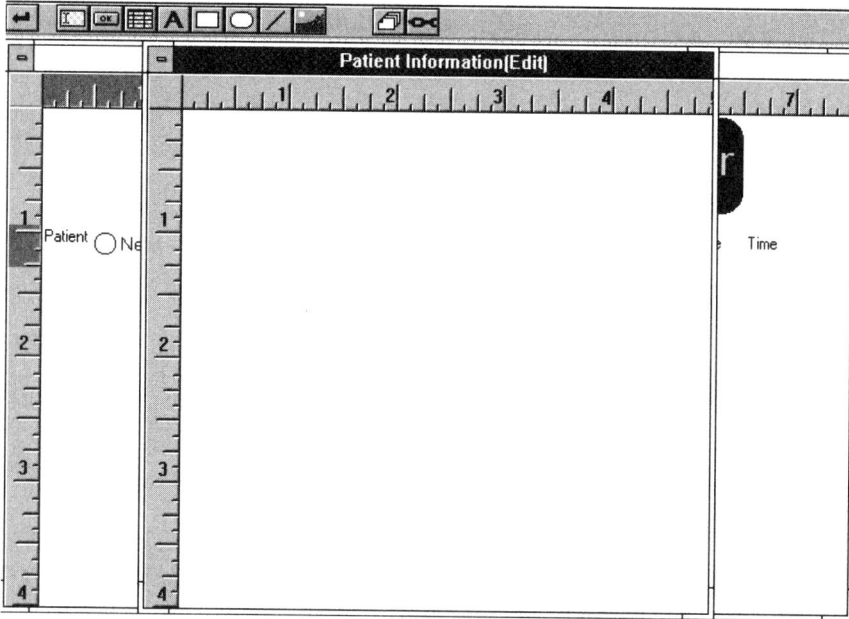

6-6
The resized patient information form.

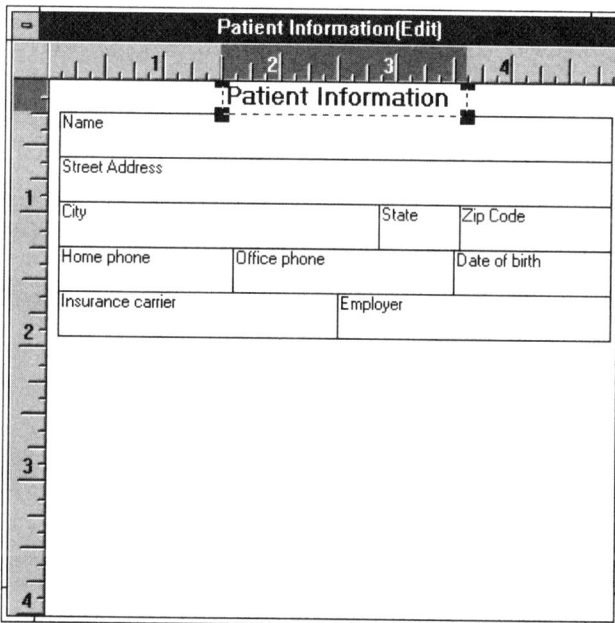

6-7
The arrangement of fields on the patient information form.

One type of field is the picture field. You want to assign this field type to fields whose contents are very specific and limited. They are also useful for preventing incorrect data from being entered in a field. A good example of a picture field is a telephone number, which, in the U.S., always consists of a three-digit area code and a seven-digit local number. With a picture field, you

Defining picture fields

Alignment...
Label **F**ont...
Val**u**e Font...
Color...
Borders...
Line **W**idth...
Pr**o**tection...
Value Tree
Event Tree
Fiel**d**...
Name/**T**ext...
Help...

6-8 *The property list with Field Type selected.*

can instruct the program to accept only numbers, and only the correct number of digits in the correct format.

Let's make that Home Phone field a picture field. Point to the field and click the right mouse button. The property list will be displayed (see FIG. 6-8).

Click on Field Type, and when the Field Type window shows up click in the diamond-shaped box next to Picture (see FIG. 6-9). Press OK, and the Picture String window will pop up, waiting for you to type in the string, or "picture," that will define (and constrain) this field (see FIG. 6-10).

Keep in mind that several specific characters have special significance in picture fields. To see what they are, click on the Help button in this window (see FIG. 6-11). Note particularly the match characters: If you insert the # symbol, the program will accept only a digit in that location; if you insert the & symbol, the program will accept only a letter and convert it to uppercase, etc.

6-9
The Field Type window with Picture selected.

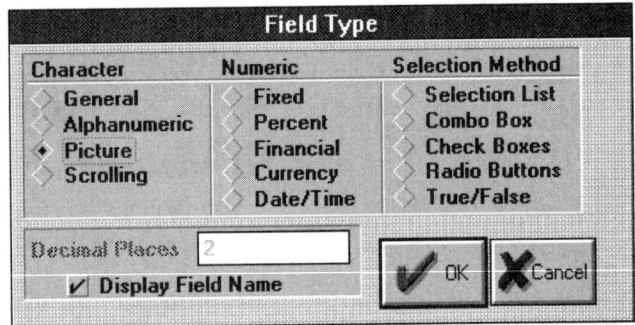

Field Type

Character	Numeric	Selection Method
General	Fixed	Selection List
Alphanumeric	Percent	Combo Box
♦ Picture	Financial	Check Boxes
Scrolling	Currency	Radio Buttons
	Date/Time	True/False

Decimal Places 2
☑ Display Field Name

✔ OK   ✘ Cancel

6-10
The Picture String window.

Picture String

Picture [   ]

✔ OK   ? Help   ✘ Cancel

Close the Help screen, click in the Picture String box, type in the following string:

(###) ### - ####

and then click on OK (see FIG. 6-12). When you return to the patient information form, the Home Phone field will be selected, and some new characters:

(___) ___ - ____

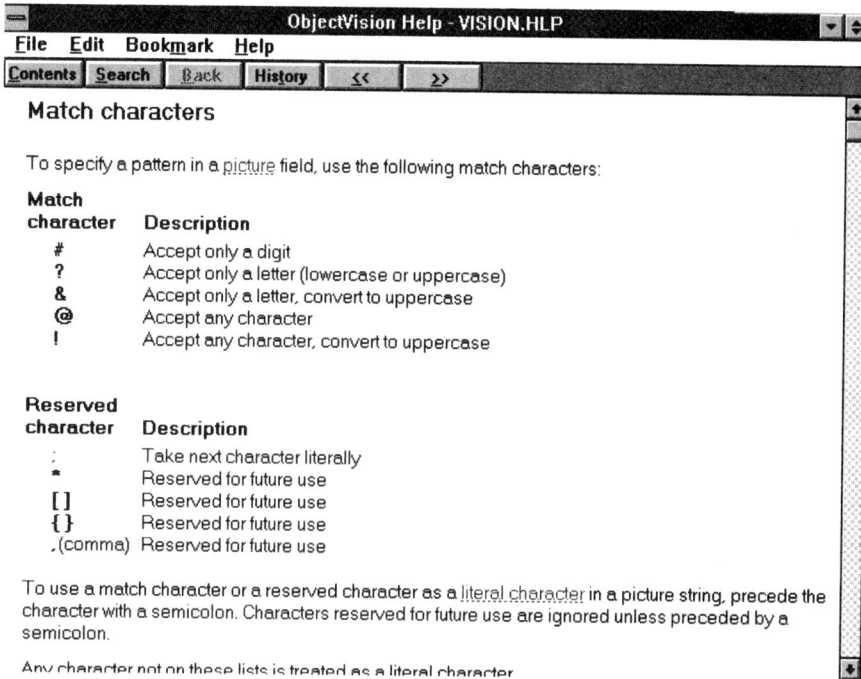

Match characters

To specify a pattern in a picture field, use the following match characters:

Match character	Description
#	Accept only a digit
?	Accept only a letter (lowercase or uppercase)
&	Accept only a letter, convert to uppercase
@	Accept any character
!	Accept any character, convert to uppercase

Reserved character	Description
;	Take next character literally
*	Reserved for future use
[]	Reserved for future use
{}	Reserved for future use
,(comma)	Reserved for future use

To use a match character or a reserved character as a literal character in a picture string, precede the character with a semicolon. Characters reserved for future use are ignored unless preceded by a semicolon.

Any character not on these lists is treated as a literal character

6-11
The Help screen for the Picture String window.

6-12
The Picture String window with the telephone-number string entered.

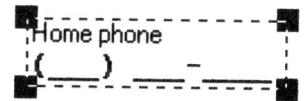

6-13 *The Home Phone field with its new format.*

will have been added (see FIG. 6-13). The underscores mark the locations where the numerals or digits should be inserted. No other numbers will be accepted in this field, and no characters other than numerals will be accepted at all.

Want to make Office Phone a picture field as well? You can repeat the procedure you just learned, or you can take a nifty shortcut: Click on the Office Phone field to select it, and then press F4. (You can also select Object from the Properties menu, and then select Repeat from the Object menu. But pressing F4 is easier.) This procedure works for only one property at a time; you can't reproduce all of a field's properties in another field with this technique.

Using the Repeat function

Other types of picture fields

You can also make the State and Zip Code fields picture fields. You want to limit entries in the State field to two uppercase letters, so the string to enter in the Picture String window is &&, which means the field will accept only two letters (no numbers) and convert them to uppercase (see FIG. 6-14).

6-14
The Picture String window for the State field with the correct string entered.

Picture String

Picture &&

✔ OK   ? Help   ✗ Cancel

In a similar fashion, you can make the Zip Code field a picture field that accepts only five digits (let's forget the Postal Service's nine-digit zip codes for now) by entering ##### as the picture string (see FIG. 6-15).

6-15
The Picture String window for the Zip Code field with the correct string entered.

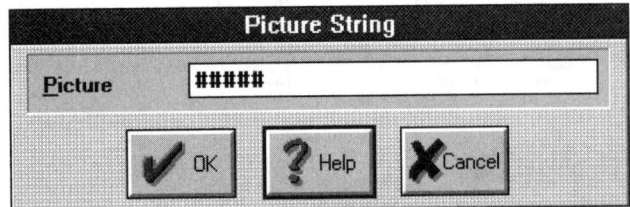

Picture String

Picture #####

✔ OK   ? Help   ✗ Cancel

That takes care of the fields for the patient information form—unless you want to add a combo box field for the Insurance Carrier field.

Adding a button object

Buttons on a form are handy for making things happen quickly and easily. For example, you might want to clear this patient information form with one stroke—perhaps because the patient moved away or died, or for whatever reason should no longer be in this physician's practice database. You can install a button to do that job.

Or perhaps you've finished filling out a patient information form, and you want to save that data to your database and move on to the next patient. Or you want to return quickly to the main, or goal, form of the application. A button will do that for you as well.

Let's create those three buttons and place them on this patient information form. To begin, click on the button tool on the object bar to open the Button Name window (see FIG. 6-16). This first button is going to be the Clear button, so type Clear in the Button Name box, and then click on OK. The mouse pointer will change into a miniature button tool with a crosshair. Position the crosshair where you want the upper left-hand corner of the button to be, and

—Button tool

6-16
The button tool with the Button Name window.

click the left mouse button. The Clear button will appear on your patient information form at the location you've designated (see FIG. 6-17).

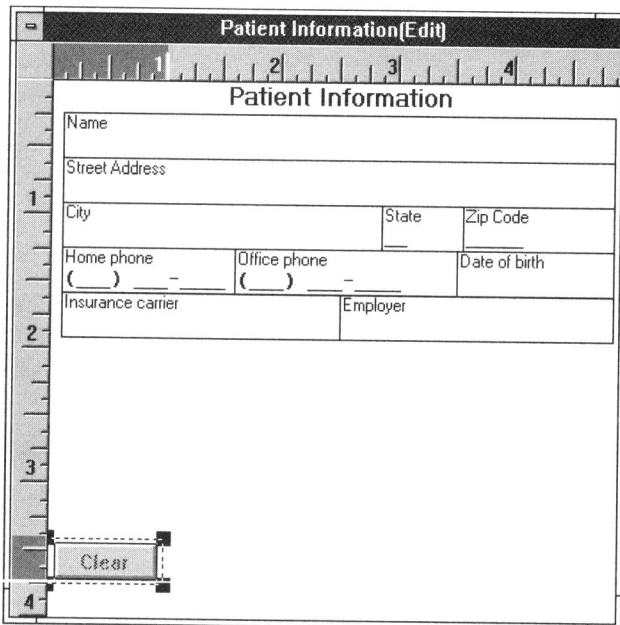

6-17
The Clear button placed on the patient information form.

Following this same procedure, create a button called Save and Clear, another one with the name Return to PV Form. Place them adjacent to the first button on the form, and make any size adjustments necessary to read all of the text on the buttons. Press the Close Tool button to return to runtime mode, and your patient information form, at its current stage of evolution, should resemble FIG. 6-18.

That's all there is to placing buttons on a form. Of course, you can click on them until your mouse squeaks and nothing will happen, because making those buttons work is a whole other story. We'll get to that soon; first, however, you're going to get acquainted with table objects.

6-18
The patient information form with three new buttons.

7 *Working with table objects*

Part of what will need to be included on the form is vital data: a record of the patient's weight, respiratory rate, pulse rate, and blood pressure at the time of the visit.

Of course, you could supply fields for filling in that information (and you will), but that information is an important part of the patient's history over time, as he makes repeated visits to the physician. It would be handy, therefore, to have a record of the vital data on the date of each visit in some sort of table, so that the physician could see at a glance, for example, what had happened to the patient's weight and blood pressure over the last five years.

Well, ObjectVision makes it easy for you to put a table like that on one of the forms in your application—but you'll need to put it on the patient information form (because the patient visit form is for recording the vital data from one visit only, not the whole history).

The table object provided in ObjectVision is easy to use and versatile. It lets you set up as many columns and rows as you want; you can also format columns and assign field types, fonts, column headings, etc. But enough talk; let's do it.

You're going to create a table for vital data on the patient information form; it will allow the physician to record the date of each visit, along with the

Form
Se**l**ect...
C**l**ear

7-1 *The*
Form menu
with Select
selected.

patient's pulse, respiratory rate, weight, and blood pressure. That means five columns, and we'll create four rows for data entry.

With ObjectVision open and your budding application loaded, pull down the Form menu and choose Select (see FIG. 7-1). When you do, the Form Name window will open, with the names of the two forms created so far (see FIG. 7-2). Select the patient information form, click OK, and the new form you created in chapter 6 will appear (see FIG. 7-3).

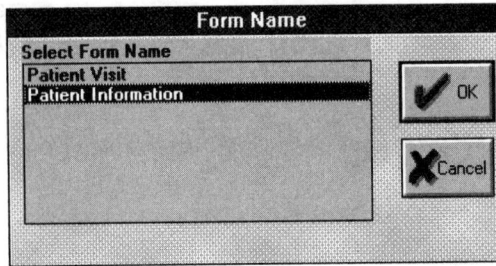

Form Name

Select Form Name
Patient Visit
Patient Information

✓ OK

✗ Cancel

7-2
The Form Name window.

Patient Information (Goal)

Patient Information

Name				
Street Address				Apartment No
City			State	Zip Code
Home phone	Office phone		Extension	Date of birth
Insurance carrier		Employer		

Clear   Save and Clear   Return to PV Form

7-3
The partially completed patient information form.

Open the Tools menu and select Form in order to shift into the edit mode and display the object bar. Now click on the table tool, the fourth button from the left in the object bar—the one that looks like a little spreadsheet. When you do, the Table Name window will pop up, waiting for you to give this new table a name. Type `Vital Data` as the name for your new table (see FIG. 7-4). Click on OK, and the mouse pointer will be transmogrified into a little table-tool icon with a cross hair. Position the cross hair just below the lower left-hand corner of the Insurance Carrier field and click. You'll see the nucleus of the vital data table, with table name, one column, and one cell for data (see FIG. 7-5).

There are four objects on the selected table that you'll use to size the table:

- When you drag the right-pointing arrow on the right, you change the number of columns to the right of Column 1.
- When you drag the right-pointing arrow on the left toward the right of your screen, you change the number of columns in front of Column 1.
- When you drag the top selection handle, you change the height of the table title area.
- When you drag the bottom selection handle, you change the number of rows.

—Table tool

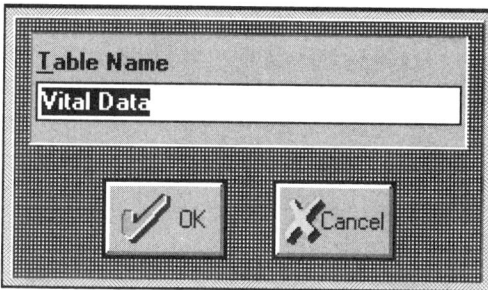

7-4
The table tool and Table Name window, with Vital Data entered as the new table's name.

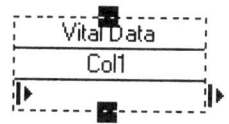

7-5 *The beginnings of the vital data table.*

It's time to create five columns for data. Point to the right-hand arrow (until your mouse pointer itself becomes a right-pointing arrow), depress the left mouse button, and drag to the right. You'll see an outline of the new row as you drag. Release the left mouse button, and your second column will appear (see FIG. 7-6). Continue until there are five columns (see FIG. 7-7). Don't worry about column widths at this point.

Adding columns to a table

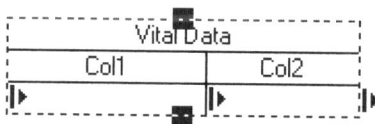

7-6
The new table with a second column added.

Now for the four empty data rows in the table. To add rows, point to the bottom selection handle until the mouse pointer becomes a selection handle, depress the left mouse button, and drag downward. As you drag, you'll see a

Adding rows to a table

Vital Data				
Col1	Col2	Col3	Col4	Col5

number in the upper left-hand corner of the table telling you how many rows you have in the table. Add four rows (see FIG. 7-8).

7-8

The vital data table with five rows.

Vital Data				
Col1	Col2	Col3	Col4	Col5

Assigning column headings, fonts, & field types

Now you'll want to give the columns their correct headings. An important thing to remember here is that columns in a table are essentially fields. They have many of the same properties as field objects, and can be edited and manipulated in much the same way. To select a column, click on the column heading; the column alone will be outlined by a dotted line with selection handles at the four corners (see FIG. 7-9).

Vital Data				
Col1	Col2	Col3	Col4	Col5

7-9

Column 1 selected.

Field Type...
Alignment...
Label Font...
Color...
Protection...
Value Tree
Event Tree
Name/Text...
Help...

7-10 *The property list for Column 1.*

Position the mouse pointer within that outlined Column 1 area and click the right mouse button. Sure enough, a property list will pop up, displaying most of the properties you're used to seeing for field objects (see FIG. 7-10).

Right now, you're going to do three things: Give the column a new heading or label, give that heading a new font, and stipulate a field type for this column.

Select Name/Text from the property list. When you do, a Field Name window will be displayed, showing that the current name for this field is Col1. Replace that by typing Visit Date, and your Field Name window will look like FIG. 7-11. Click on OK, and your new heading will appear at the top of the first column (see FIG. 7-12).

Field Name

Visit Date

[✓ OK] [✗ Cancel]

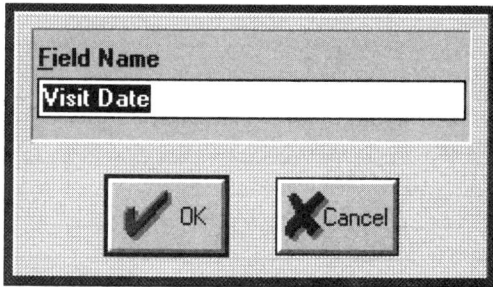

7-11
*The Field Name window
with the column heading.*

Vital Data				
Visit Date	Col2	Col3	Col4	Col5

7-12
*The first column with its new
heading.*

Right-click to bring up the property inspector again, and this time select
Label Font. The Label Font window will pop up, showing that the current
font is Helvetica 8 (your current font might be different). Change that to
Helvetica 10 Bold by clicking on the appropriate choices (see FIG. 7-13). Click
on OK, and your Column 1 heading will have a new look (see FIG. 7-14).

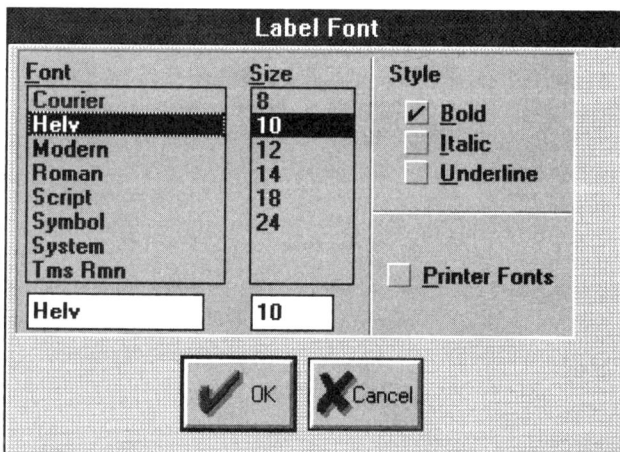

Label Font

Font	Size	Style
Courier	8	✓ **Bold**
Helv	10	☐ **Italic**
Modern	12	☐ **Underline**
Roman	14	
Script	18	
Symbol	24	
System		
Tms Rmn		

Helv   10

☐ **Printer Fonts**

[✓ OK] [✗ Cancel]

7-13
*The Label Font window with
Helvetica 10 Bold selected.*

Vital Data				
Visit Date	Col2	Col3	Col4	Col5

7-14
*The Column 1 heading in its new
font, size, and style.*

Now here's a handy little time-saver. The property repeat function, which you can activate by either selecting Repeat from the property list or pressing the F4 key, will repeat the last property you assigned. Just that one; no other. Because you just made a font assignment, click on the heading for Column 2 and then press F4—and Col2 will have a new font (see FIG. 7-15). Not a new name, because you can repeat only one property (in this case, the label font) at a time. Repeat this process for the remaining three columns. How's that for increasing your productivity?

7-15
Column 2 with the same new font assigned.

Vital Data				
Visit Date	**Col2**	Col3	Col4	Col5

Now return to that first column, select it by clicking on the column heading, and call up the property list. Select Field Type and the now-familiar Field Type window will appear (see FIG. 7-16). This column records the date of the patient's visits, so use the date/time field type. Select Date/Time, click on OK, and the Date Type window will pop up. This time choose the first format option: 8/1/90 (see FIG. 7-17). Press OK, and your column will be formatted—although you can't see any evidence of that right now.

7-16
The Field Type window with Date/Time selected.

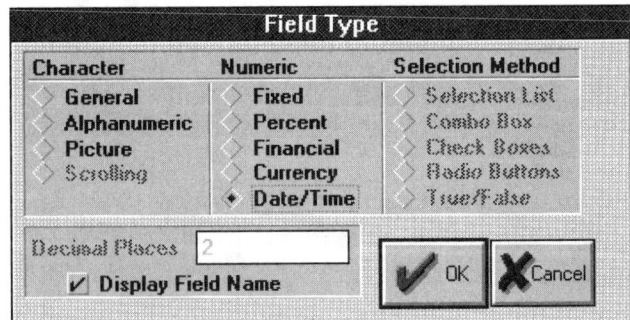

Field Type		
Character	**Numeric**	**Selection Method**
◇ General	◇ Fixed	◇ Selection List
◇ Alphanumeric	◇ Percent	◇ Combo Box
◇ Picture	◇ Financial	◇ Check Boxes
◇ Scrolling	◇ Currency	◇ Radio Buttons
	◆ Date/Time	◇ True/False

Decimal Places [2]
✓ Display Field Name
✓ OK   ✗ Cancel

To practice your newly acquired table skills, change the heading in Column 2 to Pulse, Column 3 to Respiration, Column 4 to Weight, and Column 5 to Blood Pressure, and make them all fixed numeric fields with 0 decimal places. When you're finished, your new table might look something like FIG. 7-18, with some headings not fully shown.

Adjusting column width To remedy that problem, you'll need to adjust your column widths across the form.

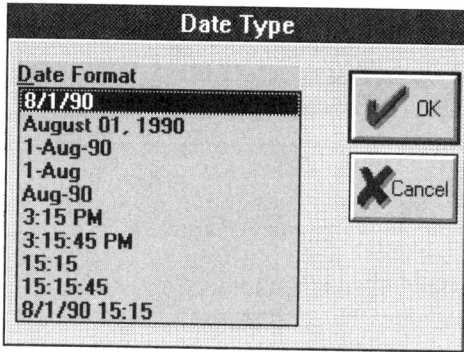

7-17
The Date Type window with 8/1/90 selected as the date format.

7-18
The vital data table with new column headings—some of which don't fit.

Click on one of the empty cells in the first column. When it's correctly selected, it will look like FIG. 7-19. Adjust the column width by dragging the selection handles to the right or left until the column is no bigger than necessary to display the column heading Visit Date. (If one of the words disappears, you'll know you went too far.) Do the same for each column until all the column headings are visible and the table is exactly as wide as the fields immediately above it (see FIG. 7-20).

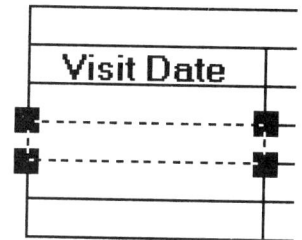

7-19 *A cell in the first column selected.*

7-20
The table with column widths adjusted.

One more thing for now—increase the height of the table title area and make the font bigger. Click on the title, Vital Data, and the table selection indicators should look like those in FIG. 7-21. This time, drag the top selection handle upward until the top of the table coincides with the bottom of the Insurance Carrier field (see FIG. 7-22).

To change the font and size of the title, click on the title and, when the table is selected, click the right mouse button. Here's a smaller property list; it will let you tinker with only five attributes of the table (see FIG. 7-23). Select Label

Changing the table title font

Vital Data				
Visit Date	Pulse	Respiration	Weight	Blood Pressure
▶	▶	▶	▶	▶

Patient Information

Name			
Street Address			Apartment No
City		State	Zip Code

Home phone	Office phone	Extension	Date of birth
(___) ___ - ___	(___) ___ - ___		
Insurance carrier	Employer		

Vital Data				
Visit Date	Pulse	Respiration	Weight	Blood Pressure

Label **F**ont...
Color...
Line Width...
Name/Text...
ScrollBar

Font, and when its window is displayed select Helvetica 12 Bold. Click on OK, and your table work is finished for the moment. Save your work by selecting Save from the File menu, and then press the close tool to return to runtime mode. Your new patient information form should look very much like FIG. 7-24.

This is looking good. The only trouble is that, although you can enter data on the forms, you can't make anything happen. For example, if you push the Return to PV Form button, you won't return to the patient visit form. You have to program these buttons—and fields and tables—to make things happen. In ObjectVision, that sort of programming is done via event trees. Guess what you're going to learn to do in chapter 8 . . .

Patient Information (Goal)

Patient Information

Name	
Street Address	Apartment No
City	State / Zip Code
Home phone / Office phone	Extension / Date of birth
Insurance carrier	Employer

Vital Data

Visit Date	Pulse	Respiration	Weight	Blood Pressure

[Clear] [Save and Clear] [Return to PV Form]

7-24
The patient information form in runtime mode, with the new vital data table.

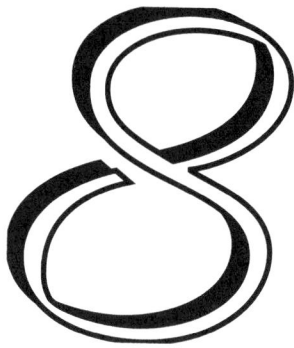

8 *Making things happen with event trees*

So far, you have two aesthetically pleasing forms in this application. It looks good, but it doesn't do anything. This chapter will show you how to change all that.

Load ObjectVision, then the patient visit form. From the Form menu choose Select, and when the Form Name window pops up, select the patient information form and click on OK. Before you do anything else, type your name, street address, city, and state into the appropriate fields (see FIG. 8-1). Now move into the edit mode by selecting Form from the Tools menu.

An event tree is a type of decision tree that triggers an action when a prescribed event takes place. For example, you can program the following command into the clear button on the patient information form: *When the button is clicked, clear all values (data) from the form.*

That's a fairly simple event tree. Move to the patient visit form and look at the first field. This is a radio button field—remember? You have two choices, and what you choose will determine what happens next. The choices are New and Prior, for new patient and prior patient. This field might be called an if . . . then field, because it says: *If the patient is a new patient then you do one thing, but if the patient is a prior patient then you do something else.* That's a somewhat more complex event tree. Let's plunge right in with those two.

8-1

The patient information form with a name and address entered in the appropriate fields.

Assigning an event tree to a button

Bring back the patient information form. You're going to take the Clear button at the bottom of the form and assign an action to it, e.g., to clear all values from the form. The event associated with this button, as with most buttons, is a click. When you click the button, something is supposed to happen.

You can get to the event tree for that Clear button in two ways. You can point to the button and click the right mouse button, which will expose the property list for that button (see FIG. 8-2). Then click on Event Tree, and the event tree for the Clear window will emerge (see FIG. 8-3). Or you can simply click twice on the Clear button, and the event tree for the Clear button will pop up.

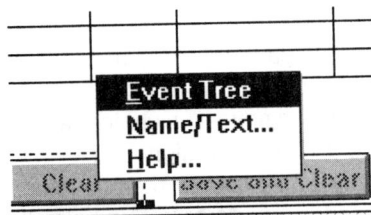

8-2

The property list for the Clear button.

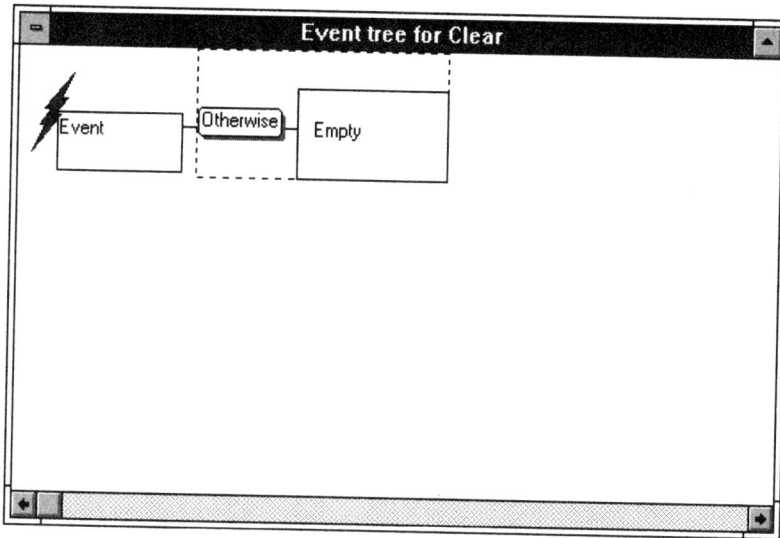

8-3
The event tree window for the Clear button.

Notice that, when you open the event tree, a new object bar appears at the top of your screen under the menu bar. This object bar has the now-familiar close tool, plus four new tools:

The event tree object bar

Branch The branch tool lets you put a branch in your event tree at a point you select (see FIG. 8-4A).

Conclusion The conclusion tool lets you put a condition and its conclusion at a point you select (see FIG. 8-4B).

Expand The expand tool lets you expand the event tree (see FIG. 8-4C). This is similar to a zoom function.

Reduce The reduce tool lets you reduce the event tree so that more of it is visible in the Event Tree window (see FIG. 8-4D).

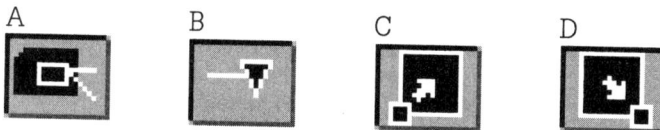

8-4
Four new tools on the event-tree object bar: A) branch, B) conclusion, C) expand, and D) reduce.

There is also a new menu bar on your ObjectVision screen. You should be familiar with some of its menus:

The event tree menu bar

File menu This is essentially the same as previous File menus, although it has a separate Print Tree option that's available if you want a printout of a specific decision tree (see FIG. 8-5).

File
Save
Save **As**...

Print Tree
Print All
Printer Setup

Close Tool

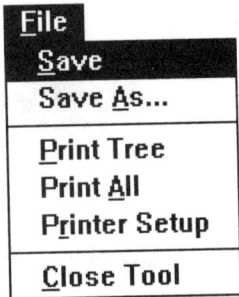

8-5 *The File menu.*

Edit
Undo   Alt+Bksp

Cut   Shift+Del
Copy   Ctrl+Ins
Paste   Shift+Ins
Clear   Del

8-6 *The Edit menu.*

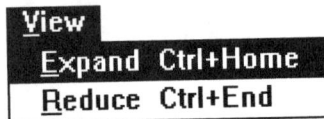

Tree
Select...
Find...

8-7 *The Tree menu.*

Objects
Branch...
Conclusion...

8-8 *The Objects menu.*

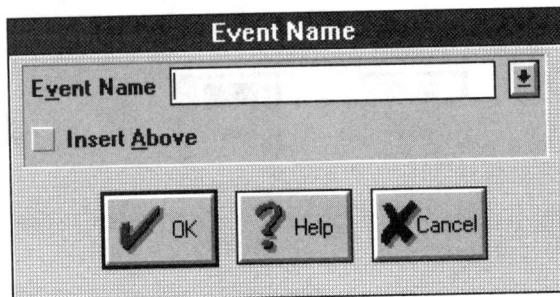

Properties
Field...
Condition...
Conclusion...
Name...

8-9 *The Properties menu.*

Edit menu   This is like those you have seen before; there are no new items or surprises here (see FIG. 8-6).

Tree menu   This is new; it allows you to either select the event tree for the field you specify, or find the next reference to that specified field in an event tree (see FIG. 8-7).

Objects menu   This gives you access to the same two tree tools as the buttons on the object bar: the branch tool and the conclusion tool (see FIG. 8-8). (Refer to the previous section, *The event tree object bar.*)

Properties menu   You've also seen this menu before; it has two elements, however, that are specific to trees: Condition, which shows you which condition (click, select, etc.) is prescribed for the current tree, and Conclusion, which tells you what happens when that condition is met (see FIG. 8-9).

View menu   This menu lets you expand or reduce your view of the event tree, just as the Expand and Reduce buttons on the object bar do (see FIG. 8-10).

View
Expand Ctrl+Home
Reduce Ctrl+End

8-10
The View menu.

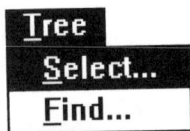

The next step is to click on the conclusion tool so you can name the event. When you do, the Event Name box will open (see FIG. 8-11). If you click on the Selection button in the Event Name box, you'll be offered three choices: Click, Select, and Unselect (see FIG. 8-12). Select Click as the action or event to trigger the result you want.

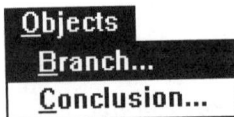

Event Name

Event Name [   ]

Insert **Above**

✔ OK   ? Help   ✗ Cancel

8-11
The Event Name box.

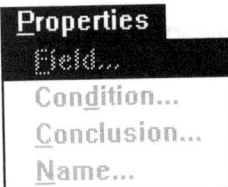

Now that you've chosen the trigger event, the program will prompt you to specify the action that should take place. You're going to enter the instructions for this action in the Action window, which in this specific case is called the Action for Clear window (see FIG. 8-13).

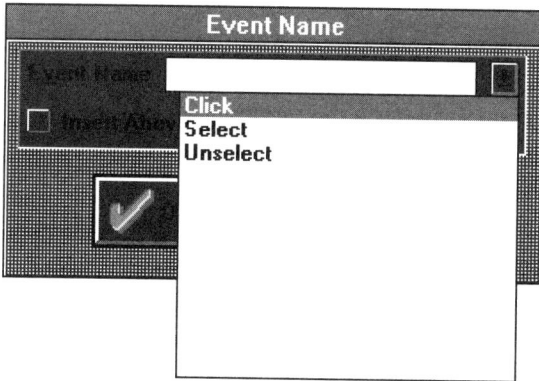

8-12
The selection list in the Event Name box.

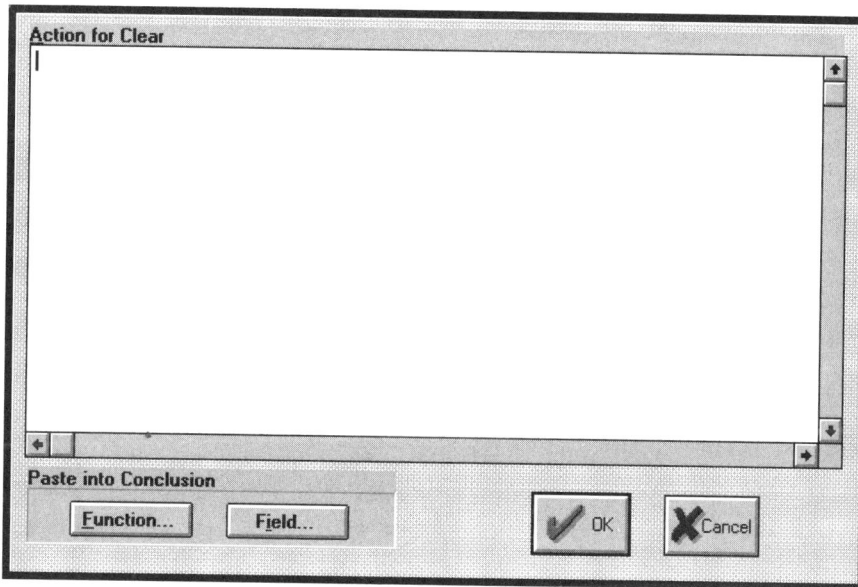

8-13
The Action for Clear window.

At the bottom of the Action for Clear window are two buttons: Function and Field. Clicking on the Function button will take you to the Function Name window, where you can select from a long list of possible actions or functions (see FIG. 8-14).

If you scroll through the function choices, you'll discover a Clear, Clearall, and Formclear option. Which is the right one to use here? Here's where the program's on-line help comes in handy. To shed some light on the three functions @CLEAR, @CLEARALL, and @FORMCLEAR, click on the Help button in the Function Name window.

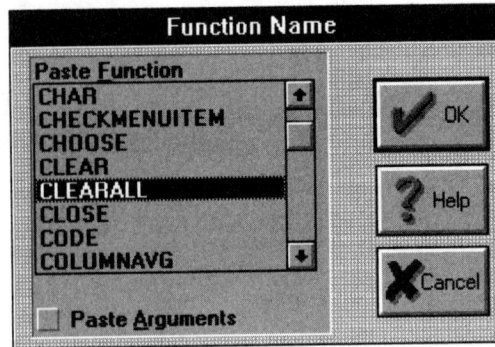

8-14
A partial listing of the functions in the Function Name window, with @CLEARALL selected.

The first thing you'll get is a window with an index of all of the @ functions (see FIG. 8-15). You might be familiar with these functions from spreadsheet software, where you use mathematical @ functions such as @SUM to perform calculations. There is a long list of various types of @ functions, many more than we'll attempt to deal with in this trial spin.

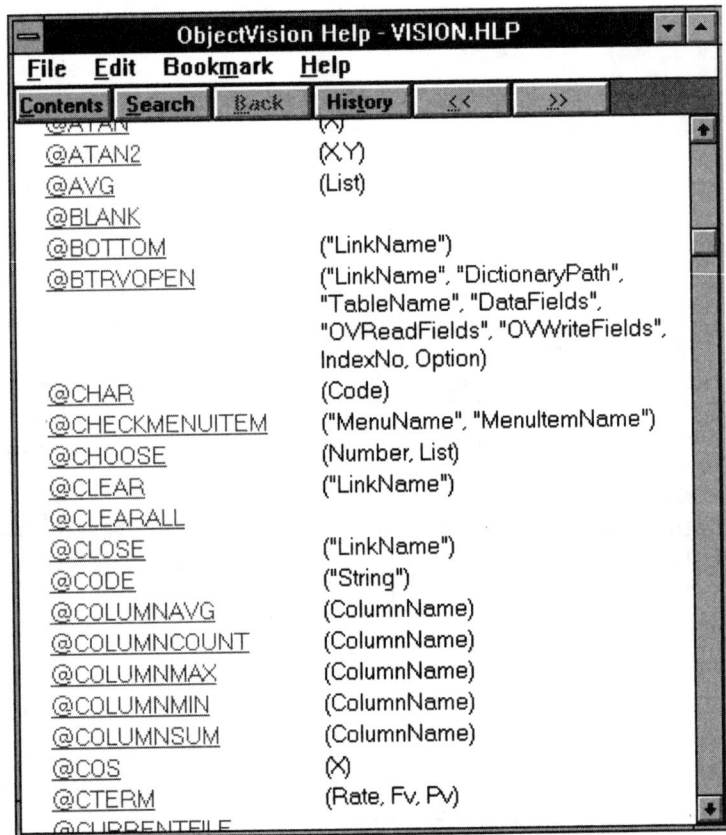

8-15
The Help screen for the Function Name window.

Simply scroll until you see the function you want, and then point and click. For example, if you point at @CLEAR (notice that the mouse pointer becomes a hand with a pointing finger as you approach one of the hot words shown in green on color screens) and press the left mouse button, a new window explaining @CLEAR in detail will pop up (see FIG. 8-16). You can use this same procedure to get explanations for @CLEARALL and @FORMCLEAR (see FIGS. 8-17 and 8-18).

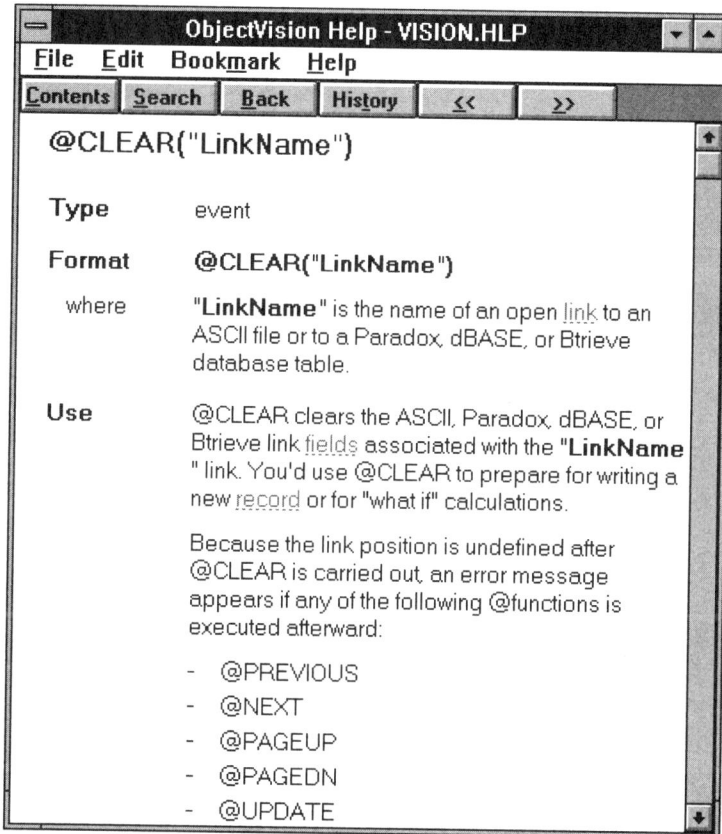

```
┌──────────────────────────────────────────────────────┐
│ ─        ObjectVision Help - VISION.HLP         ▼ ▲   │
├──────────────────────────────────────────────────────┤
│ File   Edit   Bookmark   Help                          │
├──────────────────────────────────────────────────────┤
│ Contents │ Search │ Back │ History │  <<  │   >>   │   │
├──────────────────────────────────────────────────────┤
│ @CLEAR("LinkName")                                  ▲  │
│                                                        │
│ Type       event                                       │
│                                                        │
│ Format     @CLEAR("LinkName")                          │
│                                                        │
│ where      "LinkName" is the name of an open link to an│
│            ASCII file or to a Paradox, dBASE, or Btrieve│
│            database table.                             │
│                                                        │
│ Use        @CLEAR clears the ASCII, Paradox, dBASE, or │
│            Btrieve link fields associated with the     │
│            "LinkName" link. You'd use @CLEAR to prepare│
│            for writing a new record or for "what if"   │
│            calculations.                               │
│                                                        │
│            Because the link position is undefined after│
│            @CLEAR is carried out, an error message     │
│            appears if any of the following @functions is│
│            executed afterward:                         │
│                                                        │
│            -  @PREVIOUS                                 │
│            -  @NEXT                                     │
│            -  @PAGEUP                                   │
│            -  @PAGEDN                                   │
│            -  @UPDATE                                ▼  │
└──────────────────────────────────────────────────────┘
```

8-16
The Help screen for @CLEAR.

Notice that the @CLEAR and @FORMCLEAR functions are both followed by additional text enclosed in parentheses. This additional text is called the argument, and is required in order for the function to work. In the case of @FORMCLEAR, for example, the argument is "FormName"—in other words, the program expects you to enter the name of a specific form that you want to clear. To clear the current patient information form, the correct format for the @ function would be @FORMCLEAR("Patient Information").

The @CLEAR function also requires an argument, but it's really concerned with clearing links to database tables. That isn't what we're doing right now, so @CLEAR isn't the correct function.

ObjectVision Help - VISION.HLP

File   Edit   Bookmark   Help

| Contents | Search | Back | History | << | >> |

@CLEARALL

Type   event

Format   **@CLEARALL**

Use   This function works like Edit | ClearAll—it clears all
             the values in a form except constant values returned
             by a value tree, such as @TODAY in a date field.

             DDE-linked values are not cleared.

             Calculated fields are only cleared if the fields from
             which their calculations are made are cleared—for
             example, from a tree that uses constant values. In
             this case, the trees are reevaluated.

8-17

The Help screen for @CLEARALL.

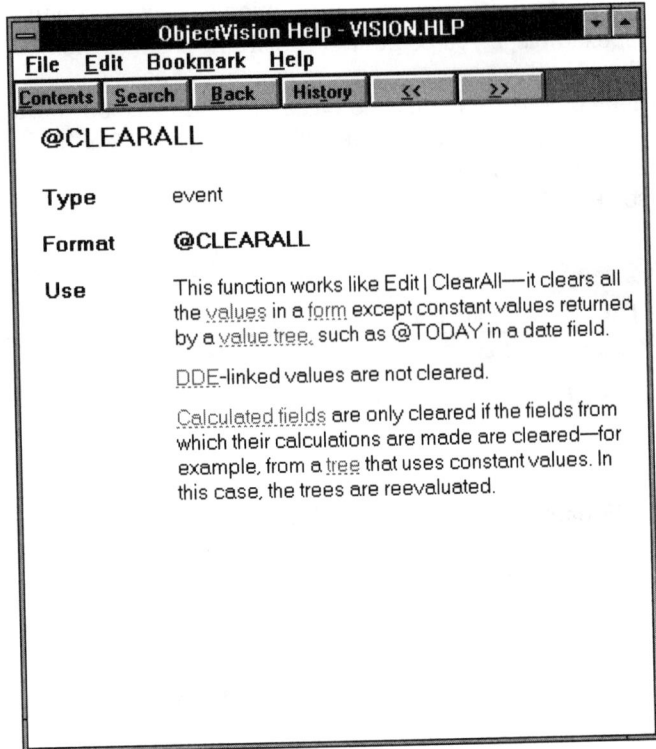

ObjectVision Help - VISION.HLP

File   Edit   Bookmark   Help

| Contents | Search | Back | History | << | >> |

@FORMCLEAR("FormName")

Type   event

Format   **@FORMCLEAR("FormName")**

where   **"FormName"** is the name of the form you want to
             clear.

Use   This function works like Form | Clear from the main
             menu except instead of clearing the current form, it
             clears the form you specify in **"FormName"**.

             If you use the value in a field as **FormName**, don't
             enclose it in quotes.

Examples

   @FORMCLEAR("Sales Order") clears the Sales Order form.

   @FORMCLEAR(Form to Clear) clears the form named in
   the field Form to Clear.

8-18

*The Help screen for
@FORMCLEAR.*

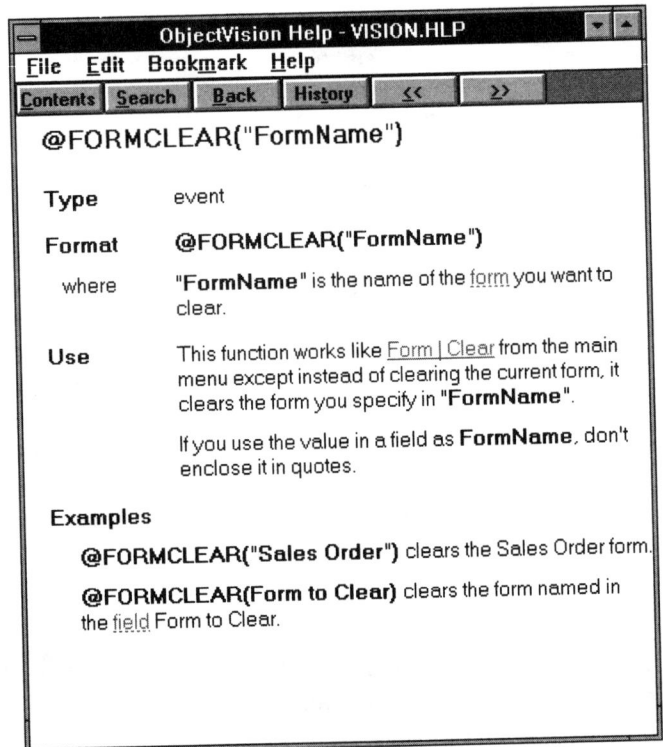

No argument is required with the @CLEARALL function; it simply clears all values in the application. Note: the Help screen says this function "clears all the values in a form . . ." In fact, it clears all values in the entire application, so watch out for this one.

Actually, @CLEARALL is the function you want to use, so select @CLEARALL and click on OK. When you do, @CLEARALL will be entered in your Action for Clear window (see FIG. 8-19). Click on OK, and the event tree for the Clear button will be complete (see FIG. 8-20).

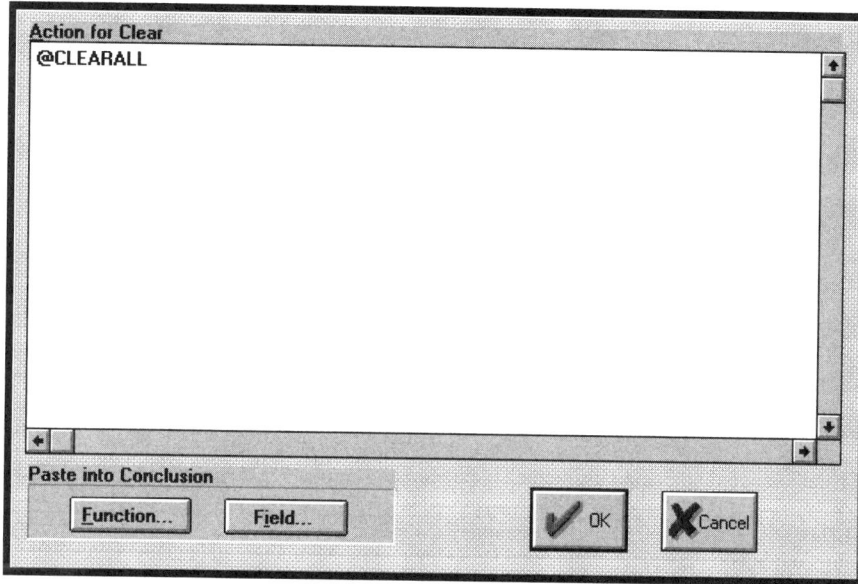

8-19
The Action for Clear window, with @CLEARALL entered as the action to be triggered by the Clear button.

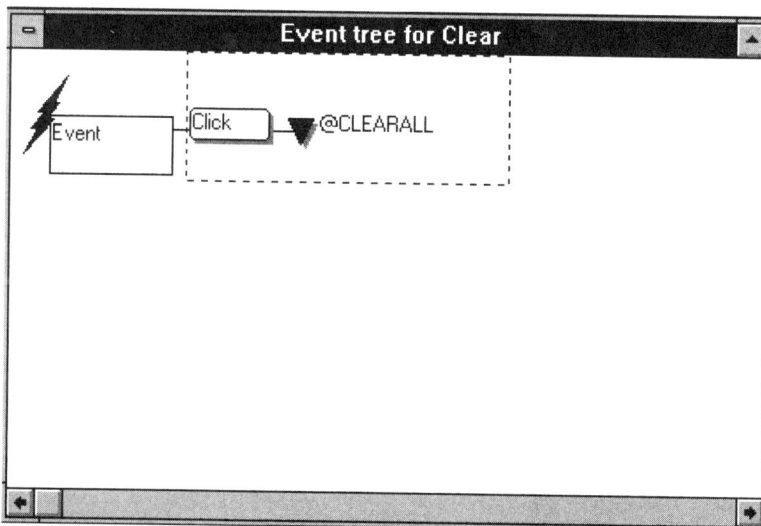

8-20
The finished event tree for the Clear button.

Close the Event Tree window, click on the Close Tool icon to return to runtime mode, and try clicking on the newly activated Clear button. When you do, it should clear the patient information form. And if you return to the patient visit form, you should find that it has been cleared as well (see FIG. 8-21).

8-21
The patient information form cleared after you press the Clear button.

Using an @ function with an argument

How's that for magic? You now have a working button; you're a real programmer.

Let's program another button, and this time we'll use an @ function that requires an argument. We'll program that Return to PV Form button.

Back at the patient information form in edit mode, click twice on the Return to PV Form button to bring up the Event Tree window (see FIG. 8-22). Now step through the procedure once more for practice; you're an old hand by now. Click on the conclusion tool and the Event Name window will pop up.

This event, like the one associated with the Clear button, is triggered by a click, so select Click as the event name (see FIG. 8-23). Click on OK, and the Action for Return to PV Form window will appear (see FIG. 8-24). Click on the Function button and scroll to find FORMSELECT in the Function Name selection list (see FIG. 8-25). Press OK, and @FORMSELECT("FormName") will be pasted in the Conclusion area of the Action for Return to PV Form window (see FIG. 8-26).

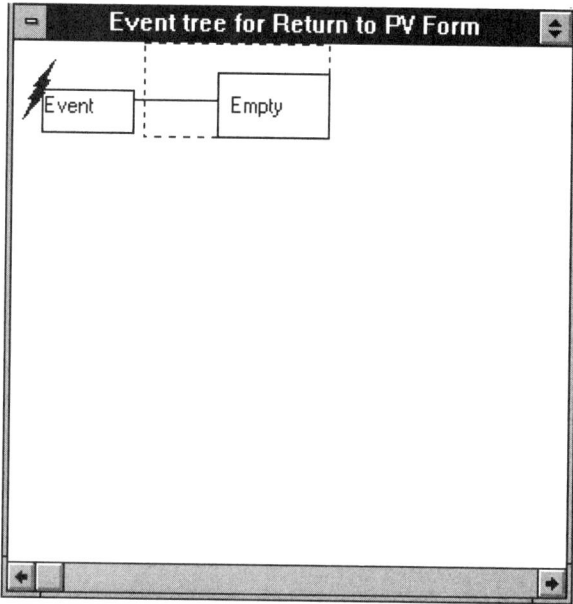

8-22
The Event Tree window for the Return to PV Form button.

8-23
The Event Name window with Click entered as the triggering event.

8-24
The Action for Return to PV Form window.

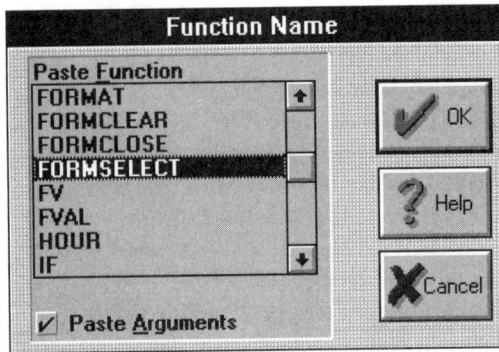

8-25
The Function Name window, with @FORMSELECT chosen as the @ function.

8-26
The Action for Return to PV Form window with @FORMSELECT pasted in.

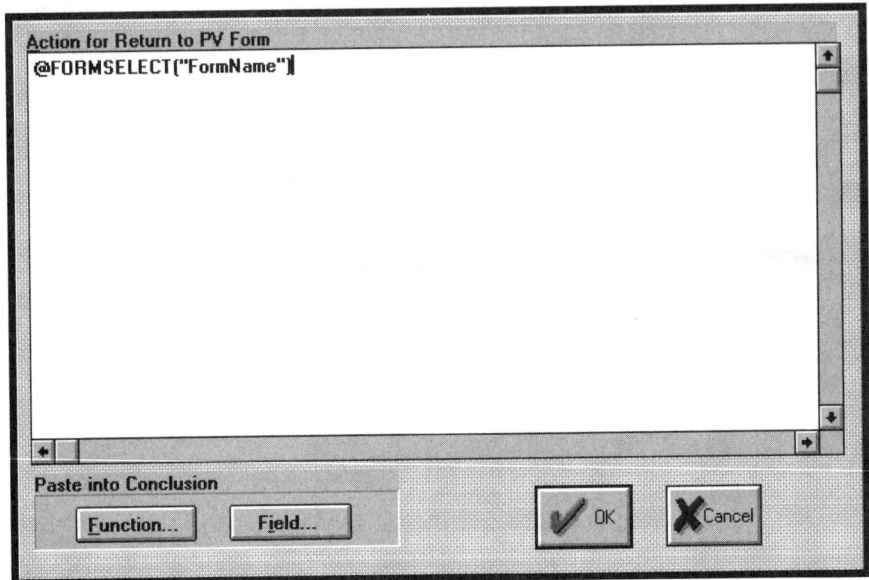

The program has highlighted "FormName" in the parentheses after @FORMSELECT; it's waiting for you to enter the argument—in this case, the name of the form (Patient Visit) that you want to return to. Be sure to put the form name in parentheses; the program won't recognize the command without them (see FIG. 8-27).

Click on OK, and your Event Tree window will reappear with the complete conclusion pasted in (see FIG. 8-28). Close the Event Tree window, return to runtime mode by clicking on the Close Tool button, and you're ready to test this newly activated button. When you click on the Return to PV Form button, you should return to the patient visit form.

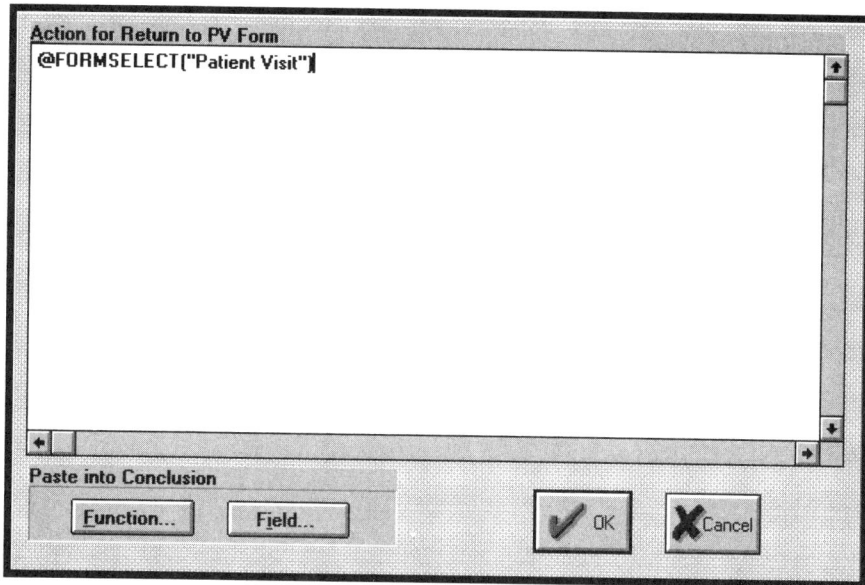

8-27
The @FORMSELECT command with the form name entered.

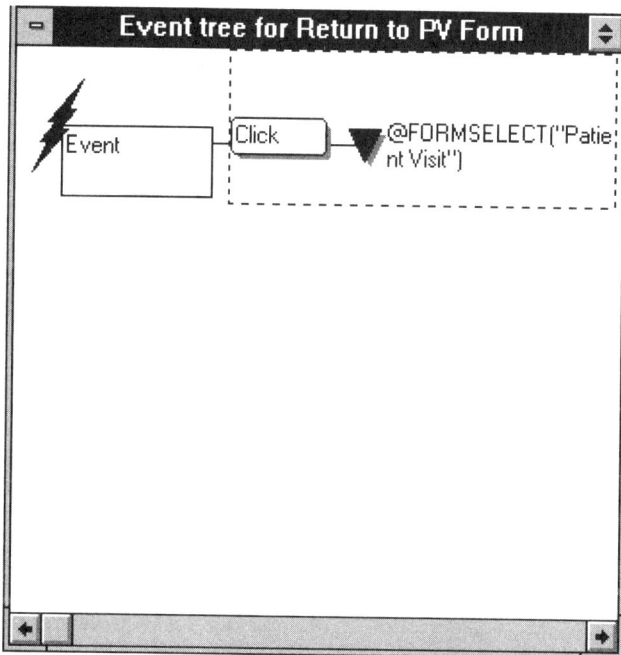

8-28
The event tree for Return to PV Form, with the complete @ function entered.

There are numerous other objects, both buttons and fields, that you might like to program right now, but they either involve values or links or both. So pat yourself on the back for reaching a new plateau in your programmer's learning curve, and we'll move on to value trees.

9 Creating value trees

If the event or action you want to program into a field, button, or some other object actually places, enters, or returns a value to some field, then the type of decision tree you need to create is called a value tree. (Remember that the term *value* refers to words or characters as well as numbers and numerical values.) Value trees can involve numerical calculations, such as the kind you might have experienced in spreadsheets with functions such as @SUM or @AVG. They can also involve calculations of the sort you don't think about much, but which are calculations nonetheless. For example, if you want to enter a date or someone's age, the expressions include or trigger simple calculations.

In this chapter, you'll create the value trees needed to enter values in three fields: Today's Date, Time, and Current Age. The Current Age field is the only one that requires a small calculation. Value trees are constructed much like event trees; let's begin with the Today's Date field.

Start up ObjectVision and load the patient visit form. To move to the edit mode, select Form from the Tools menu. Click on the Today's Date field to select it (see FIG. 9-1).

Now, if you'll recall, you can get to the Value Tree window in at least two ways. You can click twice with the left mouse button on the selected field, and the Value Tree window will appear as shown in FIG. 9-2 (you did that before to get to the Event Tree window for a button, but because this is a

Programming a field to enter today's date

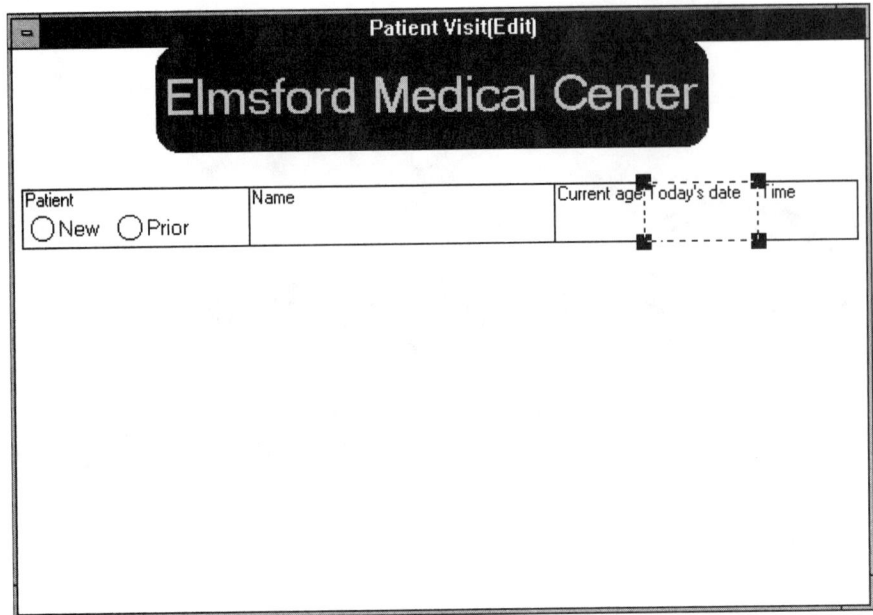

9-1
The patient visit form, with the Today's Date field selected.

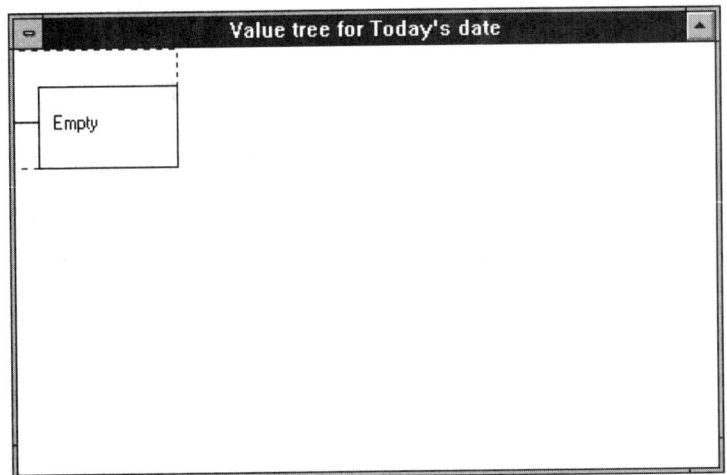

9-2
The value tree window for the Today's Date field.

field that must be filled with a value a value tree is called for). You can also click on the selected field with the right mouse button to bring up the field's property list (see FIG. 9-3). A third way is to select Object from the Properties menu, which will also display the property list (see FIG. 9-4).

By any of these means, call forth the Value Tree window for the Today's Date field. When it appears, proceed just as you did when you were creating event trees in the previous chapter. Click on the Conclusion button, and the Conclusion for Today's Date window will pop up (see FIG. 9-5). Click on the

Today's date   Time

Field Type...
Alignment...
Label Font...
Value Font...
Color...
Borders...
Line Width...
Protection...
Value Tree
Event Tree
Field...
Name/Text...
Help...

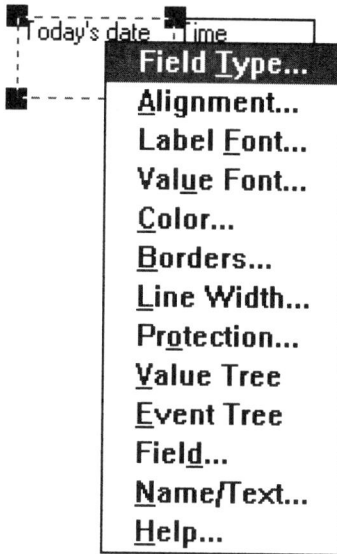

9-3
The property list for the Today's Date field.

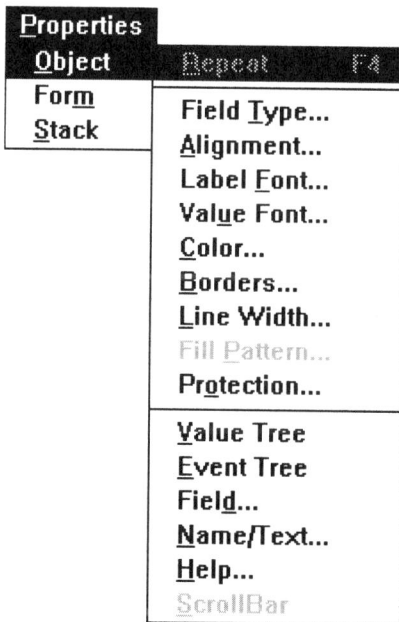

Properties
  Object   Repeat   F4
    Form
    Stack

Field Type...
Alignment...
Label Font...
Value Font...
Color...
Borders...
Line Width...
Fill Pattern...
Protection...

Value Tree
Event Tree
Field...
Name/Text...
Help...
ScrollBar

9-4
The Properties menu with object properties displayed.

Function button to bring up the Function Name window you saw when you were creating event trees, and scroll until you find the @NOW function in the selection list (see FIG. 9-6).

Click on OK, and the @NOW function will be pasted into the Conclusion for Today's Date window (see FIG. 9-7). Click on OK, and the @NOW function will

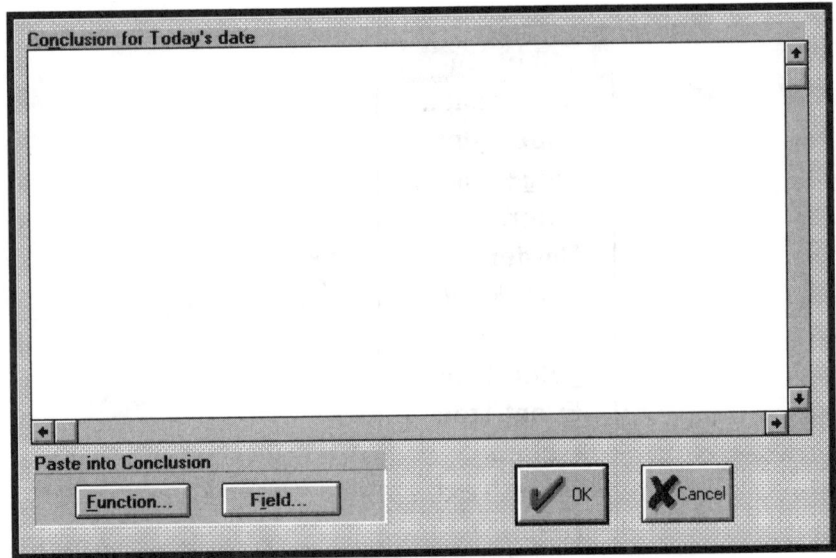

9-5
The Conclusion for Today's Date window.

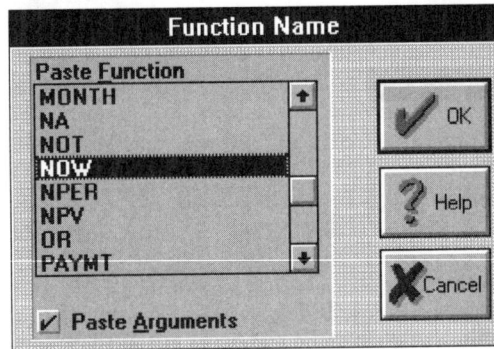

9-6
The @NOW function selected in the Function Name window.

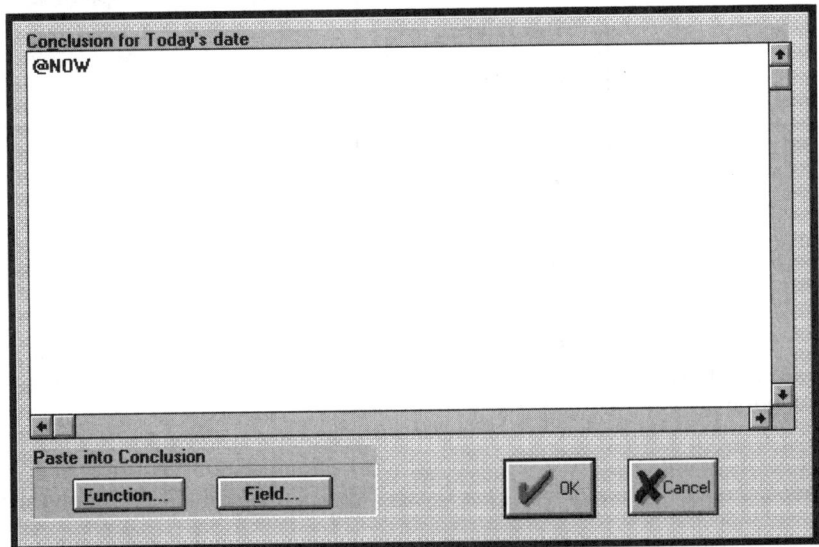

9-7
The @NOW function pasted into the Conclusion for Today's Date window.

appear in the value tree for the Today's Date field (see FIG. 9-8). Close the value tree, and the correct date should appear in your Today's Date field (see FIG. 9-9). You can return to runtime mode and try clearing the application, but the date will remain. And tomorrow, when you fire up ObjectVision and load the Patient Visit application, it will be all ready to go with tomorrow's date.

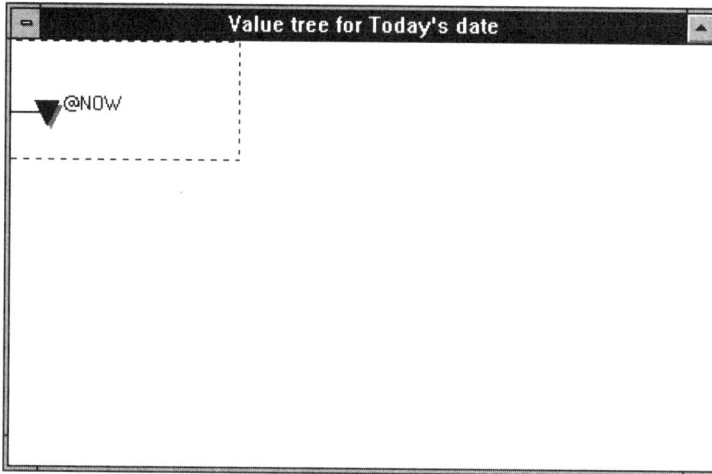

9-8
The value tree for the Today's Date field with @NOW installed.

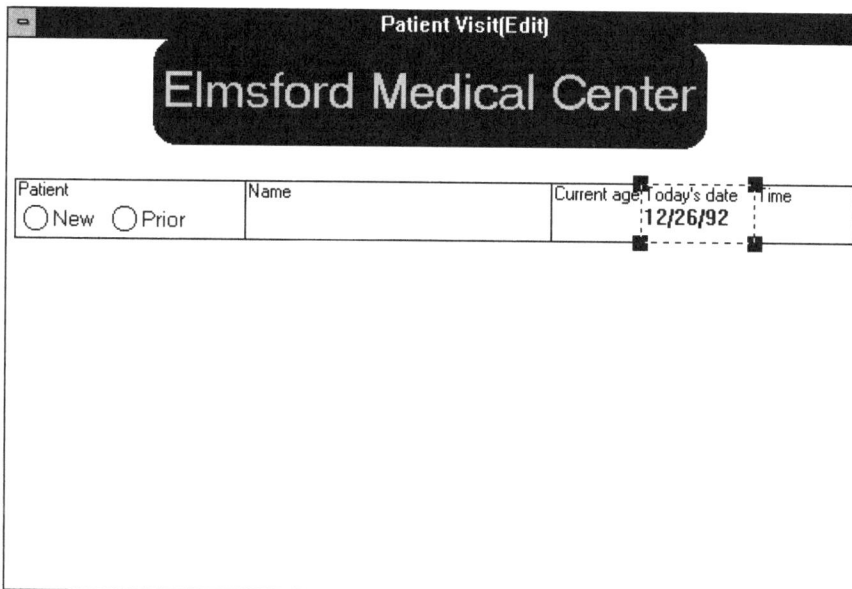

9-9
The Today's Date field with the date entered.

A word about how ObjectVision calculates dates. The program looks at your computer clock and retrieves a number corresponding to the date in this fashion: Dates from January 1, 1800 through the current date are represented by the number of elapsed days from January 1, 1900, with January 1, 1800

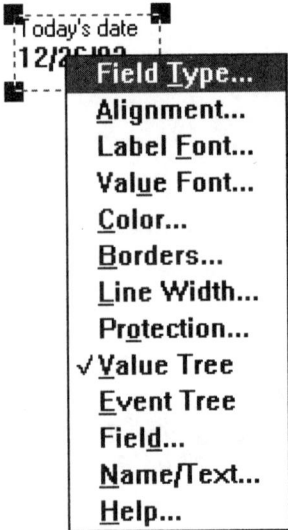

Field Type...
Alignment...
Label Font...
Value Font...
Color...
Borders...
Line Width...
Protection...
√ Value Tree
Event Tree
Field...
Name/Text...
Help...

9-10 *The Today's Date field selected and its property list displayed.*

being –36522 and January 1, 1900 being 0. Dates are calculated on the basis of 365.25 days per year, so the corresponding number for January 1, 1993 would be 93 × 365.25, or 33968.25.

Remember that back in chapter 5 you formatted Today's Date as a Date/Time field that would display the date in the mm/dd/yy format. If you unformat it, however, it should display the number you just calculated. Let's give it a whirl.

With the application in edit mode, click on the Today's Date field with the right mouse button. The Property menu should be displayed, with Field Type highlighted (see FIG. 9-10). Click on Field Type, and the program will display the Field Type window (see FIG. 9-11). The Field Type window reveals that the currently selected type is Date/Time, which is the choice you made in chapter 5. Let's change that temporarily to General field type.

Click on OK, and you'll be returned to the patient visit form, where you should be greeted by a Today's Date field that looks like FIG. 9-12. The reason for the string of # symbols is that the program is trying to fit a long number,

9-11
The Field Type window for the Today's Date field.

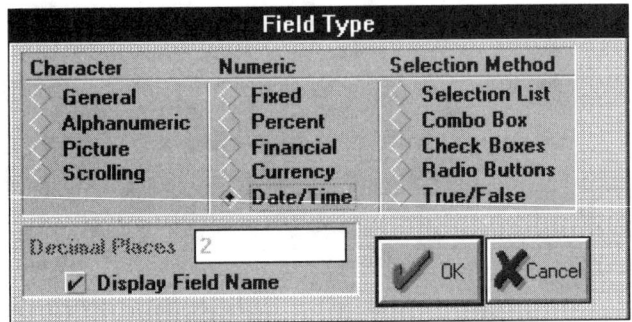

Field Type

Character	Numeric	Selection Method
General	Fixed	Selection List
Alphanumeric	Percent	Combo Box
Picture	Financial	Check Boxes
Scrolling	Currency	Radio Buttons
	◆ Date/Time	True/False

Decimal Places 2
✓ Display Field Name   ✓ OK   ✗ Cancel

9-12
The Today's Date field after reformatting. The # symbols mean that the field is too small for the long number to fit in.

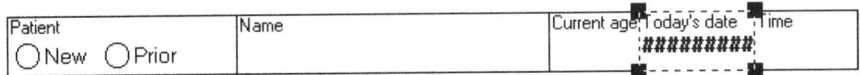

Patient	Name	Current age	Today's date	Time
○ New ○ Prior			#########	

with at least seven digits plus a decimal point, into a field that's physically too small. To verify that, try stretching the field out a bit, and you'll see the number appear (see FIG. 9-13).

Now resize the field to its original dimensions, and change the field type back to Date/Time. But keep that exercise in mind, because it will come in handy when you come to some of the other date/time calculations in this chapter.

Elmsford Medical Center

Patient	Name	Current age	Today's date	Time
○ New ○ Prior			33964.541 33	770833333

9-13
The stretched Today's Date field with the number displayed.

Programming a field to enter the current time

Just as you can create a value tree that will return the current date to a field, you can also create a value tree that will return the current time. In the previous procedure, you saw that ObjectVision computes the date in terms of the number of days elapsed since January 1, 1900. That date will be expressed in terms of an integer, or whole number, and a fraction known as a modulus.

A modulus is the remainder when one number is divided by another. If the year is expressed in terms of days by a figure such as 33962.5 and is then divided by 1, the result will be an integer (33962) plus a modulus (.5). The modulus represents a fraction of a day, which can be expressed as the time of day. For example, .5 would represent the exact midpoint of the day, or twelve noon.

One of the @ functions of ObjectVision is @MOD(X,Y), which gives you the modulus if X is divided by Y. Therefore, if you divide the date function, @NOW, by 1, the resulting integer will represent the date and the modulus will represent the time of day. So the time function you've arrived at is @MOD(@NOW,1), and that's what is going into the value tree you're about to create for the Time field.

With the patient visit form in edit mode, click twice on the Time field to display the value tree (see FIG. 9-14). When it appears on your screen, click on

Value tree for Time

Empty

9-14
The value tree for the Time field.

the Conclusion button to bring up the Conclusion for Time window (see FIG. 9-15). Press the Function button at the bottom of the window, and scroll through the selections until you find the @MOD function (see FIG. 9-16). Click on OK to paste the @MOD function into the value tree (see FIG. 9-17).

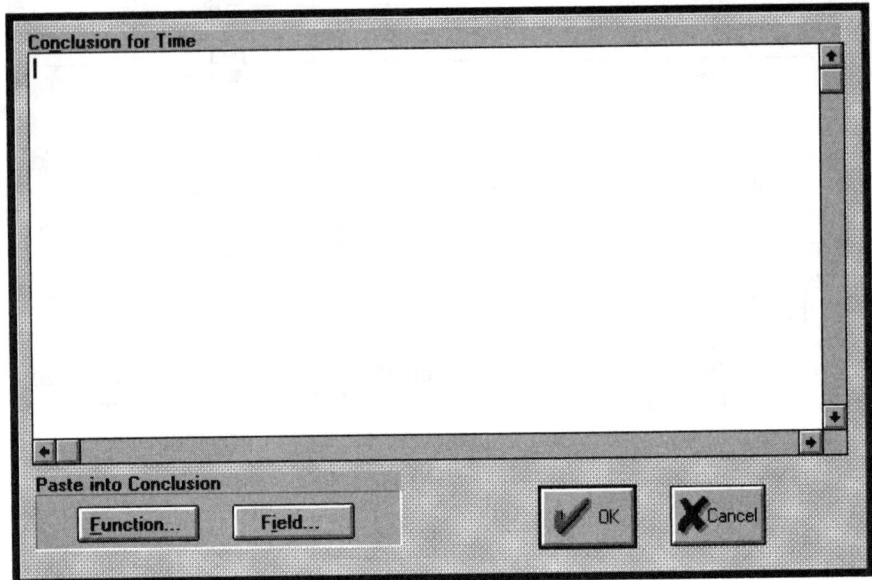

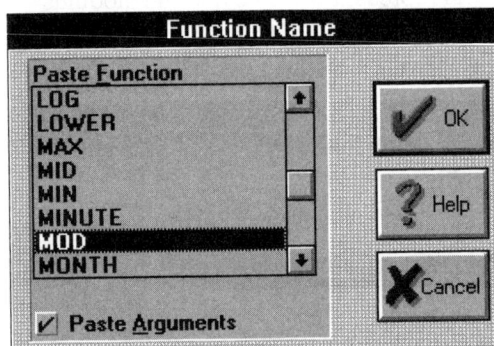

The @MOD function requires two arguments, X and Y. X is the number to be divided, and Y is the number X is to be divided by. In this case, X is another @ function (@NOW), so hit the Function button again to exhibit the Function Name window. This time, find the @NOW function, select it, and click on OK. Your value tree should look like FIG. 9-18.

There's one more step: Replace the Y with 1, which is in this case the divisor (see FIG. 9-19). Click on OK, and you've done the deed (see FIG. 9-20). When

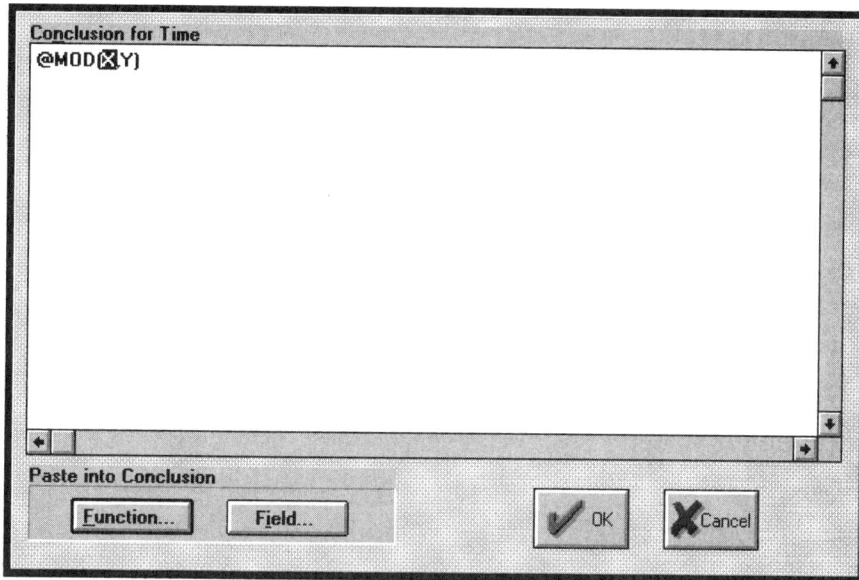

9-17
The @MOD function pasted into the Time field value tree, waiting for the X and Y arguments.

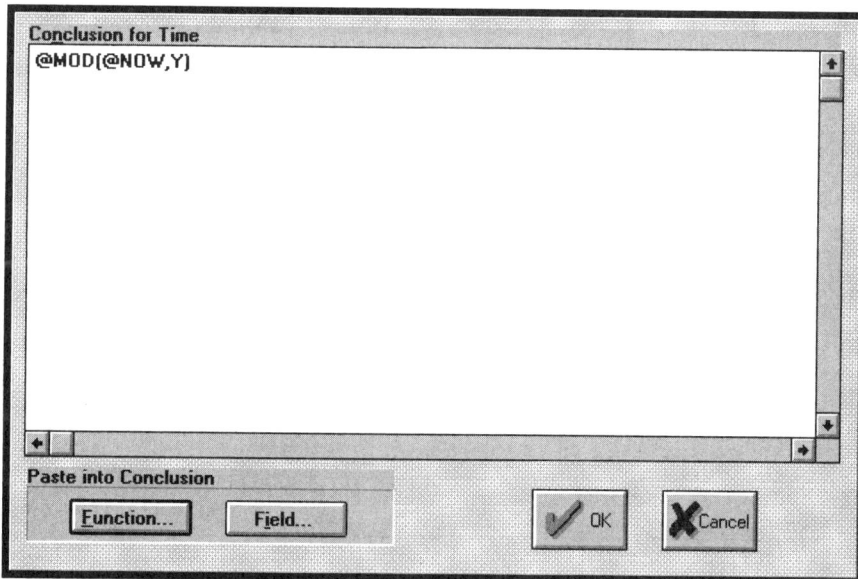

9-18
The value tree for Time with the @NOW function entered as the X argument.

you close the value tree, the current time should be entered in the Time field, and you've passed another programming milestone (see FIG. 9-21).

Now we'll turn our attention to two more fields in this patient visit form. In the patient information form, you placed a field named Date of Birth. That information has to be entered, of course, by the person filling out the form. But the patient visit form calls for the patient's current age, and that can be

Calculating someone's age

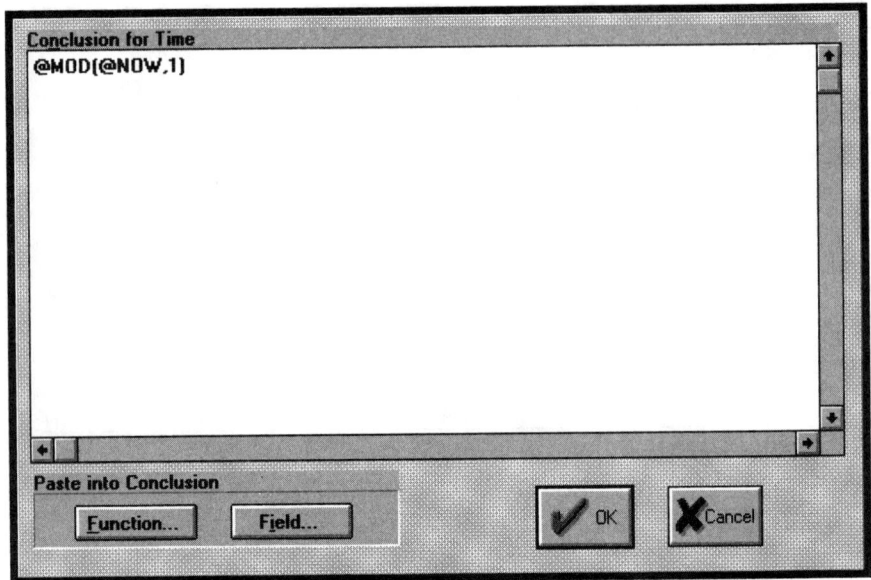

9-19
The value tree for the Time field with the @MOD expression completed.

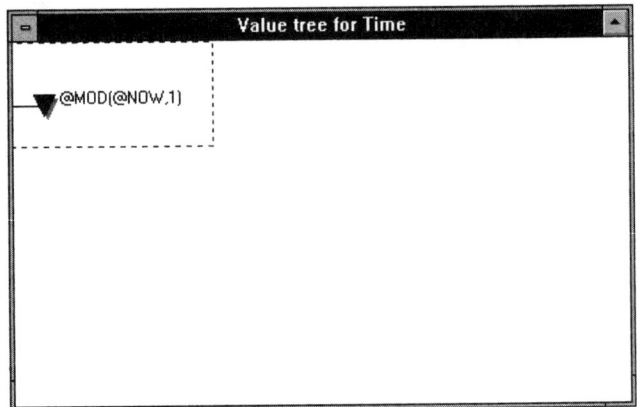

9-20
The completed value tree for the Time field.

9-21
The patient visit form with the time entered in the Time field.

Patient	Name	Current age	Today's date	Time
○ New ○ Prior			12/26/92	12:15 AM

calculated and automatically entered whenever a patient visit form is opened for a patient.

In this section, you're going to enter a birthdate in the patient information form, and then create a value tree for the Current Age field in the patient visit form that will use the birthdate to calculate the patient's current age.

With the patient visit form in runtime mode, enter the date 11/15/39 in the Date of Birth field on the patient information form (see FIG. 9-22). Then return to the patient visit form and switch to edit mode. Click twice on the Current Age field to display the value tree (see FIG. 9-23).

9-22
A date entered in the Date of Birth field.

9-23
A value tree for the Current Age window.

Now for the calculation. It's very simple—you can figure out anyone's age by subtracting the year of his birth from the current year. Your calculation is going to be a bit more precise than that; you're going to subtract the date of birth from the current date, which will give you an age in days, and then divide by 365.25 to get an age in years. Finally, you'll drop everything after the decimal point.

Here's how it goes: The current date is @NOW, so the exact age in days is @NOW – Date of Birth. To express that in years, divide by 365.25, or (@NOW – Date of Birth)/365.25. Finally, to express the age as a whole number with any fraction, use the @INT function. Here's the grand finale: @INT((@NOW – Date of Birth)/365.25). And that's what you'll insert into the value tree for the Current Age field.

Back to the value tree. Click on the Conclusion button, and the Conclusion for Current Age window will appear (see FIG. 9-24). Press the Function button and scroll until you find the @INT function (see FIG. 9-25). Click on OK, and

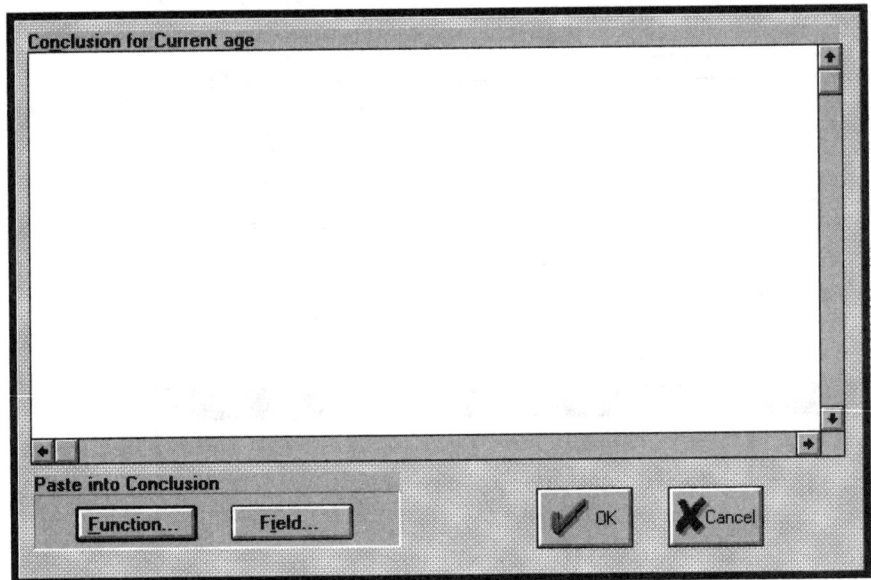

9-24
The Conclusion for Current Age window.

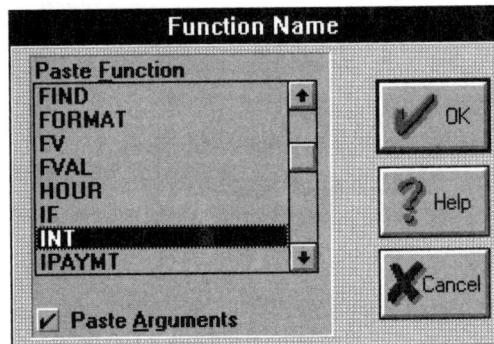

9-25
The Function Name window, with @INT selected.

the @INT function will be pasted into the Conclusion for Current Age window, waiting for its argument (see FIG. 9-26). Enter another open parenthesis and hit the Function button again. This time select @NOW and paste it into the Conclusion window (see FIG. 9-27).

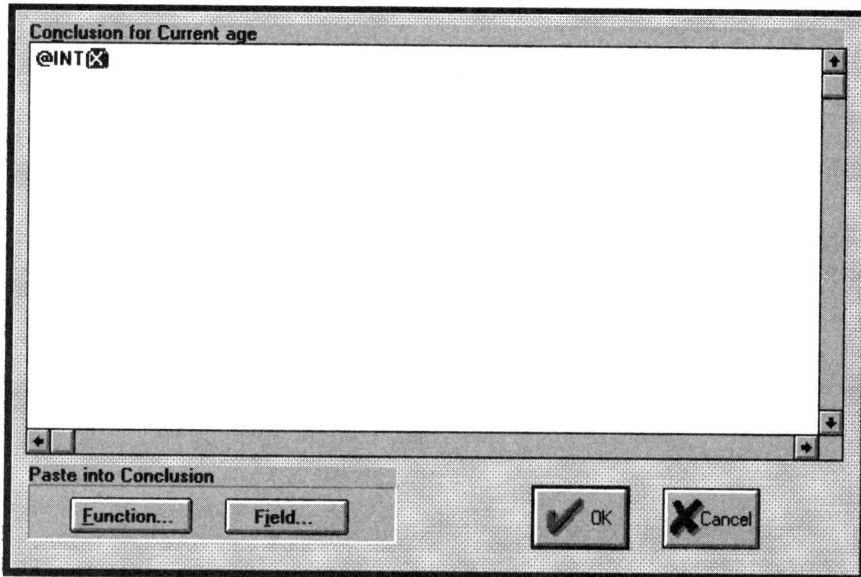

9-26
The @INT function pasted into the Conclusion for Current Age window.

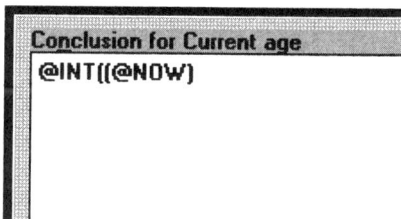

9-27
The Conclusion window with @NOW added.

Next you need to subtract the value in the Date of Birth field. You could simply type in the entire expression without extracting the @ functions and fields from the Function Name and Field Name lists, but in the interest of accuracy it's probably better to find those functions and fields in the lists. So type a minus sign, and click the Field button for the first time (see FIG. 9-28). Click on OK, and you've added Date of Birth to the expression (see FIG. 9-29). (Remember that subtracting the Date of Birth field really means subtracting the value that appears in the Date of Birth field.)

Hit the right arrow key to move the cursor to the right of the close parenthesis, and then type /365.25) to complete the formula, which should now look like FIG. 9-30.

Field Name

Apartment No
Bill payer
Blood Pressure
City
Current age
Date of birth
Employer
Employer's Address

OK

Cancel

9-28
The Field Name window, with the
Date of Birth field selected.

Conclusion for Current age
@INT[(@NOW-Date of birth)

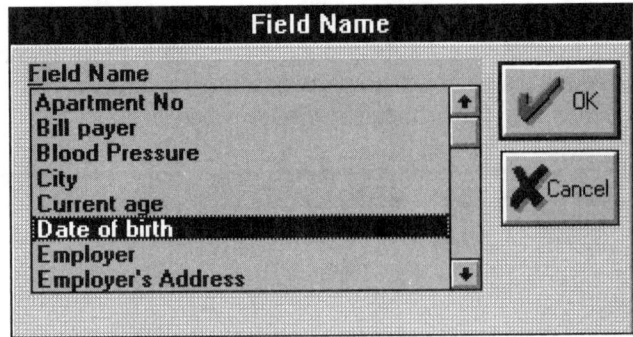

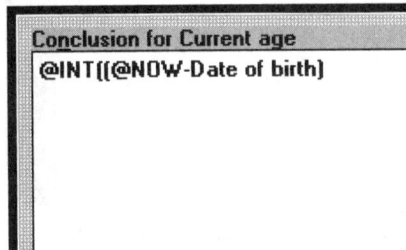

9-29
The conclusion expression
now shows that you're
subtracting the value in the
Date of Birth field from the
@NOW value.

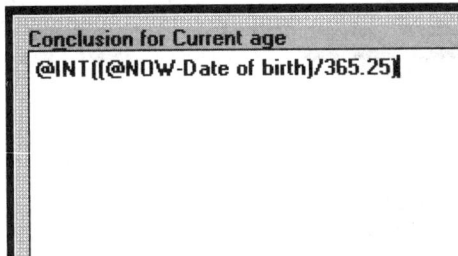

Conclusion for Current age
@INT[(@NOW-Date of birth)/365.25]

9-30
The completed formula for
calculating age and placing
it in the Current Age field.

Click on OK, and you'll see the completed value tree for the Current Age field
(see FIG. 9-31). Close the value tree, and you should discover that a person
who was born on 11/15/39 is 53 years old if you're reading this before
11/15/93 (see FIG. 9-32).

You're making admirable progress. You now have a patient visit form that
automatically fills in today's date and the time when you open the form.
When you enter a birthdate for a new patient or retrieve the data for an
existing patient, it also enters the patient's age. This is the kind of labor-
saving stuff software is supposed to do, and you're making it happen.

Being able to tap into the database of existing patients and transfer its data
into your application is just around the corner. In the next chapter, you'll
create a new Paradox database from ObjectVision, and in the chapter after
that you'll create the links between your growing application and that
database.

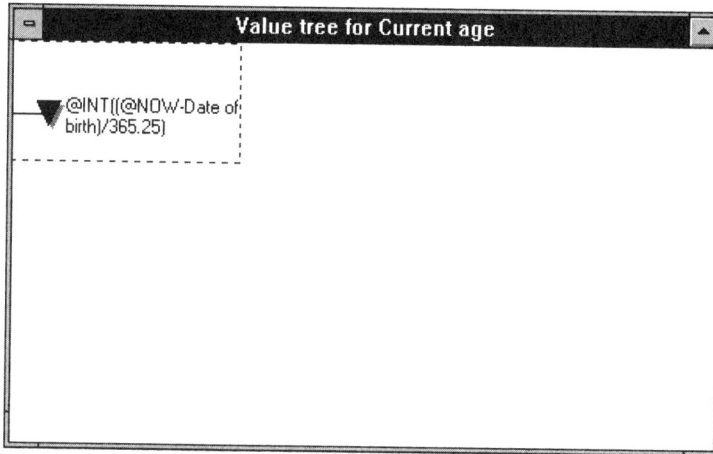

9-31
The completed value tree for the Current Age field.

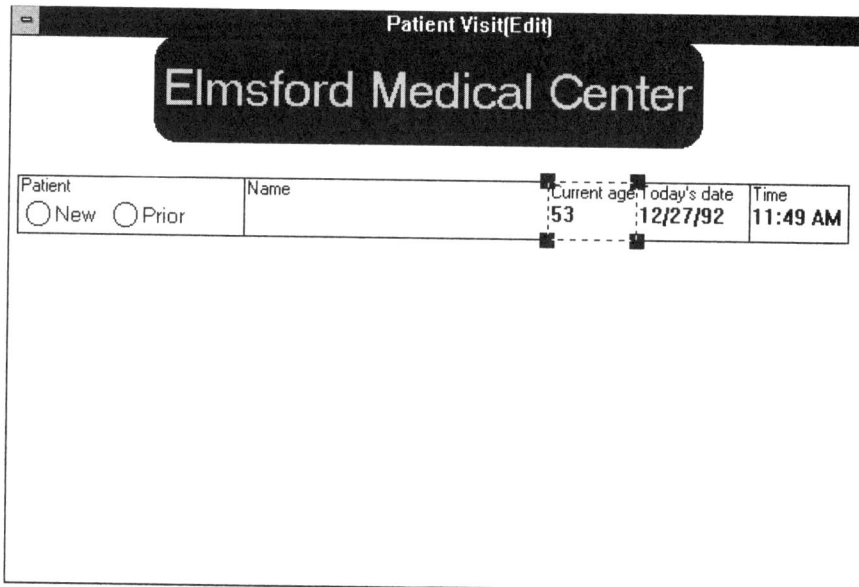

9-32
The age entered in the Current Age field.

10 Creating databases with ObjectVision

Perhaps the most powerful aspect of ObjectVision is how it allows you to link to other programs, especially powerful database programs such as Paradox and dBASE. That, of course, is a major attraction of the software; it allows you to access and manipulate tons of data, of all sorts, via an ObjectVision "front end" that you create and customize to suit your own purposes.

Not only can you access database programs with ObjectVision, but you can also create database tables that are compatible with Paradox, dBASE, Btrieve, etc. And that's what you're going to do in this chapter. For the patient visit form, you need to be able to store and retrieve data from the patient information form. You should also be able to store the patient visit form to avoid paper pileup in the physician's office. That suggests two separate databases linked by patient names. For now, you'll create only one of them—the database table for the patient information form. The fields in that table will be the same as the fields on the form.

Start ObjectVision and open your burgeoning patient visit form. Select the patient information form, open the Tools menu, and choose Links (see FIG. 10-1). The Data Links window will appear on your screen (see FIG. 10-2).

Creating the database

Select the database type you want to create (Paradox, dBASE, Btrieve, ASCII, etc.) This will probably be determined by the type of software you own. For this tutorial, we're going to set up a Paradox database table, so be sure the

Tools
Form
Stack
Links...

10-1 *The Tools menu, with Links selected.*

diamond in front of Paradox is marked. Press the Create button, and an elaborate Paradox Link Creation window will open (see FIG. 10-3).

The first step is to type in a link name, which can be any combination of up to 63 ASCII characters. To make it memorable, type:

```
Patient Information Table
```

in the box, and then click on the Create Table button. When you do, you see the Database Table Creation window, along with a listing of all of your

10-2
The Data Links window, with Paradox selected as the database type to create.

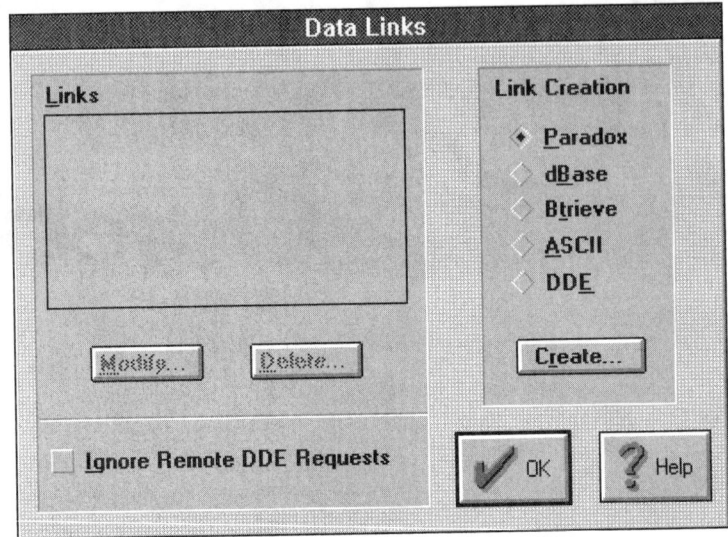

10-3
The Paradox Link Creation window.

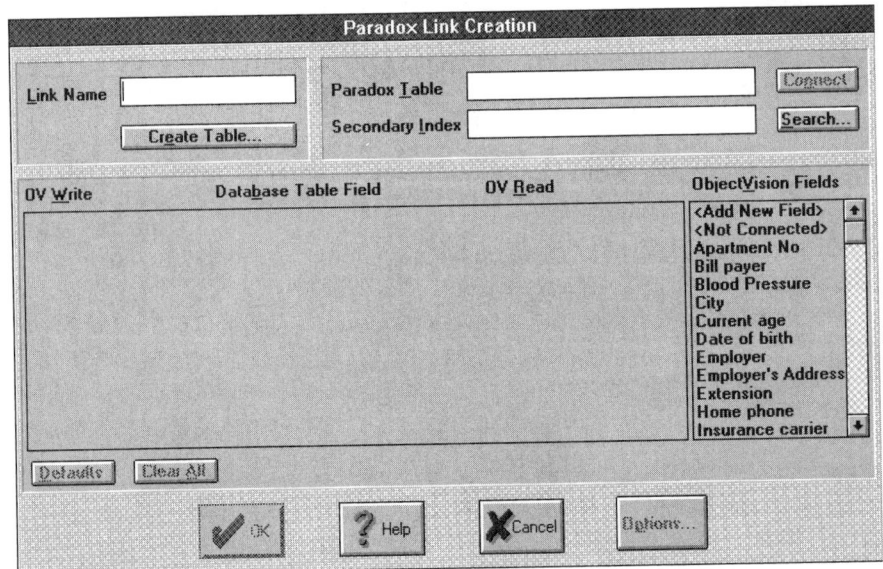

ObjectVision fields (see FIG. 10-4). The fields you want to create on this database table are the same as the ones on the patient information form: Name, Street Address, Apt. No., City, State, Zip Code, Home Phone, Office Phone, Extension, Date of Birth, Insurance Carrier, and Employer.

You won't be including the items on the vital data table—visit date, pulse, respiration, weight, and blood pressure—right now. Be careful about trying to

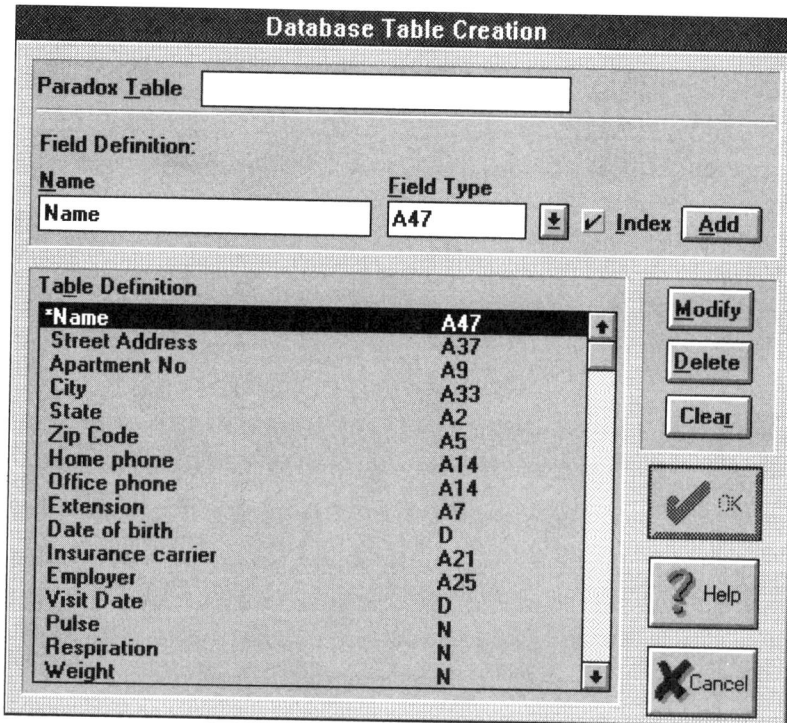

Database Table Creation

Paradox **T**able

Field Definition:

Name | **F**ield Type
Name | A47 ☑ **I**ndex **A**dd

T**a**ble Definition

*Name	A47
Street Address	A37
Apartment No	A9
City	A33
State	A2
Zip Code	A5
Home phone	A14
Office phone	A14
Extension	A7
Date of birth	D
Insurance carrier	A21
Employer	A25
Visit Date	D
Pulse	N
Respiration	N
Weight	N

Modify **D**elete **Clea**r

✔ OK

? Help

✗ Cancel

10-4
The Database Table Creation window.

put everything on a single table. It's better, and much easier to understand, if you create a number of related smaller tables.

To give the new Paradox table a name, move your cursor to the Paradox Table box at the top of the window (if for some reason it's not still there) and type PATINFO. You don't need to type an extension; the program will provide that automatically.

The fields you need should all appear on the listing in the Database Table Creation window; simply select them and choose a field type and size. Eliminate those you don't need.

In each case, the program has made a tentative selection for field type and size; in the case of the first field, Name, the selected field type is A for alphanumeric, and the proposed field size is 47 characters.

Paradox field types

There are five Paradox field types: Alphanumeric (A), Date (D), Number (N), Short numeric (S), and Currency ($). You can get an explanation about these different types by clicking on the Help button in the Database Table Creation window (see FIG. 10-5).

Note particularly that the Alphanumeric field type is followed by a number (up to three digits), which defines the size of the field in terms of the maximum number of characters it contains. Note also that Date fields can contain only dates—not times. And Paradox calculates dates differently than

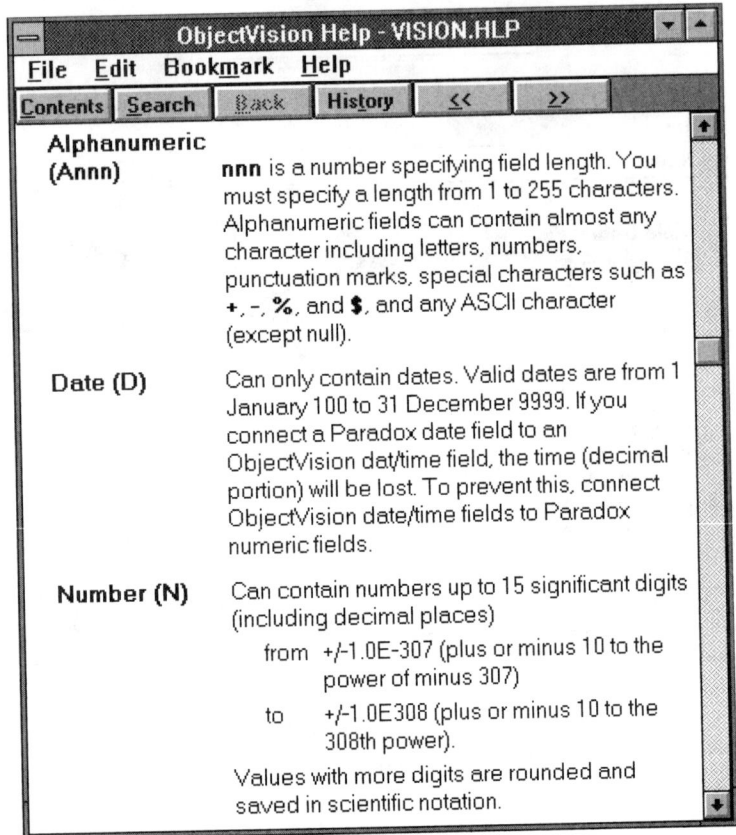

10-5

The Help screen for the Database Table Creation window, including explanations of field types.

ObjectVision Help - VISION.HLP

File   Edit   Bookmark   Help

Contents | Search | Back | History | << | >>

Alphanumeric (Annn)
nnn is a number specifying field length. You must specify a length from 1 to 255 characters. Alphanumeric fields can contain almost any character including letters, numbers, punctuation marks, special characters such as +, -, %, and $, and any ASCII character (except null).

Date (D)
Can only contain dates. Valid dates are from 1 January 100 to 31 December 9999. If you connect a Paradox date field to an ObjectVision date/time field, the time (decimal portion) will be lost. To prevent this, connect ObjectVision date/time fields to Paradox numeric fields.

Number (N)
Can contain numbers up to 15 significant digits (including decimal places)

from   +/-1.0E-307 (plus or minus 10 to the power of minus 307)

to   +/-1.0E308 (plus or minus 10 to the 308th power).

Values with more digits are rounded and saved in scientific notation.

ObjectVision does. For that reason, ObjectVision date/time fields should be entered in Paradox data tables as Number fields.

Some cautionary remarks about indexing

There's a small problem with converting ObjectVision fields to Paradox database fields. You're going to want to sort your data, which will mean selecting a field to index on. You might want to sort alphabetically by the patients' last names, or perhaps by their social security numbers. However, the ObjectVision Name field is for the full name, and that isn't very useful for indexing.

You could add another field to the ObjectVision form, or you could add a new last name field to the Paradox database table you're creating. To save time and space, we won't take either of those steps right now, but keep this kind of situation in mind as you create your own ObjectVision forms. In this instance, choose the Name field for the index, remembering that it's a flawed choice. Why? Because in order for the indexing to work as it should, you have to enter the full name exactly the same every time.

If, for instance, a patient walks in the first time and says his name is P. Joseph Gibbs, and you enter it as such on the patient information form. Then the second time he comes to the office, he says his name is Joe Gibbs. Unless you remember P. Joseph, you won't find his record on the database when you enter his name.

Here's another important thing to remember: The field you index on has to be the first one on this Database Table Creation list, and it also has to be the first one you enter in the patient information form when you're using the application. Therefore, if you wanted to modify this application for easier use, you would want to make the very first field your primary index field—social security number, last name, or something like that.

So let's get busy and create that database. ObjectVision has magically assigned field lengths (in number of characters) to the A (alphanumeric) fields. Accept the numbers it provides. Next, we want to delete the fields from Visit Date on down. That includes Visit Date, Pulse, Respiration, Weight, and Blood Pressure. Click on Visit Date to highlight it, and press the Delete button. Do the same for the four fields below.

Selecting & modifying fields for the Paradox table

Finally, click on Date of Birth so it appears in the Field Definition box, and when it does change the Field Type to N for Numerical. At this stage, the Database Table Creation window should look like FIG. 10-6. Click on OK, and you're back at the Paradox Link Creation window.

Now that you have a table defined and have also defined a linkname to get you from ObjectVision to that table, you have to connect the Paradox table fields (which could, conceivably, have different names) to the ObjectVision fields. As you might have guessed, that is what that Connect button up there is for. Click it, and your new database table fields will be listed in the center of the table, waiting for you to connect them with the appropriate ObjectVision fields (see FIG. 10-7).

There are some options here: You can elect to fill in the fields for the OV Write column, OV Read column, or both. If you enter a field in only the OV

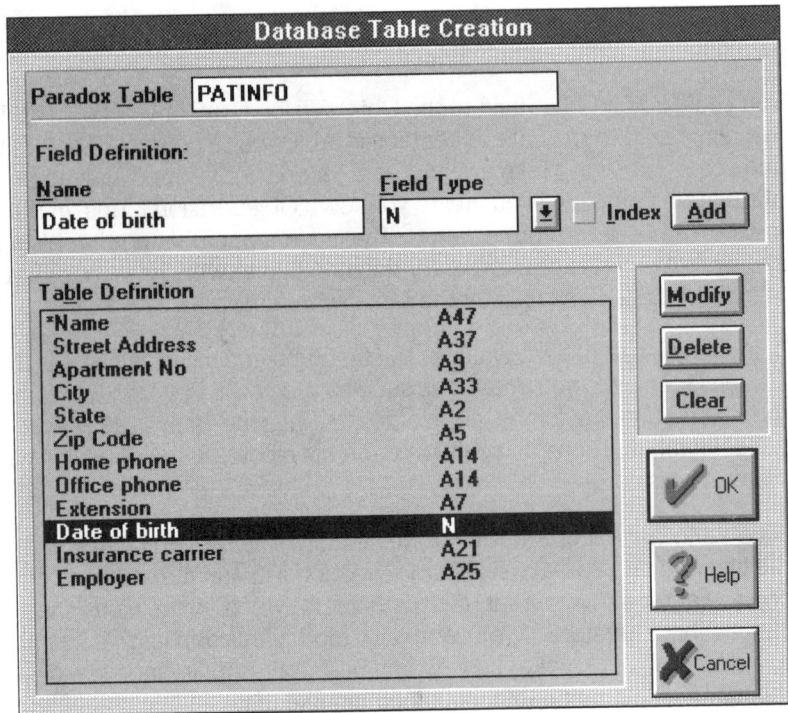

10-6

The Database Table Creation window with modifications and a Paradox table name.

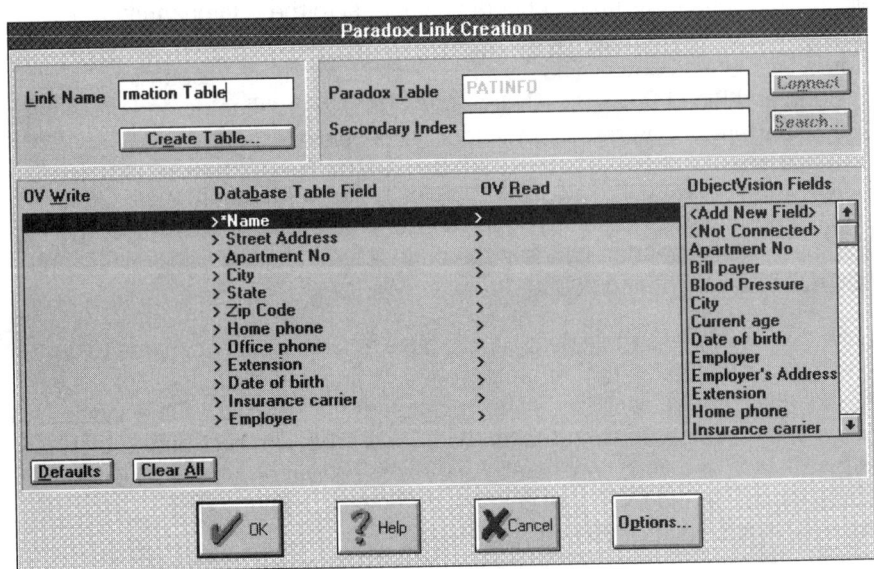

10-7

The Paradox table fields listed in the Connect box.

Write column, it means that you'll enter the data only in ObjectVision, and the data will be written to the corresponding field in your Paradox database.

If you enter a field in only the OV Read column, it means that you'll enter the data only through a Paradox data field, and it will be read by your ObjectVision application.

If you have fields in both the OV Write and OV Read columns, it means that data entry can go either way—from the ObjectVision application to the Paradox database, or from the Paradox database to the ObjectVision application. For this exercise, enter all fields in both columns.

In this example, the Paradox database fields have exactly the same names as the ObjectVision fields, so that's going to make things very easy. With the database table field *Name highlighted, scroll down the ObjectVision fields listed at the right-hand side of the window until you find Name (see FIG. 10-8). When you locate it, double-click on it and Name will appear in both the OV Write and OV Read columns. The highlighted line will then move down to Street Address (see FIG. 10-9).

Connecting ObjectVision fields to Paradox database fields

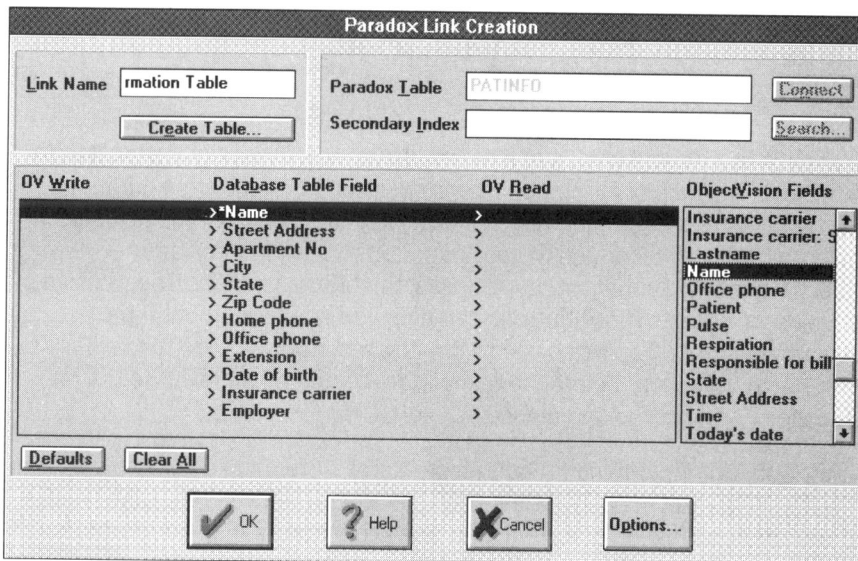

10-8
*The Paradox Link Creation window with *Name highlighted in the Database Table Field list, and Name highlighted in the ObjectVision Fields list.*

Follow this procedure until you've connected all the database fields to the ObjectVision fields. Your completed Link Creation window should now look very much like FIG. 10-10.

OV Write	Database Table Field	OV Read
Name	> *Name	> Name
	> Street Address	>
	> Apartment No	>

Paradox Link Creation

Link Name: rmation Table   Paradox Table: PATINFO   Connect

Create Table...   Secondary Index: Search...

OV Write	Database Table Field	OV Read	ObjectVision Fields
Name	> *Name	> Name	Blood Pressure
Street Address	> Street Address	> Street Address	City
Apartment No	> Apartment No	> Apartment No	Current age
City	> City	> City	Date of birth
State	> State	> State	Employer
Zip Code	> Zip Code	> Zip Code	Employer's Address
Home phone	> Home phone	> Home phone	Extension
Office phone	> Office phone	> Office phone	Home phone
Extension	> Extension	> Extension	Insurance carrier
Date of birth	> Date of birth	> Date of birth	Insurance carrier: S
Insurance carrier	> Insurance carrier	> Insurance carrier	Lastname
Employer	> Employer	> Employer	Name
			Office phone

Defaults   Clear All

OK   Help   Cancel   Options...

Now click on OK, and you'll get a pleasant surprise: ObjectVision is offering to throw in a bunch of automatic, preprogrammed buttons at no additional charge. The elves of Borland have already done all the work; you just select the buttons you want added to your patient information form, and ObjectVision will do the rest. In this case, the buttons include Top, Bottom, Previous, and Next. Those buttons can help you navigate through the records on your new table. Top takes you to the first record, Bottom to the last, Previous to the record before the one you're looking at, and next to the one after the one you're looking at (see FIG. 10-11).

Select Top, Bottom, Previous, Next, Insert, and Store. Click to create a checkmark in front of each of these choices, and when you're finished click on OK. In the twinkling of an eye (and you know how fast an eye twinkles) you'll be returned to the original Data Links window, with the link name now visible (see FIG. 10-12).

You've done it. Click on OK in the Data Links window, and your patient information form will return, this time with a whole gang of new buttons at the bottom (you might have to rearrange them to make them all fit on the screen, as shown in FIG. 10-13). We might have gone a little button-crazy

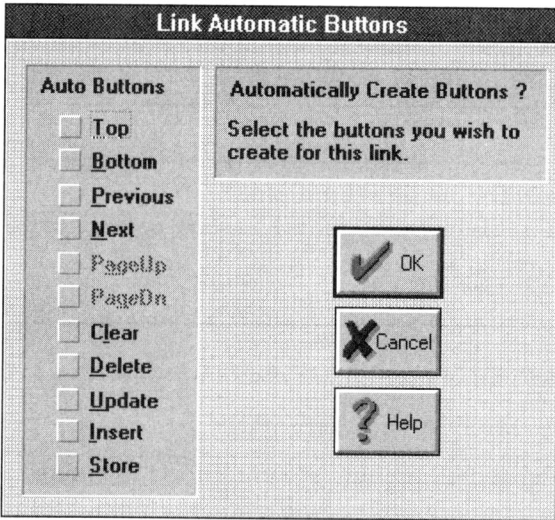

10-11
The Link Automatic Buttons window.

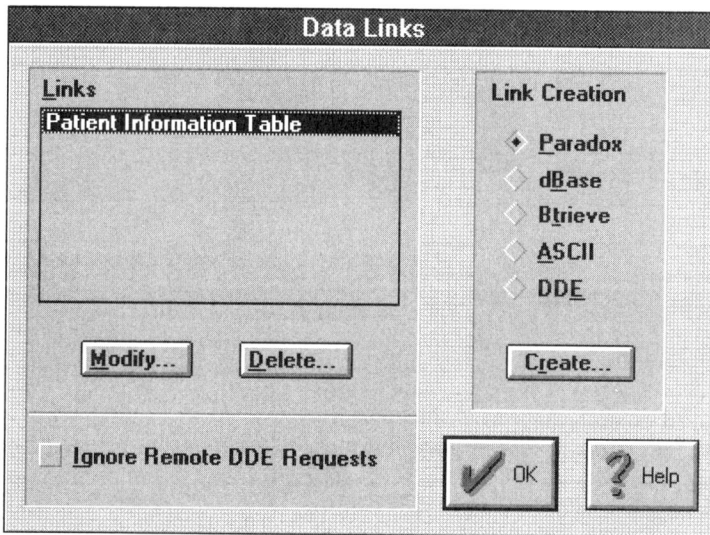

10-12
The Data Links table with the linkname.

here, but they'll be fun to play with, and you can decide in the future how many buttons, and which ones, you really need on your applications.

Before you do anything else, save your application with its powerful new links. Now—do you want to confirm that you really created a Paradox database? Well, if you have Paradox 4.0, for example, you can open it and locate the new PATINFO database in the C:\VISION directory.

Patient Information (Goal)

Patient Information

Name

Street Address	Apartment No

City	State	Zip Code

Home phone	Office phone	Extension	Date of birth

Insurance carrier	Employer

Vital Data

Visit Date	Pulse	Respiration	Weight	Blood Pressure

[Clear] [Save and Clear] [Return to PV Form]

[Top] [Bottom] [Previous] [Next]

[Insert] [Store]

10-13
The patient information form with its new array of buttons.

Here's what the steps would look like (I'm running ObjectVision under OS/2 2.0, so things might look a little different than your procedure):

If you've been operating in what OS/2 2.0 calls a WIN-OS/2 full-screen session (WIN-OS/2 is what Windows is called under OS/2 2.0) as I have, you'll need to ObjectVision and, in order to return to the OS/2 desktop, press Ctrl–Esc; a Task List window will pop up in front of the Windows Program Manager window (see FIG. 10-14), with OS/2 Desktop the third item on the task list. Click twice on Desktop and you'll be returned to the OS/2 2.0 Desktop you have customized (see FIG. 10-15).

The second icon from the bottom of the second row represents the Paradox 4.0 program. Click twice on that to launch the program, and the opening screen will appear as shown in FIG. 10-16. Click on View, and when the Table List window opens type C:\VISION to switch to the directory where ObjectVision files are stored (see FIG. 10-17). Click on OK and, sure enough, there's a table called PATINFO in the VISION directory. We're getting there (see FIG. 10-18).

Click on OK once more, and there's a real Paradox database table called PATINFO. A message at the bottom informs you that the table is empty, of

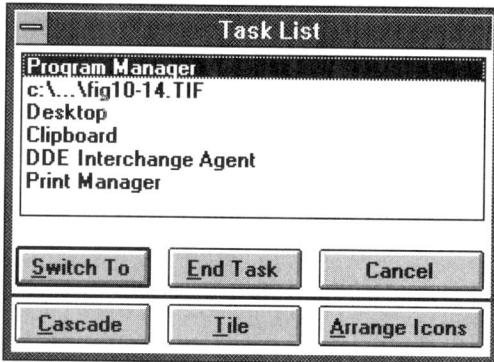

10-14
The Task List window for switching to other active programs.

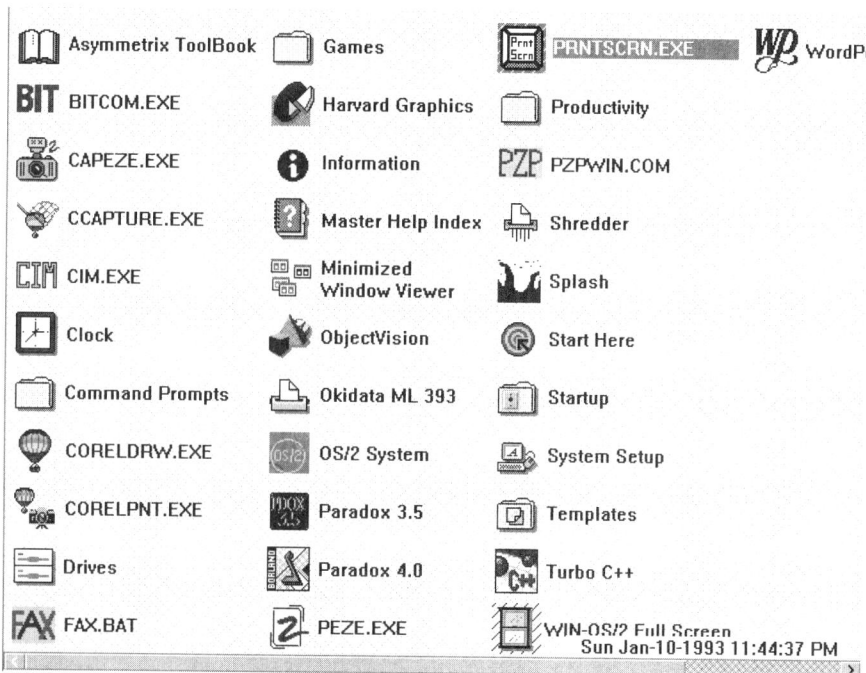

10-15
The OS/2 2.0 desktop display.

course, because you haven't entered any data. But the table is really there, and at this point you should be able to enter data that will be displayed in your ObjectVision application. Let's try (remember those Read/Write columns!).

Press F9 to edit, or add to, this table, and the program will enter a 1 in the first column for the first record. With the cursor blinking in the Name field, type:

Greenberry Swango

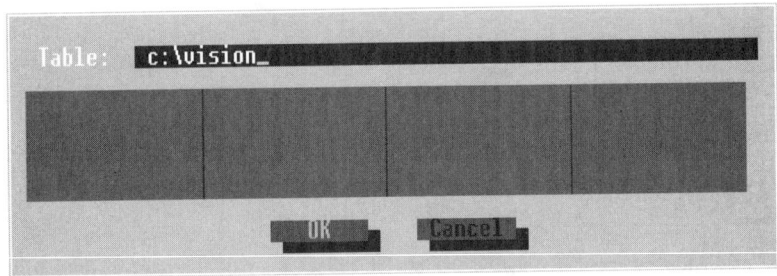

10-16
The opening screen of Paradox 4.0.

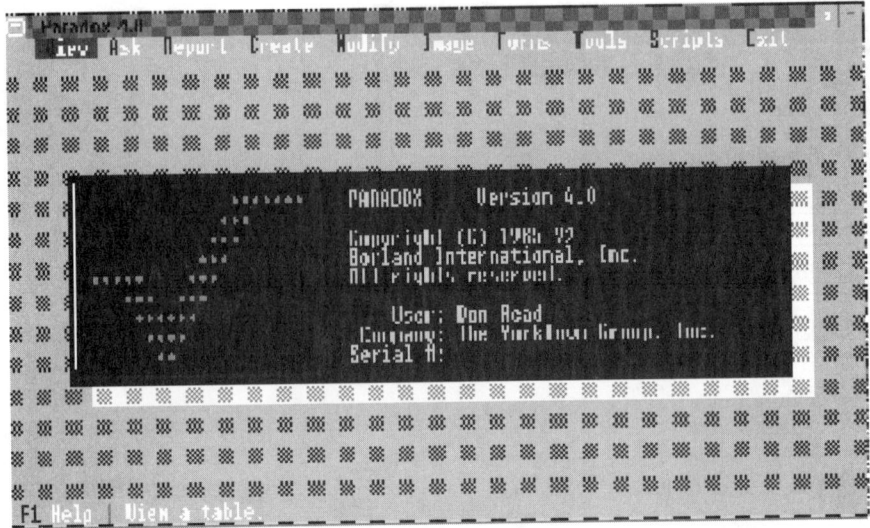

10-17
The window for viewing database tables, with the C:\VISION directory entered.

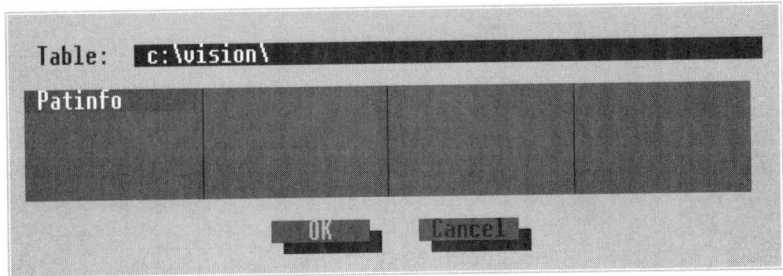

10-18
The PATINFO database name displayed in the table list window.

and press Enter. The rest of the field information is as follows:

Street Address	2014 West Broadway
Apartment No.	2
City	Louisville
State	KY
Zip Code	40604

Home Phone	502-555-5005
Office Phone	502-555-2988
Extension	423
Date of Birth	(blank—dates are a little tricky to enter at this end)
Insurance Carrier	Blue Cross
Employer	Byerly Automotive Service

Tap D for Do-It!, and the data will be entered. Click on Tools in the Paradox 4.0 menu, then on Info, and you'll see a submenu that gives you the database Structure as the first option (see FIG. 10-19). Click on Structure, type in the database table name again, and you'll see the same field listing in Paradox 4.0 that you just set up for your linked database table (see FIG. 10-20). All of this is just as it should be, of course, but isn't it fun to see that the stuff really works?

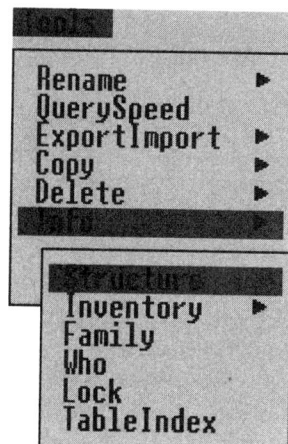

10-19 *The Tools menu with Info selected.*

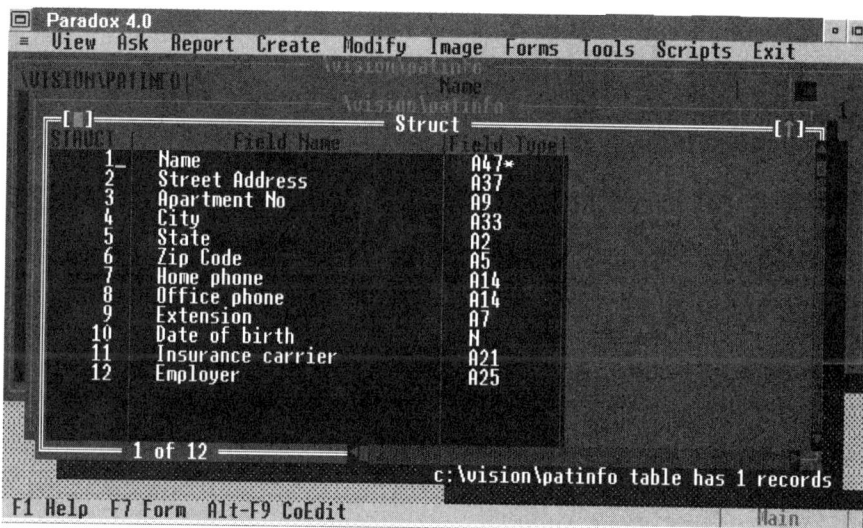

10-20 *The field structure of the newly created Paradox database table.*

Now let's go backwards. Close Paradox 4.0, return to ObjectVision and your new VISITFRM application, and select the patient information form. Let's test the new database entry and link. In the Name field of the Patient Information field, type:

Greenberry Swango

and press Enter. Miraculously, the data will all pop into the right places on the form, with the cursor blinking in the Date of Birth field—the one you didn't fill in. Enter 12/7/41 as Swango's date of birth, and the top of the form will be complete (see FIG. 10-21).

But what about that vital data table at the bottom of the patient information form? How do you plug that data into an external database? Stay tuned.

Patient Information [Goal]

Patient Information

Name			
Greenberry Swango			

Street Address		Apartment No
2014 West Broadway		2

City		State	Zip Code
Louisville		KY	40604

Home phone	Office phone	Extension	Date of birth
502-555-5005	502-555-2988	423	12/7/41

Insurance carrier	Employer
Blue Cross	Byerly Automotive Service

Vital Data

Visit Date	Pulse	Respiration	Weight	Blood Pressure

[Clear] [Save and Clear] [Return to PV Form]

[Top] [Bottom] [Previous] [Next]

[Insert] [Store]

10-21

The patient information form filled in, with the data entered in Paradox 4.0.

11 *Importing graphic objects*

Man does not live by text alone; in multimedia, there should also be an occasional graphic to spice the pudding. Happily, among the wealth of resources that ObjectVision brings to the table is the ability to import and size graphics objects. The type of graphic you want to add to an ObjectVision form will depend on the function of the form, the nature of the database(s) you're accessing, and your own aesthetic inclinations.

In the case of this patient visit form you're building, a couple of possibilities suggest themselves immediately: the logo of the medical service for whom you're designing the software and the patients' photographs. The logo would logically go on the main patient visit form, and the photograph would be appropriate for the patient information form.

You can create both the photograph and the logo with other media and scan them into the computer. As high-resolution scanners, digital photo, and video technology become more commonplace and accessible, such images are easier to come by. You could also create the logo with a computer graphics software package. Once an image exists as a computer graphics file, you can copy it onto the Windows clipboard via some application such as Paintbrush, and from there into an ObjectVision application.

Where can you get graphic images?

For the current tutorial, you'll be working only with the logo. It's contained in the file ELMSFORD.OVG, on the disk included with this book. If you don't

Getting ready to import

have the disk, you might want to try creating a replica of the logo in Paintbrush (or CorelDraw, or whatever), and copying it into your ObjectVision application via the Clipboard. Failing that, you'll have to accept the following demonstration on faith.

You're going to place the Elmsford Medical Center logo, which has been scanned, edited a bit, and saved as a bitmap file, into the top of the patient visit form. If you haven't already done so, load ObjectVision and open VISITFRM.OVD. The patient visit form, with the Elmsford Medical Center banner at the top, will appear on your screen (see FIG. 11-1).

11-1
The patient visit form.

You're going to move that banner to the right to make room for the new logo. Select Form from the Tools menu, and all the form tool icons will appear along your button bar.

Now the banner you want to move consists of two elements or fields: the rounded filled rectangle, and the text. You want to move them at the same time, however, so you have to be careful to select both elements simultaneously.

You remember the technique for selecting a number of contiguous fields at the same time? Click on the first field, and when it's surrounded by a dotted line and selection handles click on the final field in the series. You're going to do the same thing here. Click in the middle of the banner to select the text field, and it will be surrounded by a dotted line, as shown in FIG. 11-2.

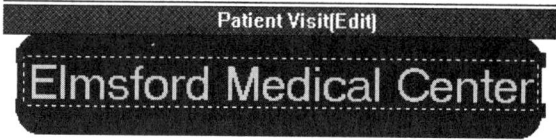

11-2
The banner text selected.

Now depress the Shift key and click on the banner outside the area of the text object. You should now see selection lines and handles for the rounded rectangle object as well (see FIG. 11-3). Drag the whole unit to the right, so your form looks something like FIG. 11-4.

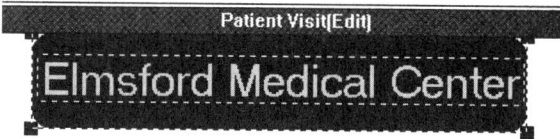

11-3
The banner with both elements selected.

11-4
The banner moved to the right to make room for the new logo.

You're now going to import a graphic object that will be placed in the top left-hand corner of the patient visit form. If you have the disk with the ELMSFORD.BMP file, you'll import it from that disk. If you don't, you can use one of the graphics files already available in ObjectVision.

There are two types of images you can import into an ObjectVision application: an image that has been copied into the Clipboard from some

Importing a non-ObjectVision graphic image

other graphics-handling application, or an image that has already been saved as an ObjectVision .OVG graphic file. (If you elect the latter option, skip down to the section *Importing an ObjectVision graphic object.*)

In the case of an outside image, which could exist in any number of graphic file formats, copy it to the Clipboard by using a Cut or Copy or some equivalent command in the software your image is loaded in. As I step through the following procedure, you can either follow along if you don't have the ELMSFORD.BMP file, or use any graphics file of your own choosing and move through the steps yourself.

If you're running in Windows, you could load Paintbrush and then load the ELMSFORD.BMP file. Let's assume the ELMSFORD.BMP file is on a disk in your A drive.

First, without closing ObjectVision, go to your Windows Program Manager by pressing Ctrl–Esc and then clicking twice on Program Manager. Find Paintbrush in your Program Manager window. It's likely to be in a folder named Accessories (see FIG. 11-5). Click twice on the icon to open the program, and when its window is maximized (opened to full size) it will look like FIG. 11-6.

11-5
The Accessories folder with Paintbrush selected.

Next, select File/Open, and when that window opens click on your A drive to show the directory of importable files (see FIG. 11-7). Select the ELMSFORD.BMP file, click on OK, and after a few seconds the logo will appear on your Paintbrush canvas (see FIG. 11-8).

Moving right along, select the pick tool (scissors with a rectangle) to define the area on your canvas that you want to copy to the Clipboard (see FIG. 11-9). Drag a rectangle around the outside of the Elmsford Medical Center logo; the logo will appear inside a dotted line, as shown in FIG. 11-10. Select Copy from the Edit file, and the image of the EMC logo should be copied to the Clipboard. To confirm that it has been, return to your Windows Program

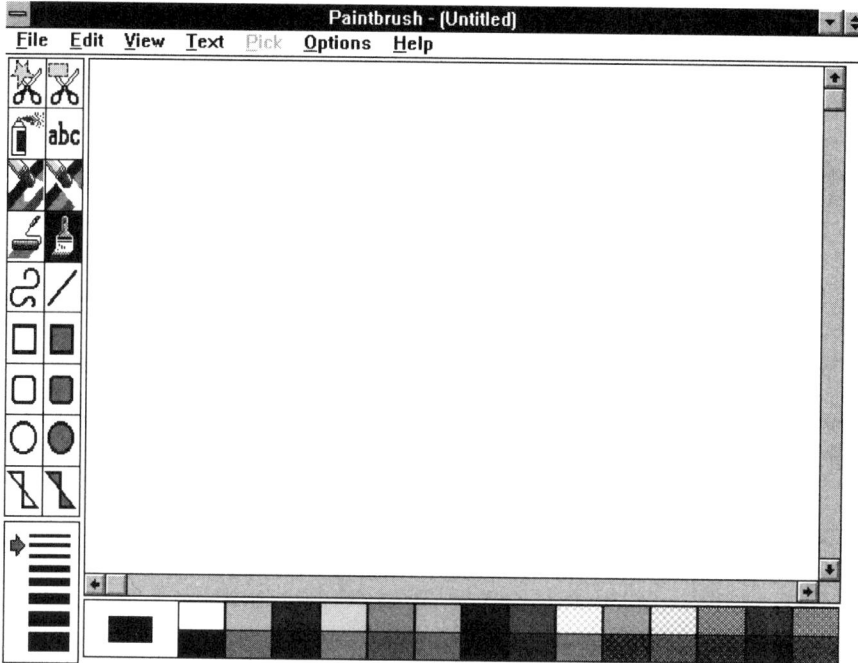

11-6
The Paintbrush opening screen.

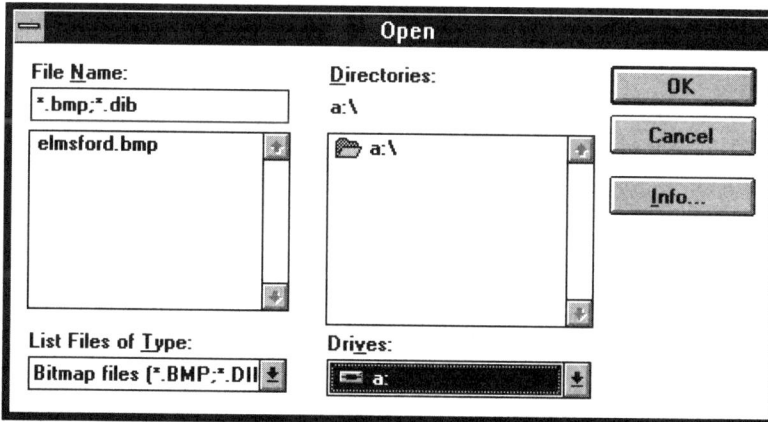

11-7
The Open File window in Paintbrush showing the bitmap files on drive A.

Manager and find the Clipboard Viewer, shown in FIG. 11-11. Open the Clipboard Viewer, and you should see an image of the EMC logo (possibly somewhat distorted) (see FIG. 11-12).

That's all there is to getting the image into your Clipboard. All that remains is to paste it into your patient visit form. Return to ObjectVision by pressing Ctrl–Esc and clicking twice on ObjectVision - VISITFRM.OVD.

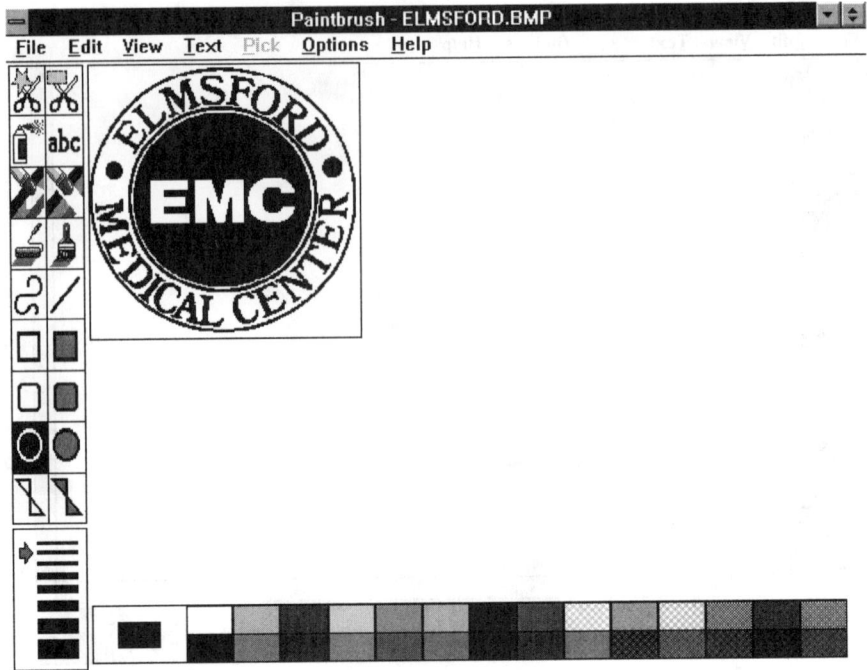

11-8
The Elmsford Medical Center logo on the Paintbrush canvas.

11-9 *The pick tool selected.*

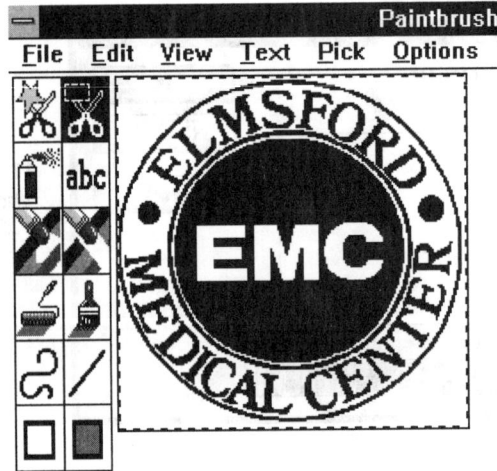

11-10
The Elmsford Medical Center logo circumscribed by the pick tool.

Back at the patient visit form, your object bar should still be available, so press the Graphics Object button. An ObjectVision window will open, asking you whether you want to use the Clipboard graphic or an existing ObjectVision graphic (see FIG. 11-13). If you want to use the Clipboard graphic (and in this case you do), click on YES. The next window will ask you to give a filename to the clipboard graphic; ObjectVision will provide the .OVG

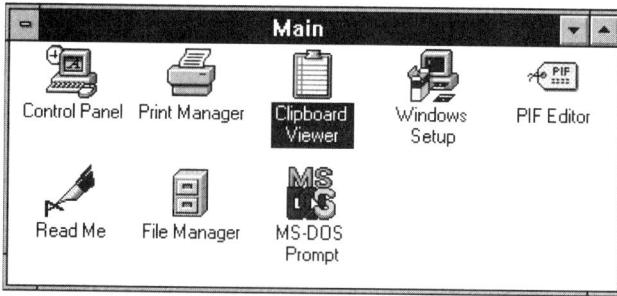

11-11
The Clipboard Viewer icon in the Main folder of the Program Manager window.

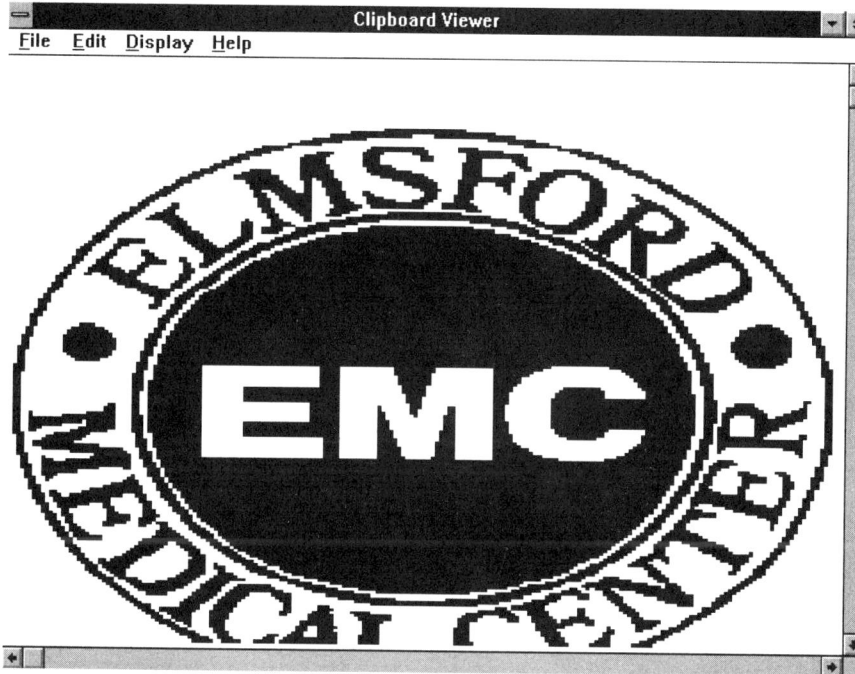

11-12
The EMC logo in the Clipboard.

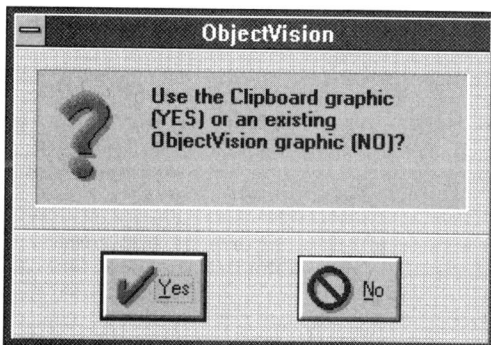

11-13
The Graphics Choice window.

extension (see FIG. 11-14). Type elmsford in front of the extension and click on OK. A dotted square representing the graphic will appear on your patient visit form; move it to the upper left-hand corner of the form and click the left mouse button to place the image.

11-14
The window for naming your Clipboard graphic.

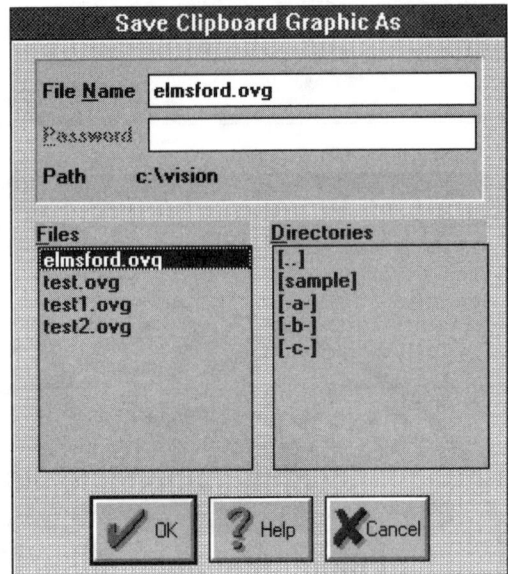

Save Clipboard Graphic As

File **N**ame elmsford.ovg

Password

Path   c:\vision

Files
elmsford.ovg
test.ovg
test1.ovg
test2.ovg

Directories
[..]
[sample]
[-a-]
[-b-]
[-c-]

✓ OK   ? Help   ✗ Cancel

Changing the size & borders

The logo now pasted into your form is probably somewhat oversized, as shown in FIG. 11-15. Use the selection handles to size the graphic just as you did the fields; when you finish, you'll probably want the result to resemble FIG. 11-16.

One thing remains: Unless you've set the defaults differently, ObjectVision will put a border around the graphic image. Let's get rid of it. Point to the new EMC logo and click the right mouse button. A small property list will pop up (see FIG. 11-17). Select Borders, and a small window will present you with the Borders options (see FIG. 11-18). Click on the box in front of Outline to remove the check, and then press OK. Press the close tool in the object bar to return to runtime mode, and your patient visit form should sparkle with its new logo.

In the case of a scanned graphic such as this, the quality will depend on a number of factors independent of ObjectVision, including the resolution of the scanner and the software you use to manipulate the image.

Importing an ObjectVision graphic object

In addition to importing graphics files from the Clipboard, you can also import existing ObjectVision graphics files. You can recognize them by their .OVG extensions. Be sure you have saved your VISITFRM.OVD file before you start this maneuver.

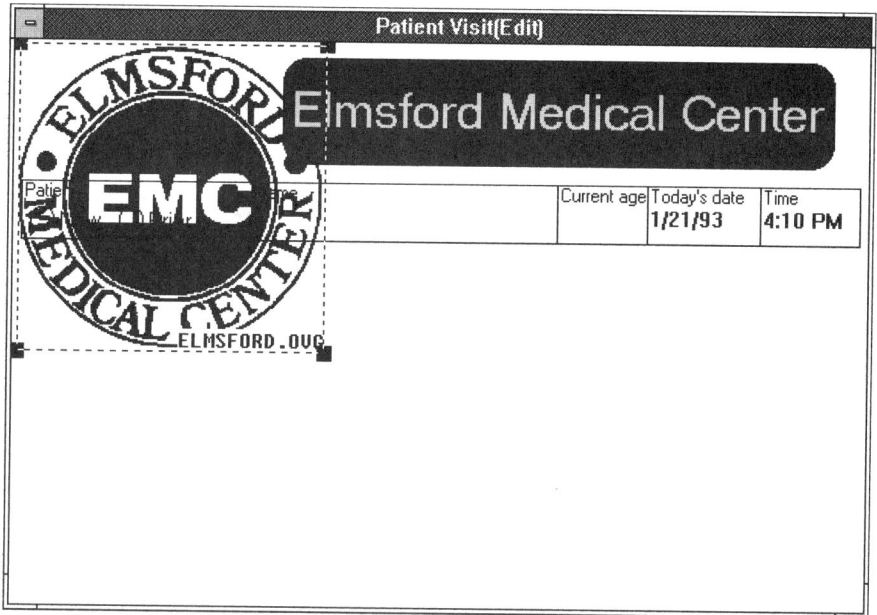

11-15
The oversized EMC logo pasted into the patient visit form.

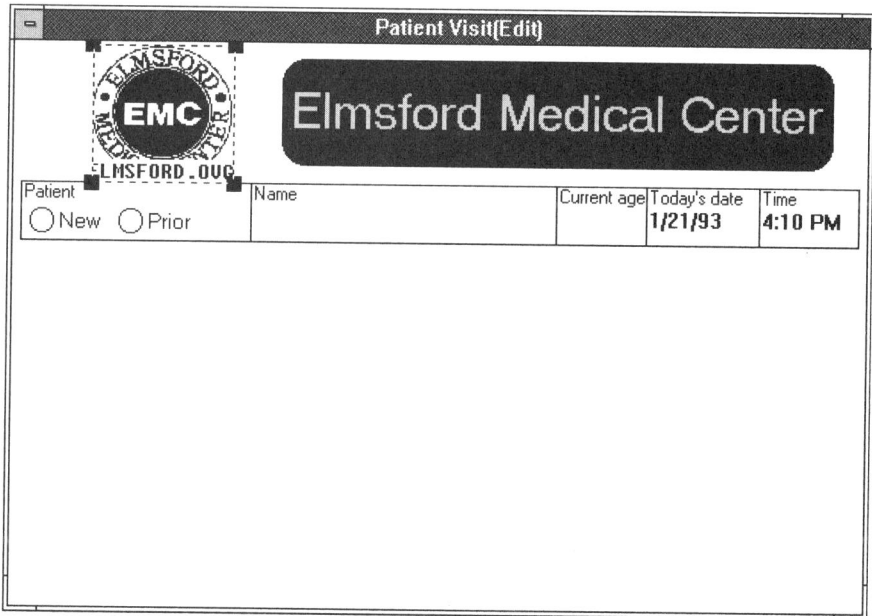

11-16
The logo placed and sized.

If you went through the previous exercise and imported the EMC logo from the Clipboard, you should begin by erasing it. With the patient visit form on your screen, select Form from the Tools menu.

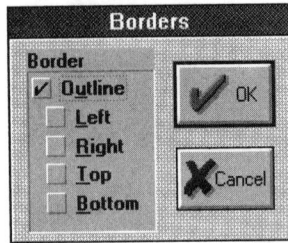

11-18 *The Borders options window before Outline is turned off.*

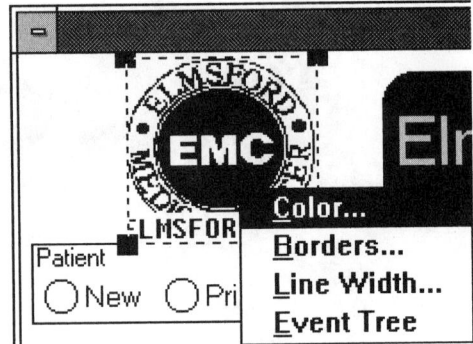

11-17 *The property list for the EMCgraphics object.*

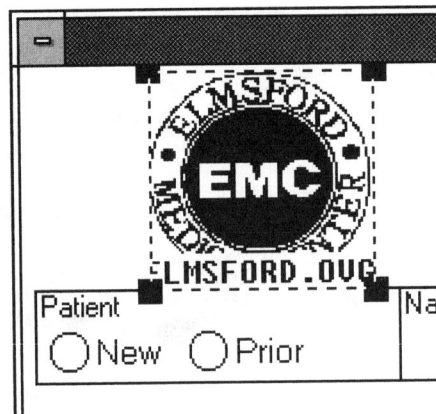

11-19
The EMC logo selected.

Next, click on the EMC logo to select it; it will be surrounded by a dotted rectangle with selection handles at the corners, as shown in FIG. 11-19. Choose Cut from the Edit menu and the logo will disappear.

Now click on the graphics tool in the object bar; a window will tell you that there is currently no graphic in the Clipboard, and ask whether you want to use an ObjectVision graphic (see FIG. 11-20). Click on Yes, and the Open Graphic File window will list any .OVG files that you might have in the C:\VISION directory (see FIG. 11-21).

There are a number of .OVG files provided by Borland in the C:\VISION\SAMPLE directory. Click twice on the directory list, and you'll see a group of .OVG files that go with the ObjectVision sample applications, under Files (see FIG. 11-22).

The graphic in this list that sounds most appropriate for a medical center is the one titled ANTIACID.OVG. Let's take that one. Point and click to select it and then press OK. A dotted rectangle indicating the size and location of the

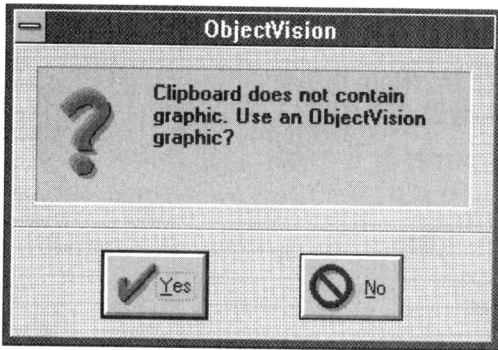

11-20
The Graphics Query window.

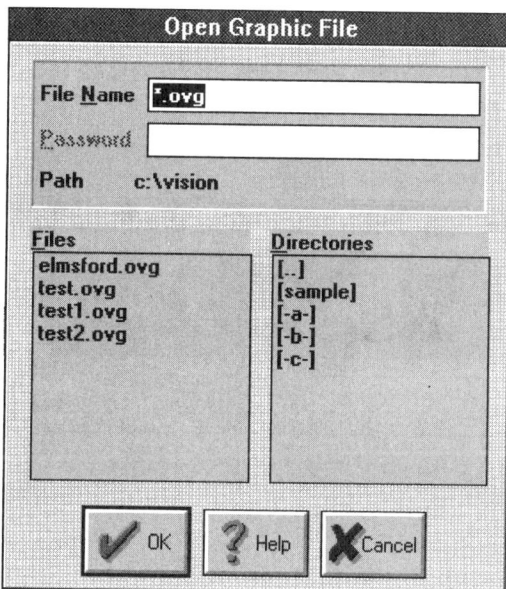

11-21
The Open Graphic File window, listing ObjectVision graphics files in the C:\VISION directory.

graphic will appear on your patient visit form (see FIG. 11-23). Drag the rectangle up to a position in front of the Elmsford Medical Center banner, and size it to fit. When you're set, click the left mouse button to place the image (see FIG. 11-24). This might be an overly graphic graphic for the Elmsford Medical Center, but it serves its purpose.

To remove the border from the graphic, point to it and click the right mouse button. When the property list pops up, click on Borders and then remove the checkmark in front of Outline in the Borders window. Click on OK, and your job should be finished.

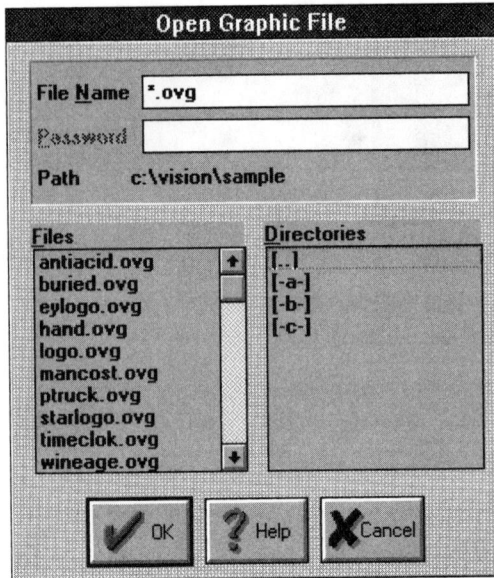

11-22
A listing of the .OVG files in the C:\VISION\SAMPLE directory.

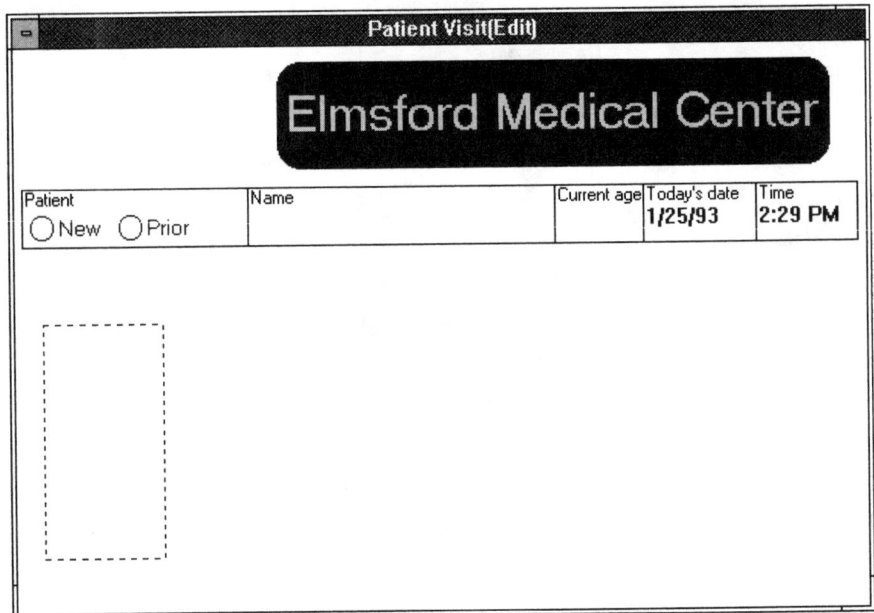

11-23
The dotted rectangle marking the location and size of the new antiacid graphic.

To see the final result, click on the close tool at the left end of the object bar. The form tools will disappear, and you should see your patient visit form in runtime mode with your spectacular new graphic logo (see FIG. 11-25).

By following one of the two procedures outlined in this chapter for importing graphic files, you can add, position, and size almost any kind of graphic image to your ObjectVision applications.

11-24
The antiacid image sized and placed in front of the Elmsford Medical Center banner.

11-25
The patient visit form with its new graphic logo.

12 More about the properties of objects & fields

In chapter 5 you did some basic work with the properties of objects. You might recall, however, that the property list for a field is rather lengthy, so there are a number of items I didn't cover. Now that you've advanced in ObjectVision sophistication, we'll take a look at the additional touches you can add with property lists.

I've taken the patient visit form and fleshed it out to nearly its complete version. You can see the screen version in two parts in FIGS. 12-1 and 12-2. Go ahead and add these remaining fields if you want; you now have the skills you need to add and size them. The form has been designed so that, in its printed version, it will fill an 8½×11-inch sheet of paper in the vertical or portrait format, and the printed version should look like FIG. 12-3.

Don't add all the bells and whistles this form needs to perform in all its glory (although you can get the fully functioning form by returning the coupon that comes with this book). You need to make a few enhancements first, in order to demonstrate the operation of some more of the elements of the property lists.

The on-screen version of the form is easily legible; the printed version, on the other hand, is filled with crabbed little fonts that are unnecessarily difficult to

12-1
The top of the patient visit form with all fields added.

12-2
The bottom of the finished patient visit form.

Elmsford Medical Center

Patient ○ New ○ Prior	Name		Current age	Today's date 2/1/93	Time 11:55 AM

| Pulse: | | Respiration: | | Weight: | | Blood pressure: | |

| Last date seen | Place of service |

Reason for visit

Patient's history

Examination

Medical decisions

Patient progress

Medications

Recommendations/referrals

Medical necessity for ancillary diagnostic procedures

Diagnosis

Time (length of visit)	Expected date to return for follow-up	Signature of attending physician
		Date

12-3
The printed version of the patient visit form in its current state.

read. As part of this tutorial exercise, you're going to enlarge both the label fonts and the value fonts. You'll also:

- Remove all but the top field borders.
- Add Help text to the Medical Decisions field.
- Add a background color for the entire form, plus a different background color for every other line.

- Add an event tree to the last field so that entered data can be stored and cleared in readiness for the next patient's data.
- Align the field values.

Removing field borders

Assume that you've launched ObjectVision, loaded the VISITFRM.OVD file that contains this application, and added the new fields shown in FIGS. 12-1 and 12-2.

Note: The second line, with Pulse, Respiration, Weight, and Blood Pressure, actually contains eight fields. The four field labels are actually text fields, and the four fields where those values appear are actually labeled Today's Pulse, Today's Respiration, Today's Weight, and Today's Blood Pressure. The program is instructed not to show the field labels.

Begin by removing all but the top borders from all fields except the four vital data fields—Pulse, Respiration, Weight, and Blood Pressure—in the second line. The first step is to select all the fields on the form. Remember that you can select all contiguous (connecting or adjacent) fields by clicking on the first field, holding down the Shift key, and clicking on the last field.

You can also select as many fields or objects as you want, contiguous or not, by keeping the Ctrl key depressed as you click on the fields or objects. That's what you're going to do now: By holding down the Ctrl key and clicking where appropriate, select the following fields: Patient, Name, Current Age, Today's Date, Time, Last Date Seen, Place of Service, Reason for Visit, and Patient's History (see FIG. 12-4).

12-4
The patient visit form with several fields selected.

Now point to any one of the selected fields and click the right mouse button. A property list will pop up (see FIG. 12-5). Select Borders and, when the Borders menu appears, turn off the checkmark in front of Outline and add one in front of Top (see FIG. 12-6). Click on OK or press Enter, and the job should be done. To confirm that it is, click on the Pulse text object and you should see that all the visible fields have only top borders, except those fields and text objects in the second line (see FIG. 12-7).

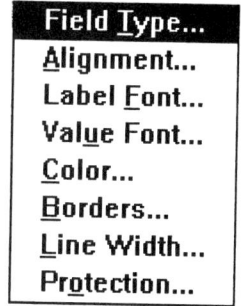

12-6
The Borders window, with Top checked.

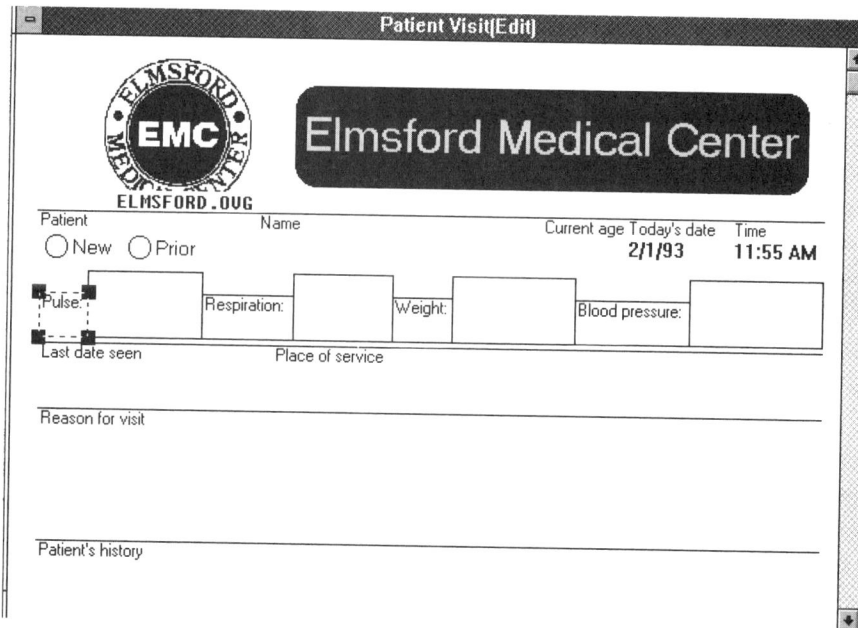

12-5 *The Field property list.*

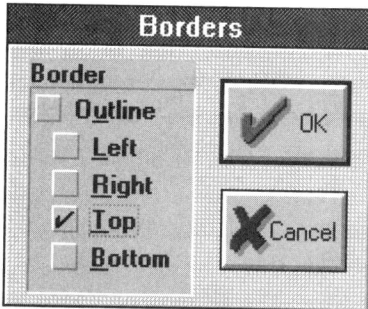

12-7
The upper part of the patient visit form with left, right, and bottom borders removed from most fields.

Now, with the Pulse text object still selected, depress the Ctrl key and select the Respiration, Weight, and Blood Pressure text objects as well (see FIG. 12-8). Again, point to any one of them and click the right mouse button. After selecting Borders from the property list, remove the checkmark in front of Outline and then click on OK. Click on a field outside the second row to deselect the text objects, and your form should resemble FIG. 12-9. In a similar

12-8
The four text objects in the second line selected.

12-9
The text objects with borders removed.

fashion, remove the left, right, and bottom borders from all the fields below, leaving them with only top borders. That concludes your work with the Borders property.

Changing label & value fonts

I mentioned earlier that the type sizes for both the labels (field names) and values (data entered in the fields) were too small to be easily readable on the printout. For that reason, you're going to make these fonts a couple of sizes larger.

Let's start with the label fonts. Select all field objects on the form and then click the right mouse button to display the property list. This time, select Label Font. When the Label Font window is shown, it will probably reveal that you've been using Helv (Helvetica) 8 pt., or something like that, as your label font (see FIG. 12-10). Let's bump the size up a notch to Helv 10. After you select 10 and click on OK, your labels will probably look like those in FIG.

12-10
The Label Font window, showing Helv (Helvetica) 8 as the current typeface and size for the field labels.

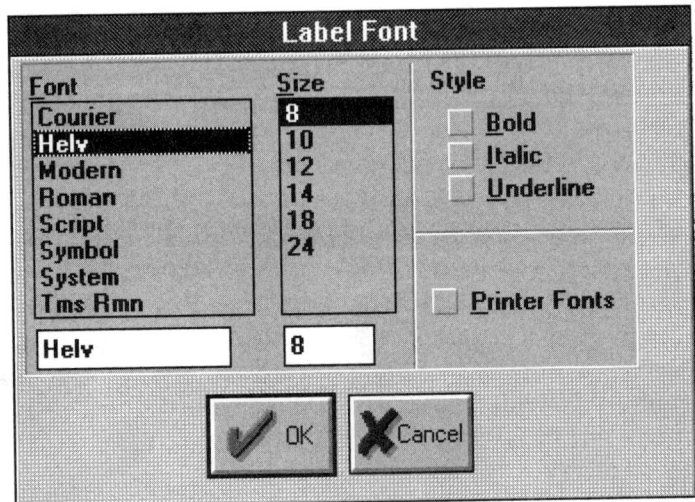

12-11. This larger type might cause some problems; observe how the value has been squeezed downward in the Today's Date field. You might have to do some resizing to remedy that situation.

You can also increase the size of the type in the text objects on the second line. Select the four objects, point to one, click the right mouse button, and select Label Font from the property list. Choose Helv 10 as the new font and press OK. Once again, the larger typesize is likely to necessitate some rearranging, as you see in FIG. 12-12. You don't need large boxes for the vital data values, so you can shrink the boxes, stretch the text objects, and end up with something that looks like FIG. 12-13.

12-12
The expanded fonts result in some crowding.

12-13
The Vital Data line readjusted for the larger text.

Next, change the value font (the font for the data entered on the form) and increase its size as well. Figure 12-14 shows the form after some data has been entered in the first line and all fields involving data entry have been selected. Click the right mouse button to display the property list that is common to all of these selected fields, and select Value Font from the menu. The Value Font window will pop up (see FIG. 12-15).

12-14
The patient visit form with some data entered and data-entry fields selected.

12-15
The Value Font window, with no font selected.

Choose the Tms Rmn (Times Roman) font, 12 point. Your Value Font window should now look like FIG. 12-16. Click on OK, and the values will be presented in their new size and typeface (see FIG. 12-17).

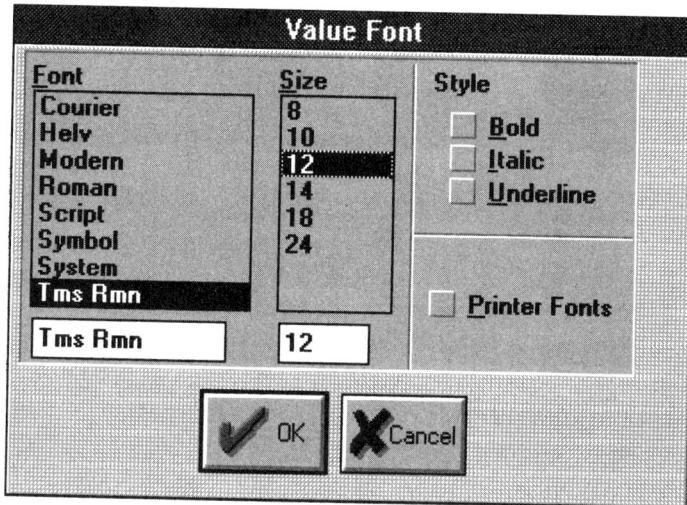

12-16
The Value Font window with 12-point Times Roman type selected.

12-17
The form with its new value font and size.

If your form is like mine, you might have field-size problems and have to play "shrink and stretch" with some of the field sizes to make everything fit—but no one told you that creating new Windows applications was going to be all creativity and glamour. Easy, yes; elegant, sometimes; glamorous—almost never.

Adding help text to a field Because you're creating a new Windows application, it's likely that those who use your application will need help—just as you might need help from time to time with software applications that you use. Of course, there's Windows Help and ObjectVision Help. But what about help with questions that are specific to your patient visit application? Well, the programmers at Borland thought of that, and made it possible for you to insert help text as one of the properties of a field.

We'll take the field named Medical Decisions for this demonstration. A doctor, or his assistant, might well come to that field and wonder precisely what sort of information or data was required. On the information sheet sent out with the letter about these patient visit forms, the New York State Medical Society expands on the sort of response that's appropriate or expected here. You can create a Help window that contains the NYSMA text verbatim. Here's how:

With your patient visit form still in edit mode, click on the Medical Decisions field to select it (see FIG. 12-18). Display the property list in the customary fashion by pointing to the selected field and clicking the right mouse button. A fairly extensive property list will pop up, and the last item on the menu is Help (see FIG. 12-19). Click on Help, and the Help Text window will pop up, ready for you to add almost as much text as you want (see FIG. 12-20). Using the standard Windows text-editing techniques, change the phrase Medical Decisions to all uppercase, type a colon and a space at the end, and then enter the following text:

```
Enter the number of possible diagnoses, the possible
treatment options, analysis of medical records and
diagnostic tests, risks of complications and/or morbidity
or mortality.
```

12-18
The Medical Decisions field selected.

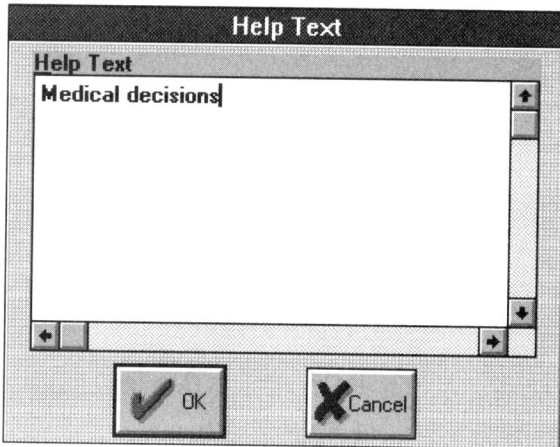

12-20
The Help Text window.

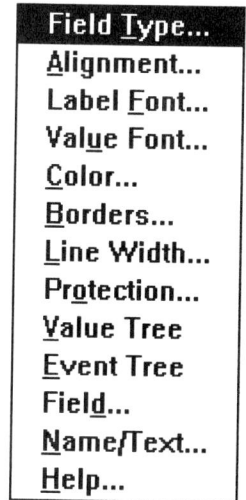

12-19 *The property list for the Medical Decisions field, with Help at the bottom.*

When you're finished, the Help Text window should look like FIG. 12-21. The text isn't wrapped at the moment, but it will all be nicely boxed up when you need it. Click on OK after you've checked your text for typing errors, and you'll be back to the patient visit form with no changes visible. So what did you accomplish? Click on the close tool and you'll find out.

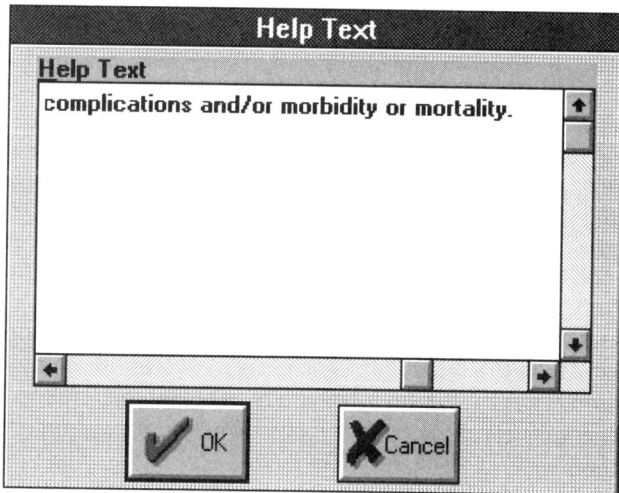

12-21
The Help Text window showing the end of the explanatory text.

Now that you're back in runtime mode, be sure that the Medical Decisions field is selected; you can tell by the box that surrounds it (see FIG. 12-22). Are you ready for this? Press F1, the standard Help key. Sure enough, there's your own little Medical Decisions Help message, neatly boxed and formatted (see FIG. 12-23). You're becoming a sophisticated programmer! Click again and the Help message will disappear into cyberspace.

12-22
The Medical Decisions field selected in runtime mode.

Examination

Medical decisions

Patient progress

12-23
The Medical Decisions Help window.

Examination

Medical decisions Help

MEDICAL DECISIONS: Enter the number of possible diagnoses, the possible treatment options, analysis of medical records and diagnostic tests, risks of complications and/or morbidity or mortality.

Medical decisions

Patient progress

Adding color to a form

Now that you're creating jazzy applications, there's no reason that they should remain drab black and white. You can change the color of the entire form, and also the color of individual fields. Let's get colorful.

To change the color of the entire form, lay a filled rectangle on top of the form and the color of the rectangle becomes the background color of the form. In the form edit mode, select the filled rectangle tool. When the rectangle cursor appears, place the crosshairs in the upper left-hand corner of your form and click the left mouse button. The small default version of the filled rectangle will be displayed in that corner, as shown in FIG. 12-24. (Your version might not look exactly like mine.)

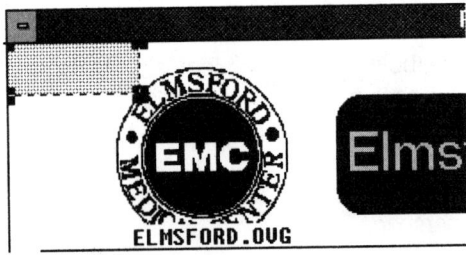

ELMSFORD.OVG

12-24
The default version of the filled rectangle.

Drag the lower right-hand corner of the rectangle until it covers the entire patient visit form. When you release it and return to the top of the form, your whole form should be covered by the rectangle. It might appear shaded, as in FIG. 12-25.

12-25
The entire form covered by the filled rectangle.

With the rectangle still selected (you should see four selection handles at the four corners of the rectangle; be careful that you're not looking at another field that was inadvertently selected), click the right mouse button to exhibit the property list for the rectangle (see FIG. 12-26). Click on Color and, when the Color window pops up, press the selection button on the Background field. That will display a palette of background color options (see FIG. 12-27).

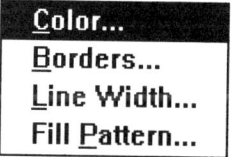

12-26 *The property list for the filled rectangle, with Color selected.*

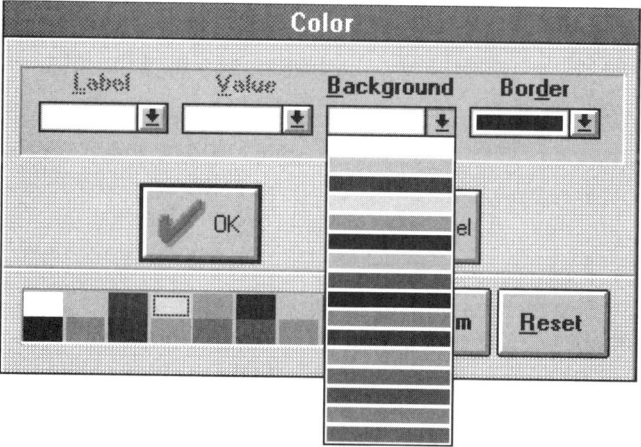

12-27
The Color window with the background palette displayed.

Choose a light yellow if you have it; if you don't, choose anything you please. Press OK, and your form should be transmogrified into a spectacle of rich lemon yellow. (There's no point in trying to demonstrate this in a black-and-white illustration.)

But don't stop there. Let's make every other line lime green by using the Field Property menu. Select the first line by clicking first on the Patient field and then, with the Shift key depressed, clicking on the Time field (see FIG. 12-28). Now, while holding down the Ctrl key, select all fields in lines 3, 5, 7, etc. Point to any one of the selected fields and click the right mouse button, and the property list that's common to all the selected fields will pop up (see FIG. 12-29).

12-28
All fields in the first line selected.

12-29 *The property list for the selected fields.*

Notice that some options you saw on other property lists are missing from this one. For example, there's no Event Tree option, nor is there a Value Tree option. The reason is that, when multiple fields are selected, the only property options available are those that can be assigned to all of the fields at once.

Select Color from this property list and, when the Color window shows up, open the Background palette and select the light green or lime green color and press OK. Your form should return in green and yellow stripes (see FIG. 12-30).

I've had you create this stripey form primarily to make a point—that it can be done. However, you might want to do something like this for practical reasons. For example, computer printout paper has, for a long time, come with different colors in alternating rows. The reason is that it's often easier to

12-30
The new form, with many colors.

read and keep track of data in long horizontal rows if the rows immediately above and below are colored differently. Or maybe you just have a thing about zebras. In any case, you've now mastered another item on the property menu. Before you forget it, save your file.

When you finish filling out a form, you'll normally want to do two things: save the data you've entered on the form, and clear the form for new data entry. You can accomplish both of these (and many more) with a single event tree. Let's go to the final field in this form—Expected Date to Return for Follow-Up—and give it a multipurpose event tree.

Building a multipurpose event tree

In edit mode, select the Expected Date to Return for Follow-Up field (see FIG. 12-31). With the mouse pointer in the field, click the right button to display the property list (see FIG. 12-32). Select Event Tree from the menu, and the Event Tree window will open, ready for you to construct the tree (see FIG. 12-33).

12-31
The Expected Date to Return for Follow-Up field selected.

Field Type...
Alignment...
Label Font...
Value Font...
Color...
Borders...
Line Width...
Protection...
Value Tree
Event Tree
Field...
Name/Text...
Help...

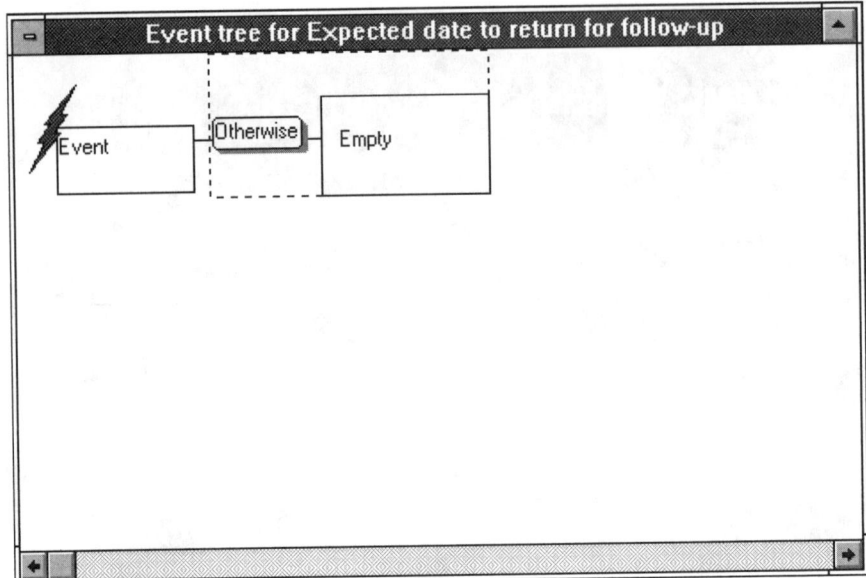

12-32 *The property list for the Expected Date to Return for Follow-Up field, with Event Tree highlighted.*

12-33 *The Event Tree window for the selected field.*

12-34 *The conclusion tool.*

Click on the conclusion tool (see FIG. 12-34). When the Event Name window opens, click on the selection button to reveal your choices: Change, Select, and Unselect (see FIG. 12-35). Your choice here is Unselect. Here's why: When your cursor either arrives at a field or selects it, it's time to enter data. When you enter the data and press Enter, you unselect the field and move on to the next one. That's the point at which you want to store all data and clear the form, hence the choice of Unselect.

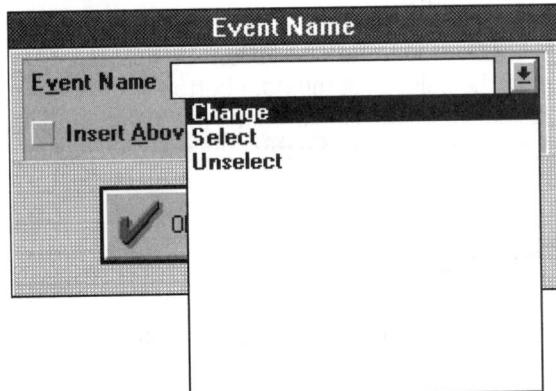

12-35
The Event Name window with event options displayed.

After you've selected Unselect (sort of a Zen moment in ObjectVision), click on OK. The program will now open the Action window; there are two things you need to do here. First, click on Function and, when the Function Name window pops up, find STORE and select it (see FIG. 12-36). Click on OK, and the @ function will be pasted into the Action window, waiting for you to supply a linkname—the name you gave the link that connects you to that Paradox database you created back in chapter 10 (see FIG. 12-37). The link name you assigned in chapter 10 was Patient Information Table, so type:

"Patient Information Table"

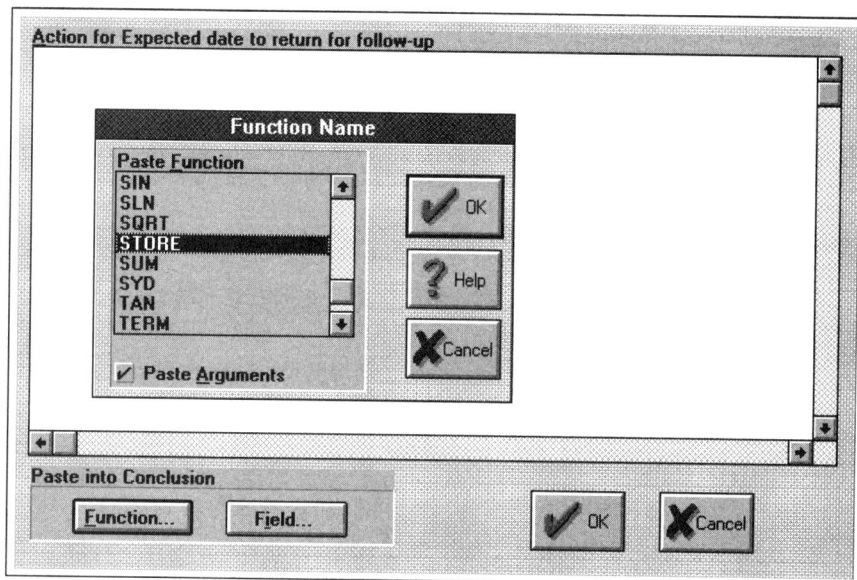

12-36
The Function Name window with @STORE highlighted.

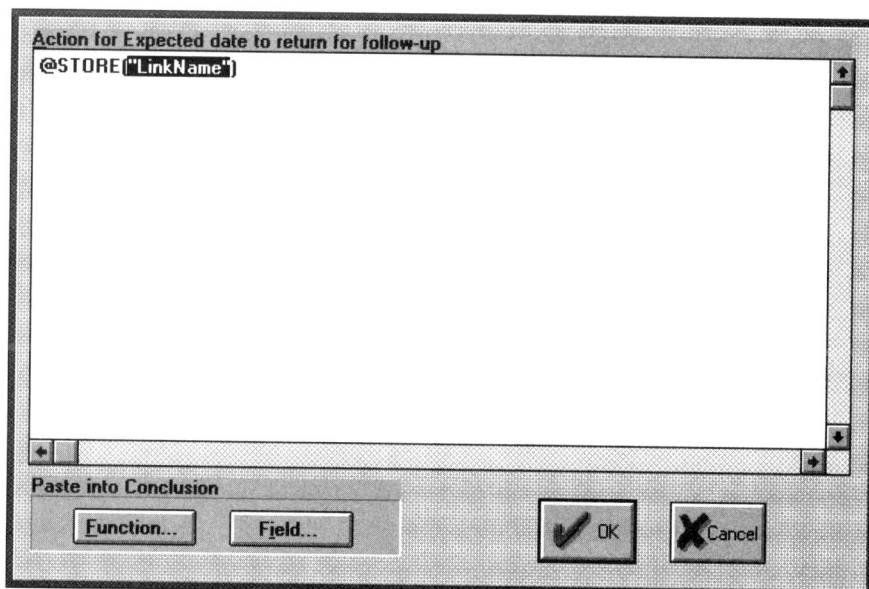

12-37
The @STORE function pasted into the Action window, waiting for a linkname.

Don't forget the quotation marks. Then hit a right arrow or your End key to get outside the parentheses.

There's still another action to be entered into this window, and it has to go on the next line. You can't hit Enter, however, because that's the same as clicking on OK. Instead, press Ctrl–Enter, and that will do the job for you.

Go once again to the Function button at the bottom of the window; this time select FORMCLEAR and click on OK (see FIG. 12-38). The program will paste this second @ function into the Action window and wait for you to name the form. Type:

```
"Patient Visit"
```

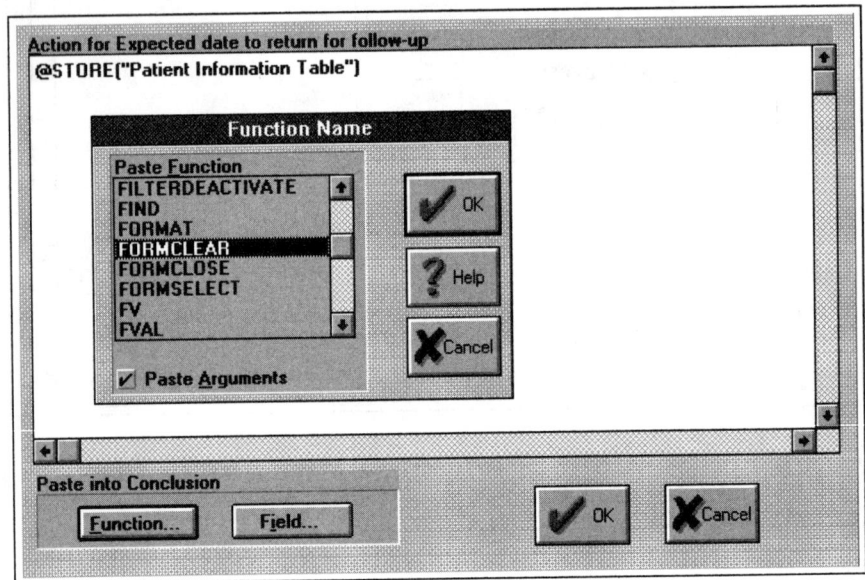

12-38
The Function Name window with @FORMCLEAR selected.

(Don't forget the quotation marks.) Your Action window should now look like FIG. 12-39. Click on OK, and your completed event tree will be returned, as shown in FIG. 12-40.

Can't quite read everything in that list of conclusions or actions? Open the View menu at the top of the screen (see FIG. 12-41). Click on Expand, and the top (and only) branch of your event tree will be enlarged so you can now read everything (see FIG. 12-42). Handy trick.

Close the Event Tree window, click on the close tool, and enter some data in your form to test the operation of this new event tree. Don't forget to save your file with this new change.

Action for Expected date to return for follow-up

```
@STORE("Patient Information Table")
@FORMCLEAR("Patient Visit")
```

Paste into Conclusion

Function... | Field... | ✓ OK | ✗ Cancel

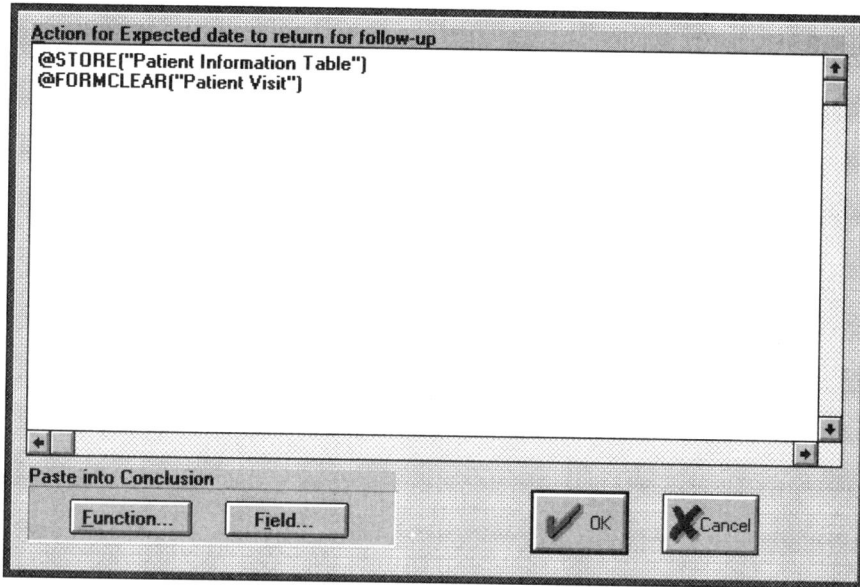

12-39
*The Action window with
two actions entered.*

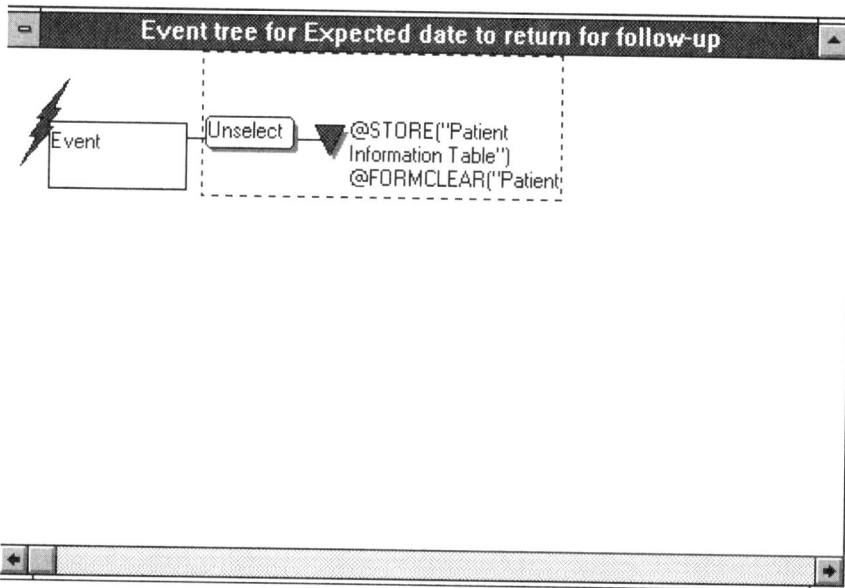

Event tree for Expected date to return for follow-up

Event — [Unselect] ▼ @STORE("Patient
Information Table")
@FORMCLEAR("Patient

12-40
*The completed event tree
for the Expected Date to
Return for Follow-Up field.*

View
Expand Ctrl+Home
Reduce Ctrl+End

12-41
*The View menu, with
Expand selected.*

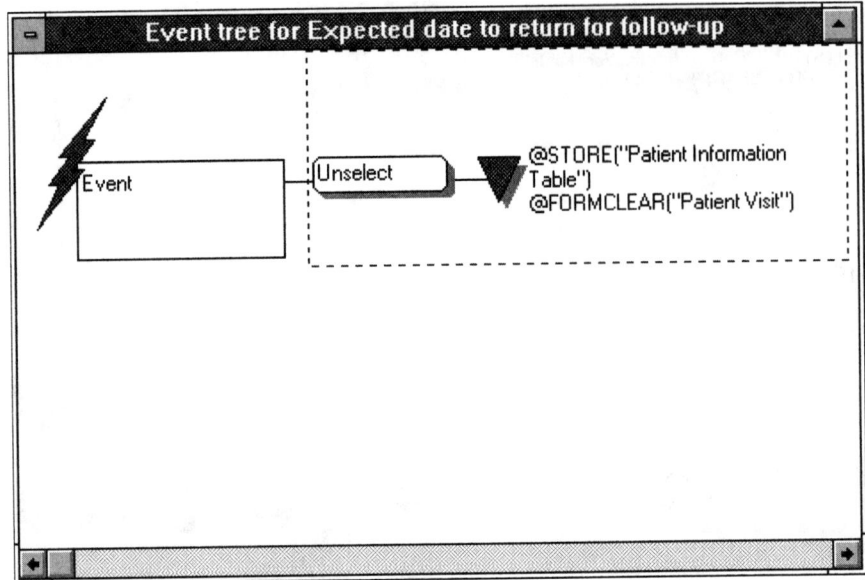

Event tree for Expected date to return for follow-up

Event | Unselect | @STORE("Patient Information Table") @FORMCLEAR("Patient Visit")

12-42
The event tree branch expanded so that all information is legible.

Editing an event tree

OK. So you have this exotic new patient visit form. You carefully fill in the data for each field and, as you finish the last field (Expected Date to Return for Follow-Up), you type in the follow-up date, give a triumphant slap to the Enter key, and watch as the form clears and stands ready to receive the data on the next patient. And then you realize that you had intended to print the form, and it's going to be a pain to retrieve and/or replace the data.

Don't despair; the situation isn't beyond remedy. You can get back into that event tree and insert a print command so the program will store, print, and clear all in one fell swoop.

Back in the edit mode once more, select the Expected Date to Return for Follow-Up field and display the property list by pointing and clicking the right mouse button. There should be a check next to Event Tree, indicating that an event tree has been created for this field. Click on Event Tree, and the event tree for the current window should appear (take a look back at FIG. 12-40).

Properties
Field...
Condition...
Conclusion...
Name...

12-43 *The Properties menu, with Conclusion highlighted.*

This time you want to store, print, and clear—in that order—which means you need to insert a print command between the @STORE function and the @FORMCLEAR function. To edit this window, open the Properties menu from the menu bar at the top of the screen (see FIG. 12-43). Select Conclusion from the menu, and the now-familiar Action window will reappear (check back to FIG. 12-39). Move the cursor to the end of the @STORE line and press Ctrl–Enter. This will insert a new line.

Press the Function button, and scroll through the @ function options in the Function Name window until you find PRINTFORM (see FIG. 12-44). Select PRINTFORM, click on OK, and the function will be pasted into your Action window, waiting for you to insert the form name once more. Type:

```
"Patient Visit"
```

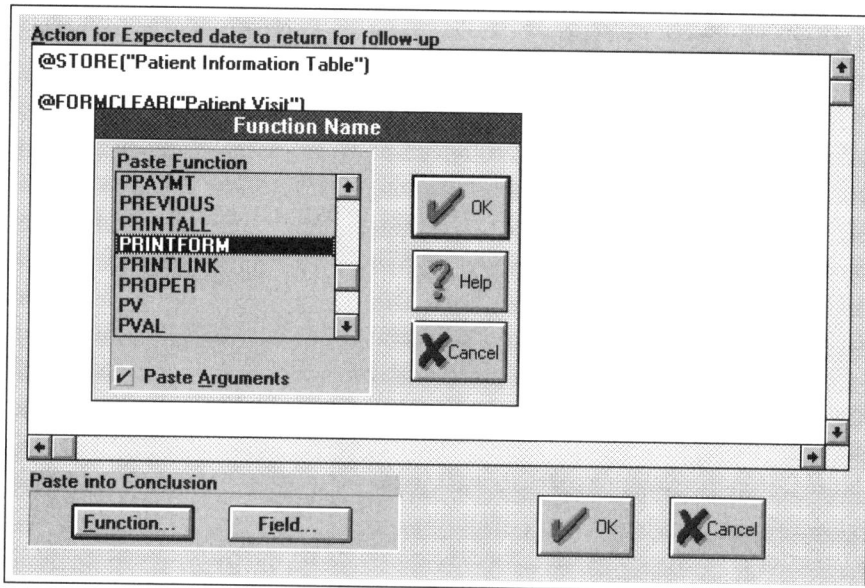

12-44
The Function Name window, with @PRINTFORM highlighted.

(Again, be careful not to omit the quotation marks.) Click on OK or press Enter and your revised Event Tree window, in its expanded view, should look like FIG. 12-45. Click twice on the close box in the upper left-hand corner of the window to close it. When you're finished, click on the close tool to return to runtime mode and give this second draft of your program a trial run.

Is this an elegant solution? No, but it's one solution, and it provides the demo you need at this point. It isn't elegant because it doesn't give you the option of not printing; a better solution would be to build the store, clear, and print instructions into some buttons on the form. But you've learned some more about using property lists for a field, and that, after all, was the point.

Now let's take a look at one more field property you can adjust—Alignment. With this function, you can determine the placement of values within a field. Nothing radical here; it's the usual left, right, center, or full justification that you've run into in word processing and other places.

Aligning values within a field

In FIG. 12-46 you see the top of the patient visit form with some data about a fictitious patient entered in some of the fields. With the program in edit

12-45
The revised event tree for the Expected Date to Return for Follow-Up window.

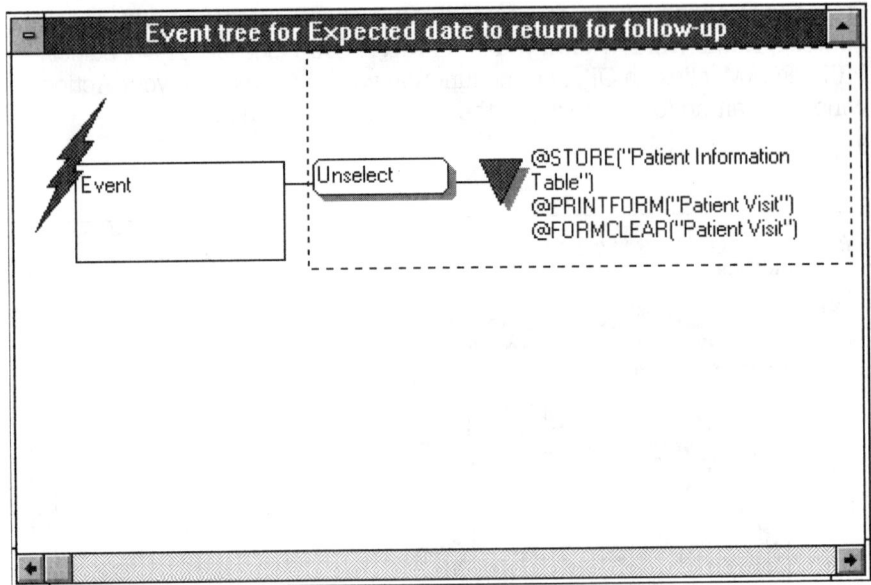

12-46
The top of the patient visit form with some data entered.

mode, select all of those data fields by holding down the Ctrl key and successively clicking on the fields you want to include (see FIG. 12-47).

Display the property list by pointing to any one of the selected fields and clicking the right mouse button (see FIG. 12-48). Select Alignment, and the

12-47
The form with several data fields selected.

Alignment window will offer you four alignment choices: Left, Right, Center, and Justified (see FIG. 12-49). Left, Right, and Center are probably obvious; Justified is what is referred to in word processing software such as WordPerfect as full justification—i.e., the text is aligned with both the left and right margins. Click on OK, and you'll see the results: The fields with a lot of text are spread from side to side, and the fields with short answers are justified left because they were in effect stopped and fixed in place by the Enter key—the equivalent of a hard Return in a word processing program (see FIG. 12-50).

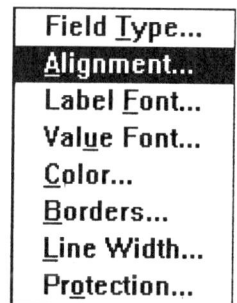

Field **T**ype...
Alignment...
Label **F**ont...
Val**u**e Font...
Color...
Borders...
Line Width...
Pro**t**ection...

12-48
The Properties menu with Alignment highlighted.

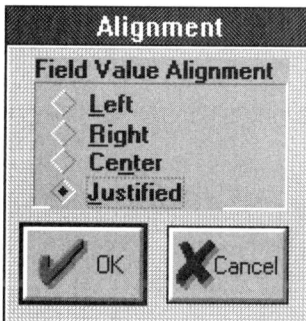

Alignment

Field Value Alignment
◇ **L**eft
◇ **R**ight
◇ **C**enter
◆ **J**ustified

✓ OK   ✗ Cancel

12-49
The Alignment window with Justified selected.

This looks pretty good—but what if you wanted those short answers centered? Well, just select them as a separate group, choose Center alignment, and you'd end up with something like FIG. 12-51. There are no rules about these things. Whatever works best, is easiest to read, or is most

12-50
The data fields with fully justified alignment.

12-51
Short-answer fields with center alignment.

responsive to your (or your users') aesthetic sense is what you should go with.

In this chapter, I've covered most of the field properties that you can assign or modify. You've probably begun to get a sense of the vast possibilities of this program—and in this basic tutorial, we're barely skimming the possibilities.

13 Printing & the View function

So far in this ObjectVision primer, we've focused on screen output, i.e., the way the program looks on your computer monitor. But what if you want a printout, called a *hardcopy*? After all, the patient visit application you've been designing is intended to automate the creation of a form that's printed and mailed to some company whose motto is "better things for better living through paperwork." So you—and all of your proctologist, pathologist, cardiologist, and endocrinologist friends and colleagues—have to get this jazzy new form all decked out and printed up.

If you've printed from other Windows applications, you'll find no surprises here. If you open the File menu, you'll see that one of the choices is Printer Setup (see FIG. 13-1). Take that choice, and the Printer Setup window will appear (see FIG. 13-2). I'm using an Okidata ML 393 24-pin dot-matrix printer and running under OS/2 2.0, which at the time of this writing doesn't supply a driver specifically for the Okidata printer. It does, however, provide a driver for the Epson 24-pin machine, which is compatible with the Okidata. You might have a similar situation; if you can't find your specific printer, there's likely to be a printer whose settings you can use because it's nearly 100% compatible.

Setting up your printer

Press the Setup button in the Printer Setup window, and another window will give you all the setup options for the particular printer you've selected: graphics resolution, orientation (*portrait* is vertical, *landscape* is horizontal),

File menu:
- **New**
- **Open...**
- **Resume**
- **Save**
- **Save As...**
- **Print Form**
- **Print All**
- **Print Link...**
- **Printer Setup**
- **Exit**

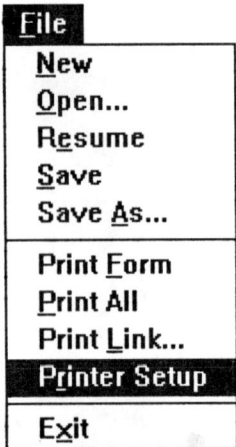

13-1 *The File menu with Printer Setup highlighted.*

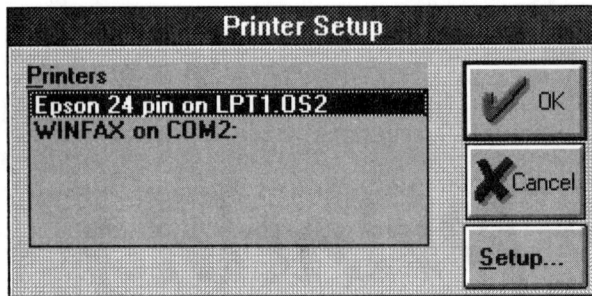

Printer Setup

Printers
Epson 24 pin on LPT1.OS2
WINFAX on COM2:

OK
Cancel
Setup...

13-2 *The Printer Setup window with an Epson 24-pin printer selected.*

paper feed type, text mode, paper width, etc. (see FIG. 13-3). Some of these options are pretty arbitrary, some are less so. For example, this form is going to print out best in portrait or vertical format—and that's the way the companies you're sending it to will expect to see it.

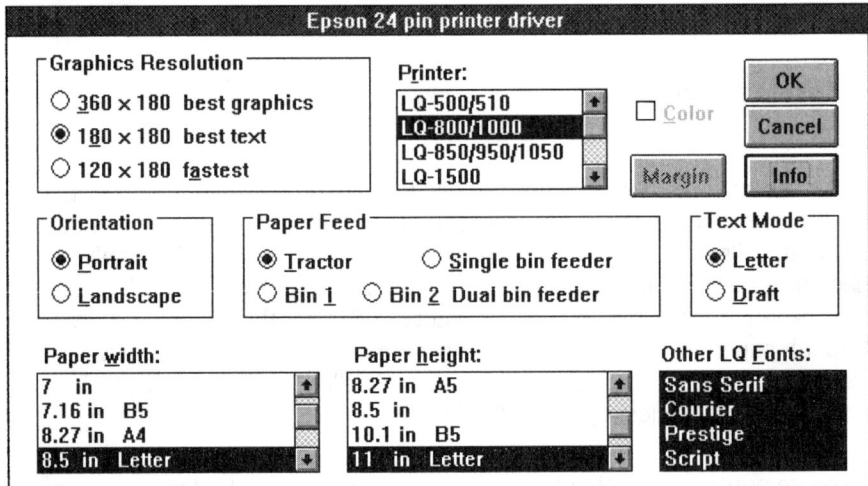

13-3 *The printer driver options for the Epson 24-pin printer driver.*

Epson 24 pin printer driver

Graphics Resolution
- ○ 360 × 180 best graphics
- ● 180 × 180 best text
- ○ 120 × 180 fastest

Printer:
LQ-500/510
LQ-800/1000
LQ-850/950/1050
LQ-1500

□ Color

OK
Cancel
Margin
Info

Orientation
- ● Portrait
- ○ Landscape

Paper Feed
- ● Tractor   ○ Single bin feeder
- ○ Bin 1   ○ Bin 2 Dual bin feeder

Text Mode
- ● Letter
- ○ Draft

Paper width:
7   in
7.16 in   B5
8.27 in   A4
8.5 in   Letter

Paper height:
8.27 in   A5
8.5 in
10.1 in   B5
11   in   Letter

Other LQ Fonts:
Sans Serif
Courier
Prestige
Script

When you've set the options to your satisfaction, click on OK and again on OK in the Printer Setup window. If you're using ObjectVision for OS/2 with a LaserJet or compatible printer, you must check (turn on) the printer-specific format option found on the print-queue page after opening the settings of the printer driver.

Printing a single form

To print the form you're working with, select Print Form from the File menu (see FIG. 13-4). A message will appear in a window telling you that the print data is being sent to the selected printer (see FIG. 13-5), and before long the wheels will spin and the printed form will come sliding out of your printer.

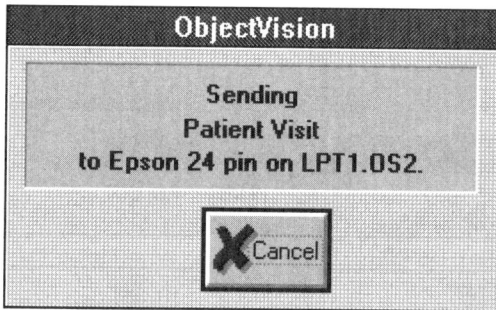

13-5
The message that data is being sent to the printer.

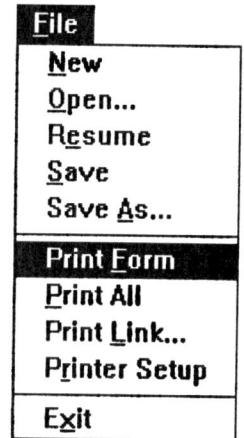

13-4 *The File menu with Print Form highlighted.*

To print every form in an application with a single action, select Print All from the File menu (see FIG. 13-6). ObjectVision will tell you once more that the designated printer is printing, and the process will continue until all forms in the application are printed.

Printing all forms in an application

The next item on the File menu is the Print Link command (see FIG. 13-7). With this command, you can go to the database that has the list of records you want to print, and print all selected records from that database. For example, you can get a printout of the patient visit form for every patient recorded in your database. Print Link will "respect" filters and restricted ranges, and therefore print only those records that are passed through the link to the form.

Using the Print Link command

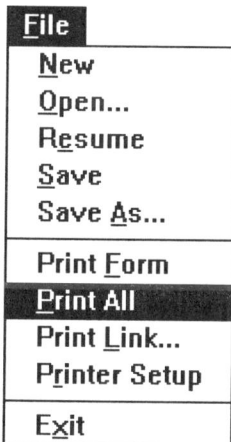

13-6 *The File menu with Print All highlighted.*

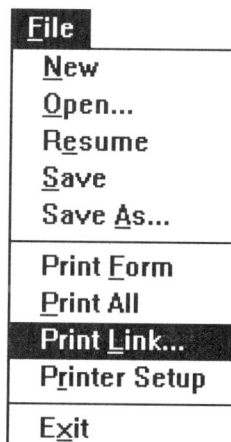

13-7 *The File menu with Print Link highlighted.*

Printing trees

There's one more type of printout you can get that doesn't currently show up on the File menu. You can print any tree, or all of the trees in an application. To see how this works, select Form from the Tools menu and then click on the Current Age field to select it (see FIG. 13-8). Now click on that field with the right mouse button to display the property list, and you'll see that ValueTree is checked (see FIG. 13-9).

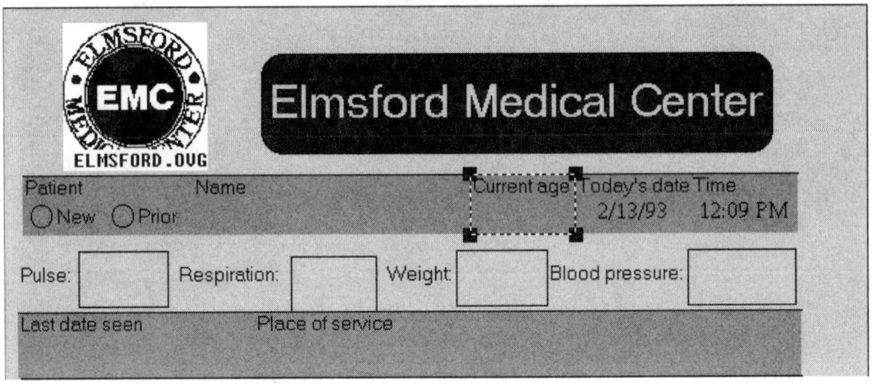

13-8
The Current Age field selected.

Select Value Tree from the list, and the value tree for that field will show the tree you created back in chapter 9 (see FIG. 13-10). Now open the File menu, and you'll see a couple of new choices: Print Tree and Print All (see FIG.

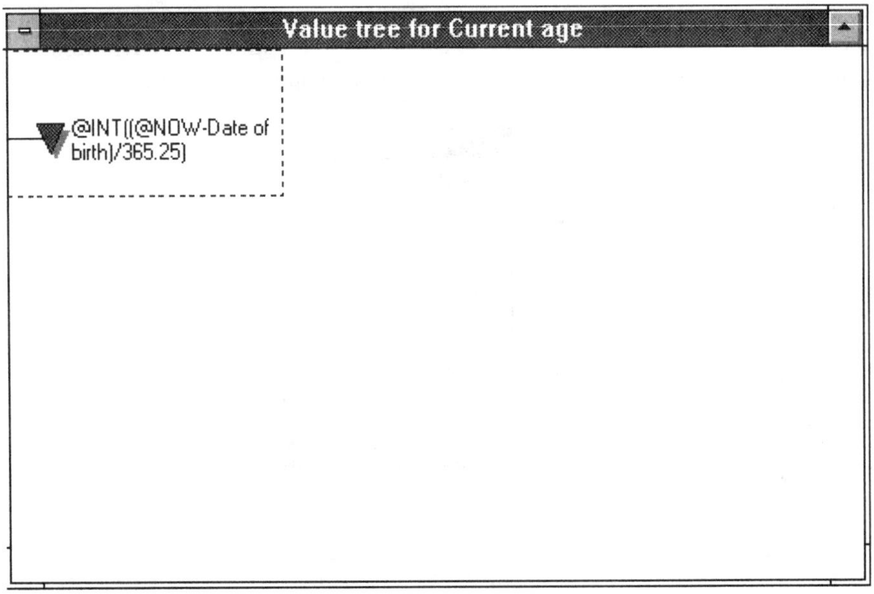

Field Type...
Alignment...
Label Font...
Value Font...
Color...
Borders...
Line Width...
Protection...
√ **Value Tree**
Event Tree
Field...
Name/Text...
Help...

13-9 *The property list for the Current Age field, with a check indicating that there's a value tree.*

Value tree for Current age

▼ @INT((@NOW-Date of birth)/365.25)

13-10 *The value tree for the Current Age field.*

13-11). Select Print Tree, and the command structure for that value tree (not the window itself) should come off your printer.

If you select Print All, the program will print out every value tree (not the event trees) associated with the form. Printing event trees—singly or en masse—works the same way as printing value trees. If the complete conclusion expressions don't appear in your Event Tree window, you can use the Expand and Contract buttons to change the resolution so everything you want to see is visible. The Print Tree command will then print whatever is shown on the screen.

Sometimes what you see on the screen isn't the same as what you get from the printer. For a reasonably accurate preview of what your printed copy will look like, you can use the Printer option on the View menu.

For example, if you load the Address Book application that's included with the sample files (ADDRESS.OVD) and select the Screen option from the View menu, the opening screen of the application will appear as shown in FIG. 13-12. Note that the value font (the font for the data entered on the form) appears to be some version of the System font. If you go into edit mode, however, and look at the properties for one of the data fields, you'll see that the stipulated font is Courier, as shown in FIG. 13-13. (At least that's what it is in my version of the program.)

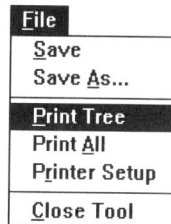

File
Save
Save As...
Print Tree
Print All
Printer Setup
Close Tool

13-11 *The File menu with Print Tree highlighted.*

Using the View function

Address Book (Goal)

Name		Top
Philippe Kahn		Previous
Title/Position		Next
President/CEO		Bottom
Company		Lookup...
Borland International, Inc.		Find...
Address		Birthdays
1800 Green Hills Road		Store

13-12
The opening screen of the Address Book application.

Name
Philippe Kahn
Title/Position
President/CEO
Company
Borland International, Inc.
Address
1800 Green Hills Road
Address2
P.O. Box 660001
City   State Zip Code
Scotts Valley CA   95067-0001
Country   Relationship
              ☒ Business ☐ Personal
Work Telephone   Ext   Home Telephone
(408) 438-5300
Fax Telephone   Birthday   Anniversary

Notes
Borland makes the hottest Windows
development products, including
ObjectVision and Turbo Pascal for
Windows. Stay in touch to get all
info on product updates!

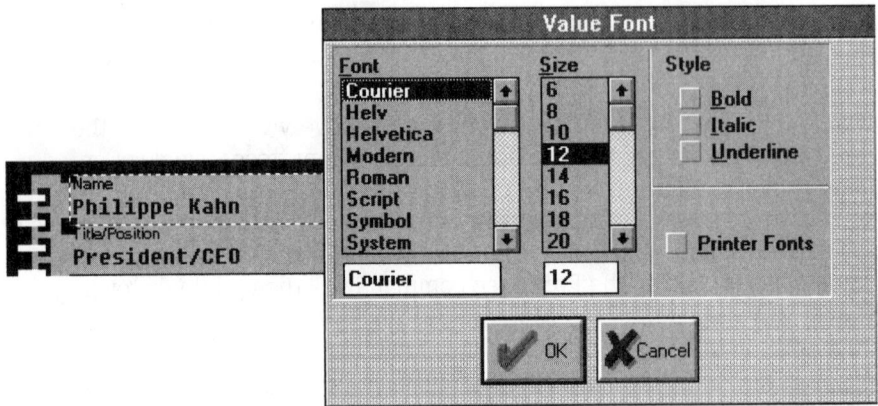

13-13
The Name field selected, with the value font shown as Courier 12.

If you select the Print option from the View menu, you'll see that the values, or data entries, are displayed in the Courier font. Also notice that, especially in the edit mode, the address book "page" no longer quite fits on the screen—which is one of the main reasons for using the View/Screen option (see FIG. 13-14).

You should now be ready to view and print out your ObjectVision applications. In the next chapter, you'll work on getting those applications ready for distribution.

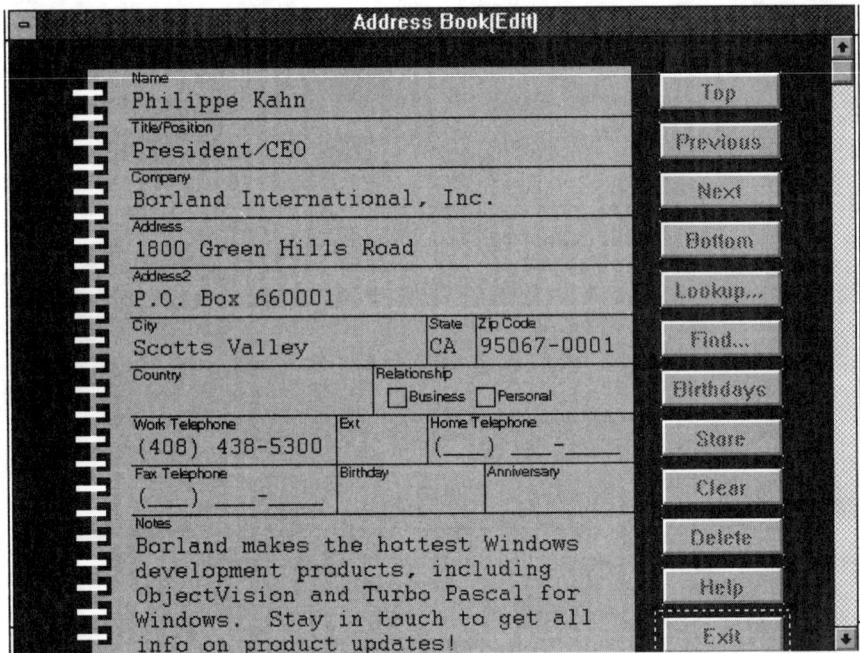

13-14
The opening screen of the Address Book application displayed in the View/Printer option.

14 *Running ObjectVision 2.1 applications*

Assume that you've completed the patient visit application (or any other application) to your satisfaction, and are now ready to supply this new application to your customers, clients, significant others, whoever. You want to hand it to them as a ready-to-run stand-alone application, not as one of several applications under ObjectVision. Can you legally do that? If so, how?

The first answer is yes. Borland has thoughtfully provided a runtime disk you can copy and then distribute with your applications.

One of the most useful things Borland has done in connection with this program is to provide an annotated file listing of the files that come with the program (including the filenames contained in the compressed files) and a brief description of those files. This is a valuable service; I don't know why more software publishers don't imitate Borland in this respect.

Creating a runtime disk

In the Tips and Techniques booklet that might have come with your ObjectVision documentation (if it didn't, call Borland customer service and order a copy), you're told that you can do a DISKCOPY of the runtime disk. If you don't want your users to have the sample applications that Borland provides on the runtime disk—or if you want to conceal the fact that the application you're distributing has been created via ObjectVision—you can delete the file named RTSMP.PAK.

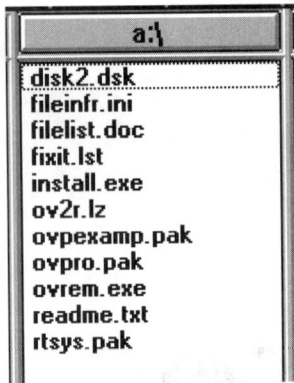

```
┌──────────────────────────┐
│            a:\           │
├──────────────────────────┤
│ disk2.dsk                │
│ fileinfr.ini             │
│ filelist.doc             │
│ fixit.lst                │
│ install.exe              │
│ ov2r.lz                  │
│ ovpexamp.pak             │
│ ovpro.pak                │
│ ovrem.exe                │
│ readme.txt               │
│ rtsys.pak                │
└──────────────────────────┘
```

14-1 *The contents of disk 2 of the three-disk Runtime and Applications Installation set (5.25-inch disks) that come with ObjectVision PRO 2.1.*

```
┌──────────────────────────┐
│            b:\           │
├──────────────────────────┤
│ disk1.dsk                │
│ elmsford.bmp             │
│ elmsford.ovg             │
│ filelist.doc             │
│ fixit.lst                │
│ install.exe              │
│ ov2r.lz                  │
│ patinfo.db               │
│ patinfo.f                │
│ patinfo.px               │
│ readme.txt               │
│ rtsys.pak                │
│ visitfrm.ovd             │
│ vistdate.db              │
│ vistdate.px              │
└──────────────────────────┘
```

14-2 *A directory of Runtime files for installing the Patient Visit application.*

Note: Follow their instructions and use the DISKCOPY command. If you use a simple COPY procedure, your installation of the runtime files might not work properly—or at least that was my experience. Borland also suggests that you then use a DOS batch file to copy your application to this new runtime disk, and then copy all the files you'll need to run your applications—files with .OVD, .OVG, and .DLL extensions, as well as any database files you might have created—to the appropriate subdirectory.

Now let's take a look at the runtime disk. If you have 5.25-inch disks, you'll have two runtime disks—two of the three-disk installation set identified as Runtime and Applications Installation disks. Note: If you're using ObjectVision 2.1 rather than ObjectVision PRO (you can purchase either the entire ObjectVision PRO package or just the ObjectVision 2.1 program), there will be only two installation disks. If you look at the disk directory for disk 2 of the three-disk set, you'll see that it contains the files shown in FIG. 14-1. Note that, in the case of this three-disk set, the RTSMP.PAK file is on disk 3.

These files will be copied to your new distribution disk, along with all of the .OVD, OVG, .DLL, and database files required by your application (see FIG. 14-2).

Here's what to instruct your client—the one who's receiving your nifty new ObjectVision application—about installing the runtime disk you supply: To install the runtime version of your ObjectVision application, start Windows and select Run from the File menu (see FIG. 14-3). When the Run window opens, type *d*: INSTALL (where *d* is the name of the drive where the runtime disk is located), and press Enter (see FIG. 14-4).

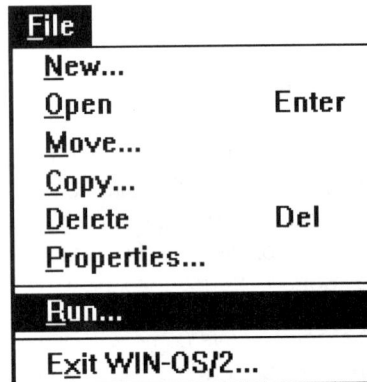

14-3 *The File menu with Run highlighted.*

As the installation program gets underway, the ObjectVision PRO Runtime Installation window will be displayed, asking you to confirm the source drive, the destination drive and directory for the system files, and the destination drive and directory for any sample files. It will also query you about some other matters (see FIG. 14-5). Make your selections and click on Install; the

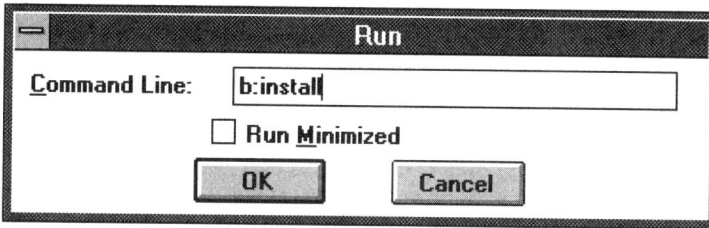

14-4
The Run window with the correct install command entered.

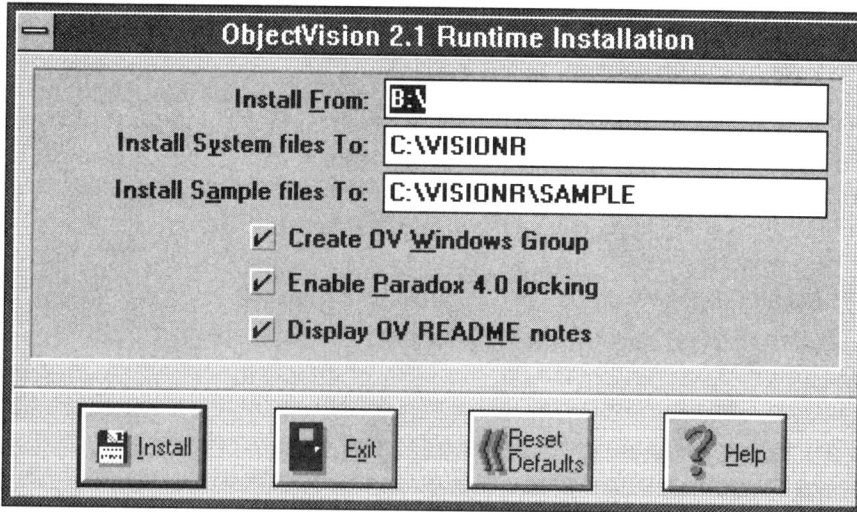

14-5
The ObjectVision 2.1 Runtime Installation window.

program will begin to unpack files and load them onto your hard drive. When the process is completed, a window will appear to confirm this and tell you where the files have been located (see FIG. 14-6).

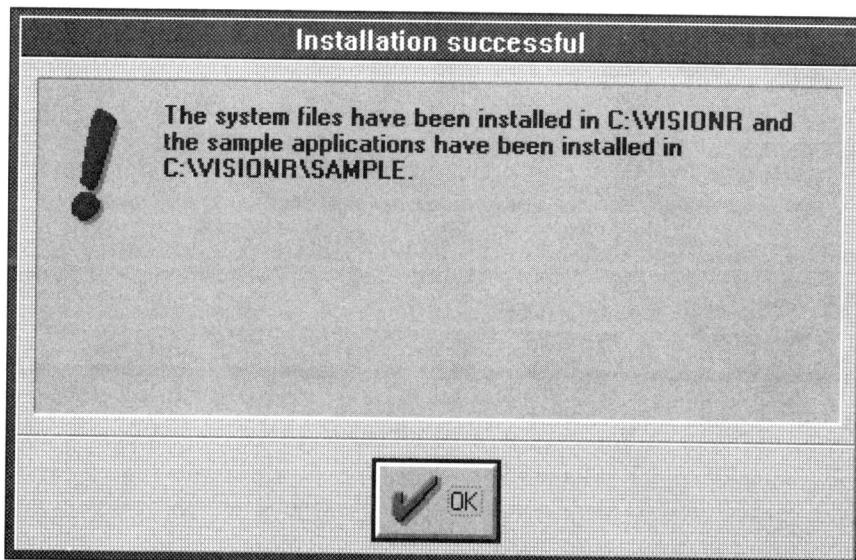

14-6
The Installation Successful window, confirming the locations of files and directories on the hard disk.

Unless you've turned it off, you'll also see a README file entitled *Welcome to ObjectVision PRO 2.1*. Click on OK, and your next message will tell you that you've just completed the installation of a whole bunch of stuff (see FIG. 14-7). Actually, you didn't install all of it, and you might not want to install the other ObjectVision PRO applications (Turbo C++ and Crystal Reports).

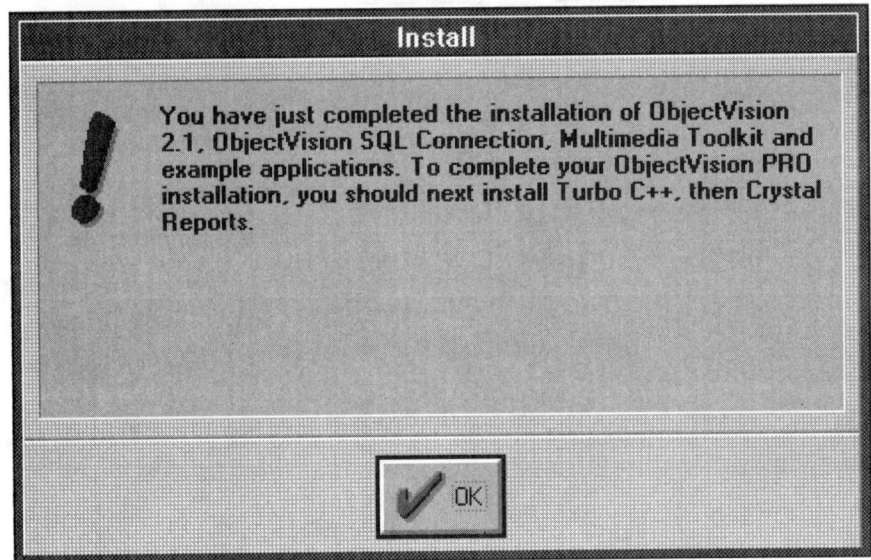

14-7
Another Install message.

During your installation, you can bypass the installation message in FIG. 14-7; don't assume that you've done something wrong if it doesn't appear. Click on OK, and you should see the icons for the runtime version of ObjectVision PRO, ObjectVision Demos, and Multimedia Demos (see FIG. 14-8).

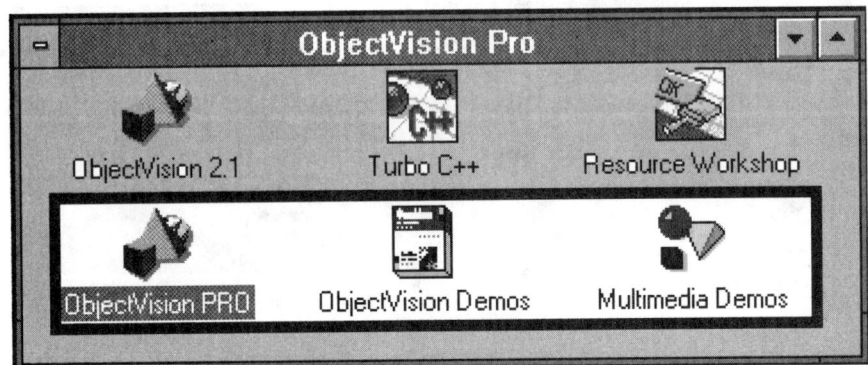

14-8
The new ObjectVision program icon and demo icons.

There's no reason for you to install the runtime version of ObjectVision on the same computer where you have the full package already installed. If, however, for whatever obscure reasons of your own, you decide to do it anyway, you'll need to go into your WIN.INI file to make a change. Before you install the runtime version, your WIN.INI file should have an entry like the following:

```
[ObjectVision]
HomeDir=c:\vision
```

In other words, there's an instruction in your WIN.INI file to set the home directory for ObjectVision to C:\VISION. If you install the runtime version, however, the instruction will be changed to:

```
HomeDir=c:\visionr
```

If you try to open ObjectVision, you'll get only the runtime version—which doesn't allow you to create or modify applications. You must, therefore, go into that WIN.INI file and change the instruction back to:

```
HomeDir=c:\vision
```

You can, of course, avoid all of this by not installing the runtime version on the hard drive of your computer.

There are a number of things you can do to customize the applications you create with ObjectVision in order to identify them as your own and not simply as some filename under ObjectVision. Some of them, such as removing the ObjectVision logo that appears when you first open the program (the one with the Roman bust and the geometric figures), are a bit beyond the scope of this tutorial—though certainly within the scope of the tools that come with the ObjectVision package. Others, such as the operation we're going to do right now, are quite simple.

Changing the opening title

When you first load up the patient visit application, your opening screen should look like FIG. 14-9. The title in the main window, at the very top of your monitor, is ObjectVision - VISITFRM.OVD. Now because ObjectVision is simply, in a sense, a language you're using to construct your program, you aren't obliged to make ObjectVision a part of your program's name, any more than you'd be obliged to include C++ or Microsoft Basic in the title of programs you write with those languages. So because the application is a product of The Yorktown Group, Inc., let's just call it Yorktown Patient Visit Form.

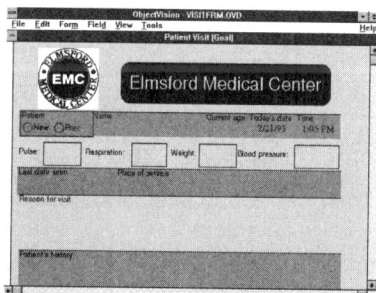

14-9
The Patient Visit application opening screen.

Tools
Form
Stack
Links...

14-10 *The Tools menu with Form highlighted.*

First, pull down the Tools menu and select Form (see FIG. 14-10). When you move into the edit mode, point to the title bar of the main window and click the right mouse button. This familiar action will bring up the property list for the title bar; in this case, there's only one item on that menu: Event Tree (see FIG. 14-11).

Click on Event Tree, and you'll open the Event Tree for Application window, just like the event tree windows you've seen before (see FIG. 14-12). The procedure is now just the same as the one you followed for event trees at the earlier stages of your work: Click on the conclusion tool (see FIG. 14-13). When the Event Name window opens, press the selection button and you'll see that you have only two choices: Close and Open. In other words, you're programming an event that will be triggered by either the opening or the closing of the application. In this case, of course, it's the opening.

14-11
The title bar with the one-item property list.

ObjectVision - VISITFRM.OVD	Event Tree

14-12
The Event Tree for Application window.

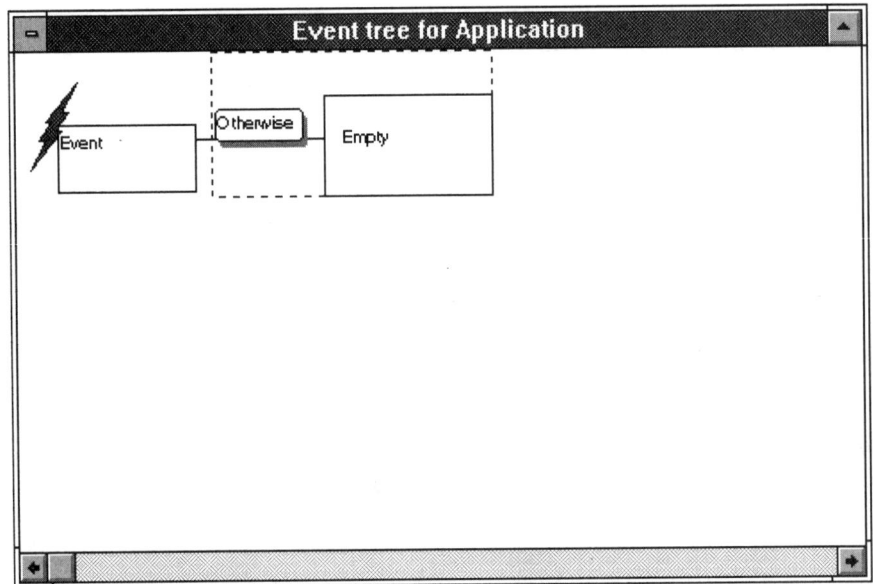

Event tree for Application

Event — Otherwise — Empty

14-13
The conclusion tool.

When the application opens, therefore, you want a new title to be entered in the title bar. So select Open (see FIG. 14-14), click on OK, and the Action for Application window will wait for you to enter the action that will be triggered by opening the application. Click on the Function button, and from the @ function listing in the Function Name window select SETTITLE (see FIG. 14-15). Make sure that Paste Arguments is checked.

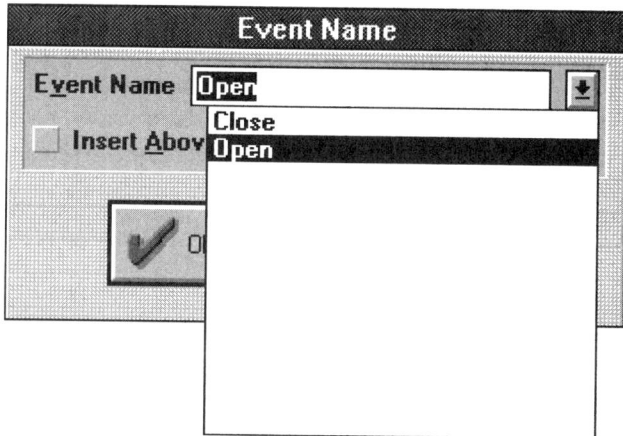

14-14
The Event Name window, with Open selected as the trigger event.

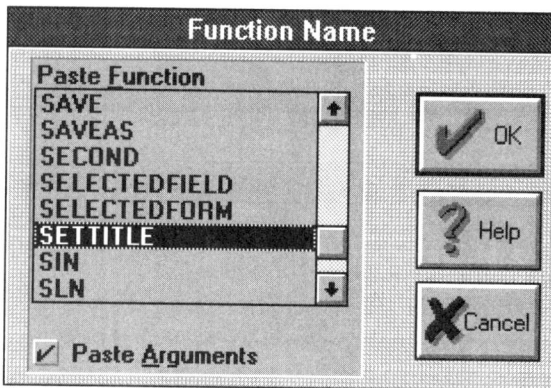

14-15
The Function Name window with SETTITLE highlighted.

Click on OK, and the @SETTITLE function will be pasted into the Action for Application window, waiting for you to enter the title. Type "Yorktown Patient Visit Form", being sure to include the quotation marks (see FIG. 14-16). Click on OK again, and the completed event tree will now include the triggering event and its consequence (see FIG. 14-17). Close the event tree window and save the file.

At this point you won't see any difference; in order to see the effect of your new event tree, you have to exit the application and reload it. When you do, your opening screen will appear with its new title bar (see FIG. 14-18).

This application is already beginning to look like your own. As you become more sophisticated in the use of ObjectVision, you can customize in many ways, giving your applications a distinctive "look and feel" to make them uniquely yours.

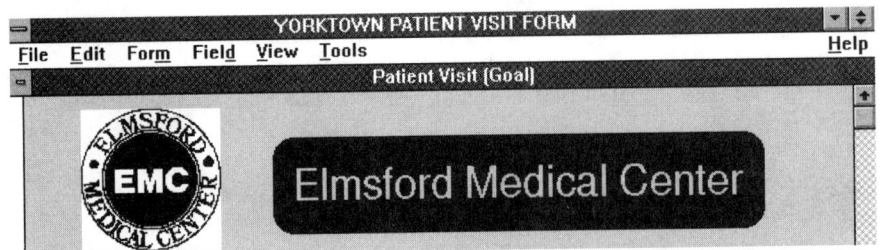

14-16
The Action for Application window, with the new title entered.

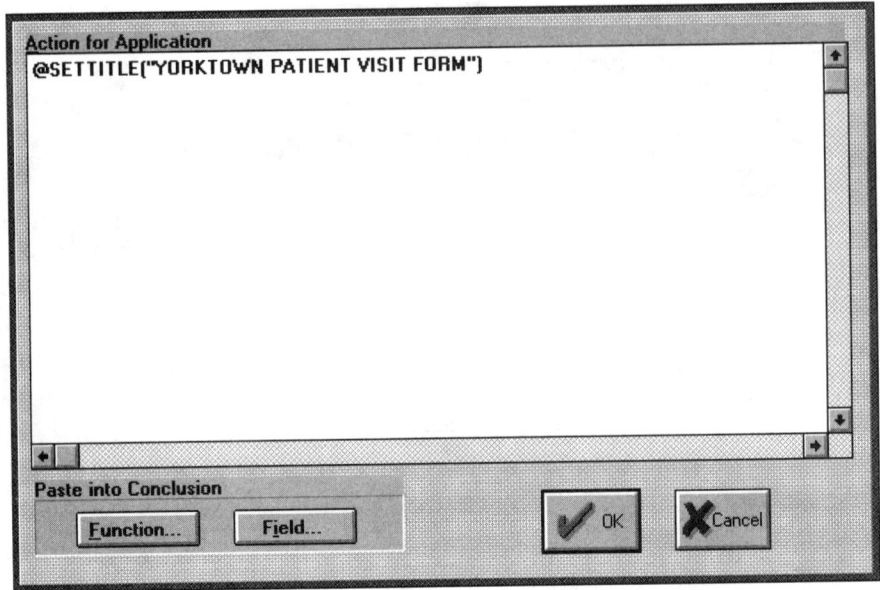

14-17
The Event Tree window with the completed event.

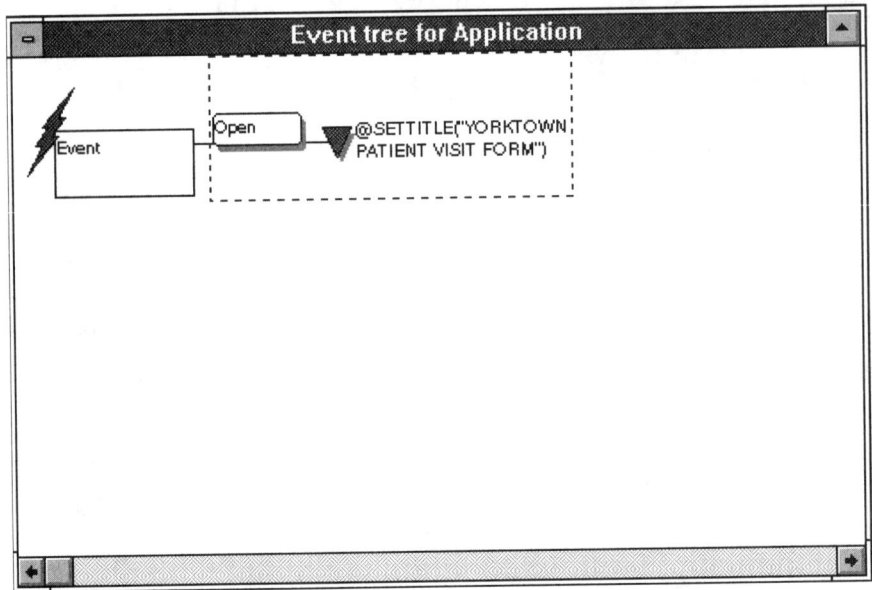

14-18
The application's opening screen with the new title bar.

15 *Advanced applications & multimedia*

Because this book is an introductory tutorial to ObjectVision, a way to get you up and running and familiarized with the software to the extent that you can—to steal a current cliché—move on under your own steam, I've stuck pretty close to the basics. You should, however, take a brief look at one of the newest and most exciting tools that ObjectVision PRO makes available: multimedia.

To use the full multimedia powers of ObjectVision, you must be using the 3.1 version of Microsoft Windows. To get beyond the most rudimentary applications of multimedia, you'll also need some additional hardware: a CD-ROM drive, a sound board, additional speakers, and possibly a video board—depending upon what you dream of doing with multimedia-enhanced or multimedia-based applications. And you had just as well dream large, because the brave new world of multimedia, full of juice and promise, is just now beginning to burst upon us.

So much for dreams and poetry; back to the rudiments. Assuming that most readers haven't yet made the additional investments in equipment, let's take an introductory peek at what kind of things you can do with nothing more than Microsoft Windows 3.1, a speaker driver, the little speaker that's already installed in your computer, and the multimedia demo files that come with ObjectVision PRO. You must be using ObjectVision Pro; if you're using ObjectVision 2.1, the multimedia files won't be available.

Getting a speaker driver from CompuServe

First, the matter of that speaker driver. It's likely you don't have one, but they're distributed by Microsoft. And one of the places where you can get one is CompuServe if you're a subscriber to the online CompuServe Information Service.

The filename for the speaker driver is SPEAKER.DRV, and if you look for it on CompuServe, you can find it on the forum called the Microsoft Connection. Here's the menu sequence:

1. Log on to CompuServe.
2. Select Computer & Software Support. This will get you to a long list of computer forums, generally listed by product name or manufacturer.
3. Select the Microsoft Connection.
4. Select Microsoft US.
5. Select Microsoft End-User.
6. Select Microsoft Software Library.
7. Select Download a File.

The filename you want to download (copy to your computer) is SPEAK.EXE, and ObjectVision will tell you that it's a binary file. If you look at the file listing via the Browse command, you'll see the following message: *This file contains the Microsoft PC Speaker Driver, SPEAKER.DRV. Also contains AUDIO.TXT, SPEAKER.TXT and License Agreement.*

After you've downloaded the SPEAK.EXE file to your WINDOWS\SYSTEM directory (where the rest of your Windows driver files are likely to be located), run the program by typing SPEAK and hitting Enter. This will decompress or unpack the files, and place the SPEAKER.DRV file in the correct directory.

Registering the Multimedia DLL

Before you can incorporate sound into applications that you create with ObjectVision, you need to follow a procedure called Registering the Multimedia DLL. The DLL, or dynamic-link library, provides a live or dynamic link between your application and the drivers and other files needed to create sound.

This gets a bit technical for the level of this book, and you'll probably want to look into the first chapter of the ObjectVision PRO User's Guide, *Writing DLLs for ObjectVision*. Under the section headed *Registering functions in a DLL*, you'll see a much more detailed discussion of the process. For now, however, I'll simply walk you through the steps required to prepare this application for multimedia.

15-1 *The Properties menu, with Stack selected and Event Tree showing as the single property.*

At the opening screen of the patient visit application, go into edit mode by selecting Form from the Tools menu. From the Properties menu select Stack; it should show the single property, Event Tree (see FIG. 15-1). Click on Event Tree, and the Event Tree for Application window will open (see FIG. 15-2).

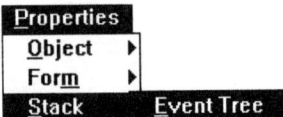

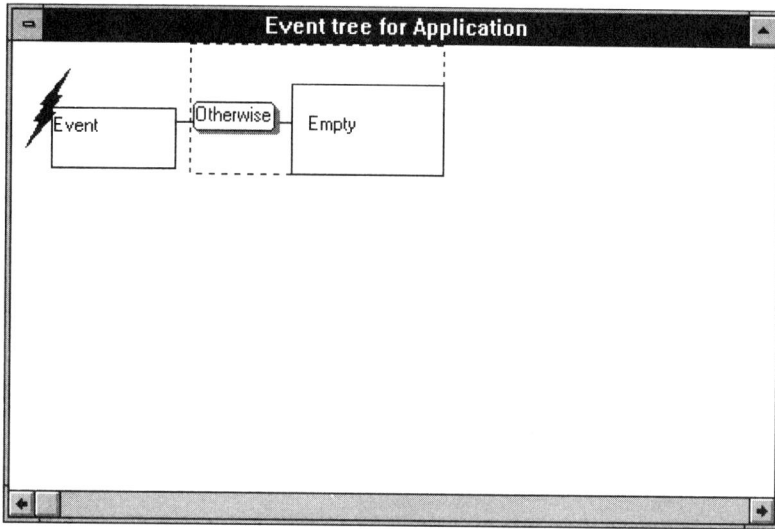

15-2
The event tree for the Application window.

This procedure will give you some experience with the Stack option on the Properties menu. An alternate way of getting to the same event tree is by right-clicking on the application title bar and then on Event Tree. Borland tech support prefers this method, but either should work for you.

You're now going to "register" OVMEDIA.DLL—the dynamic-link library that lets you play or record sound from ObjectVision applications. Click on the conclusion tool, and when the Event Name window opens select Open from the selection list (see FIG. 15-3). Click on OK, and the Action for Application window will wait for you to enter the action. Press the Function button, and

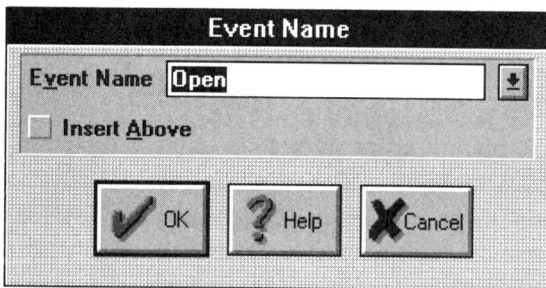

15-3
The Event Name window with Open selected as the trigger event.

select REGISTER from the list of @ functions (see FIG. 15-4). Press OK, and the @REGISTER function will be pasted into the Action for Application window (see FIG. 15-5). The @REGISTER function requires you to list several arguments. Without discussing them here, I'll simply indicate what they should be:

```
OVAlias = @MMREGISTER;
Arg Types = Jn;
ArgHelp = blank;
LibName = C:\VISION\SAMPLE\OVMEDIA.DLL;
FuncName = MMREGISTER; Type= 1
```

15-4
The Function Name window with REGISTER selected.

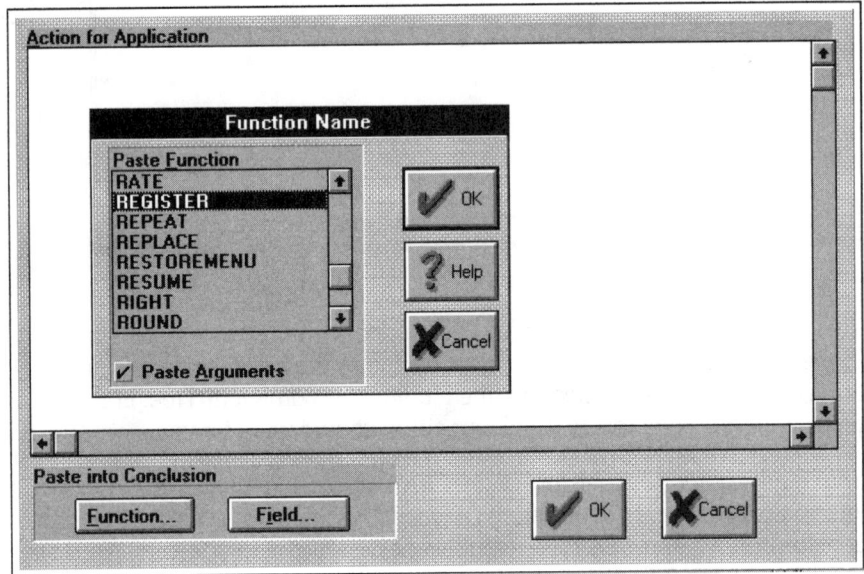

15-5
The @REGISTER function pasted into the Action for Application window, waiting for the arguments to be entered.

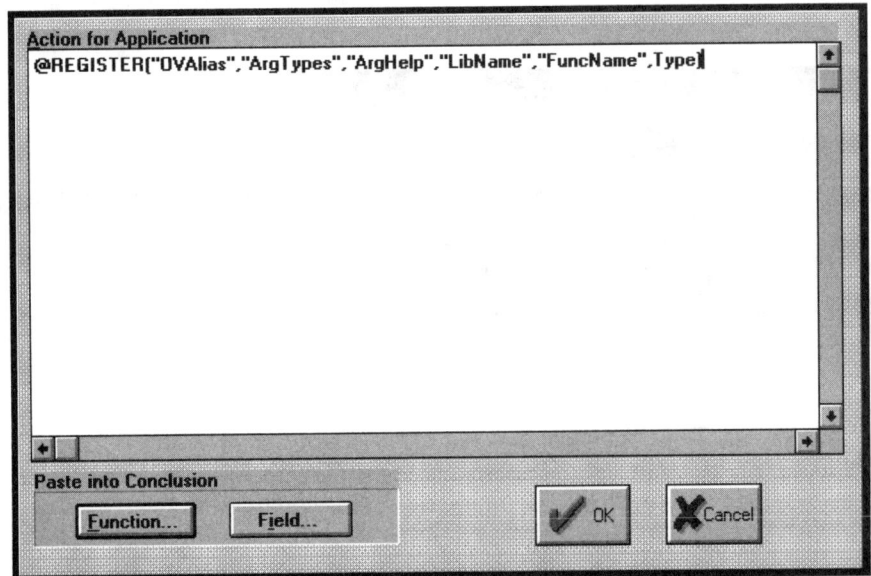

When you enter these values as the arguments for the @REGISTER function, your Action for Application window should look like FIG. 15-6.

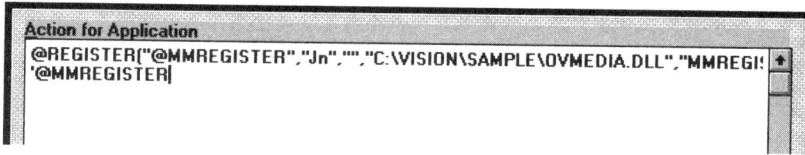

Action for Application
```
@REGISTER("@MMREGISTER","Jn","","C:\VISION\SAMPLE\OVMEDIA.DLL","MMREGIS
'@MMREGISTER|
```

15-6
The Action for Application window with the correct arguments inserted into the @REGISTER function.

Press Enter or click on OK, and ObjectVision will place the @REGISTER function in the Event Tree for Application window, as shown in FIG. 15-7. Close the window, save the altered application, then close and reopen the application. Return to the Event Tree for Application window and open the Action for Application window.

Event tree for Application

Event — Open — @REGISTER("@MMREGISTER","Jn","","C:\VISION\SAMPLE\OVMEDIA.DLL","MMREGISTER",1)

15-7
The completed event tree.

Point to the first (and only) node (the area bounded by the dotted line), and click the right mouse button. A pop-up menu will offer you the options Condition or Conclusion (see FIG. 15-8). Select Conclusion, and you'll see the Action for Application window again.

Event tree for Application

Open — @REGISTER("@MMREGISTER","Jn","","C:\VISION\SAMPLE\O...

Condition...
Conclusion...

15-8
The options for editing the first node of the event tree for the application.

This time, remove the apostrophe in front of @MMREGISTER in the second line. Click on OK, save the altered application, then close and reopen it again. Now that the registration has taken place, ObjectVision will recognize @MMREGISTER as a valid function.

Now that the preliminary setup work has been done, you can plug multimedia events into forms to your heart's content. Would you use multimedia with an application such as the patient visit form? Probably not, but I can think of a couple of possibilities.

Programming a multimedia event into a field

Suppose you were a physician and your secretary or receptionist were visually impaired? You could program spoken commands into each field. Or suppose your Brazilian secretary's English was limited and you wanted to program spoken Portuguese commands into the fields? You could do that as well.

To complete the demo, however, let's do something a little silly to demonstrate ObjectVision's multimedia abilities and complete the job of the tutorial. Let's program the Reason for Visit field so that it says "Welcome to ObjectVision" when it's selected. The multimedia function you need is in the sample files that come with ObjectVision PRO. Use the HELLO.WAV file that should have been placed in your C:\VISION\SAMPLE directory.

You're going to create an event tree for the Reason for Visit field. It will instruct the program to play the HELLO.WAV file every time the field is selected. Here's the procedure:

With the application in edit mode, select the Reason for Visit field (see FIG. 15-9). Display the property list by clicking on the field with the right mouse button, as shown in FIG. 15-10.

15-9
The patient visit form with the Reason for Visit field selected.

Select Event Tree from the Properties menu, and when the event tree for the Reason for Visit field pops up, press the Conclusion button. The Event Name window should appear; use the selection button to pick Select as the triggering event (see FIG. 15-11).

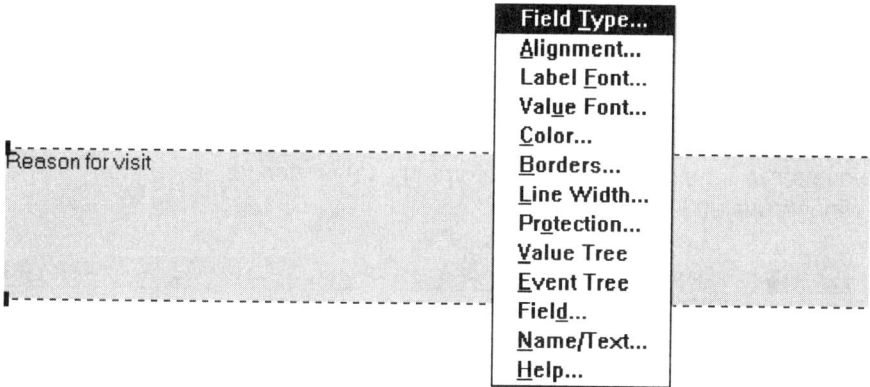

Reason for visit

| Field Type... |
| Alignment... |
| Label Font... |
| Value Font... |
| Color... |
| Borders... |
| Line Width... |
| Protection... |
| Value Tree |
| Event Tree |
| Field... |
| Name/Text... |
| Help... |

15-10
The Properties menu for the Reason for Visit field.

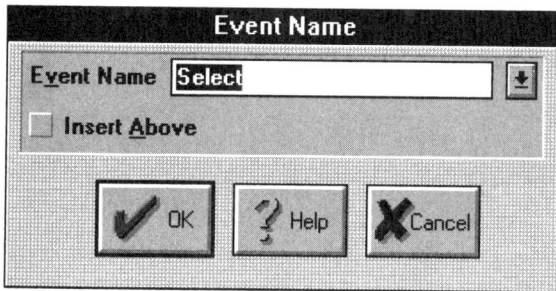

Event Name

Event Name [Select]

☐ Insert Above

✔ OK ? Help ✗ Cancel

15-11
The Event Name window with Select chosen as the trigger event.

Click on OK, and the Action for Reason for Visit window will open. When the Reason for Visit field is selected, you want to play an audio file; the @ function that performs this action is called MMPLAY. Click the Function button and select MMPLAY from the @ function list in the Function Name window (see FIG. 15-12).

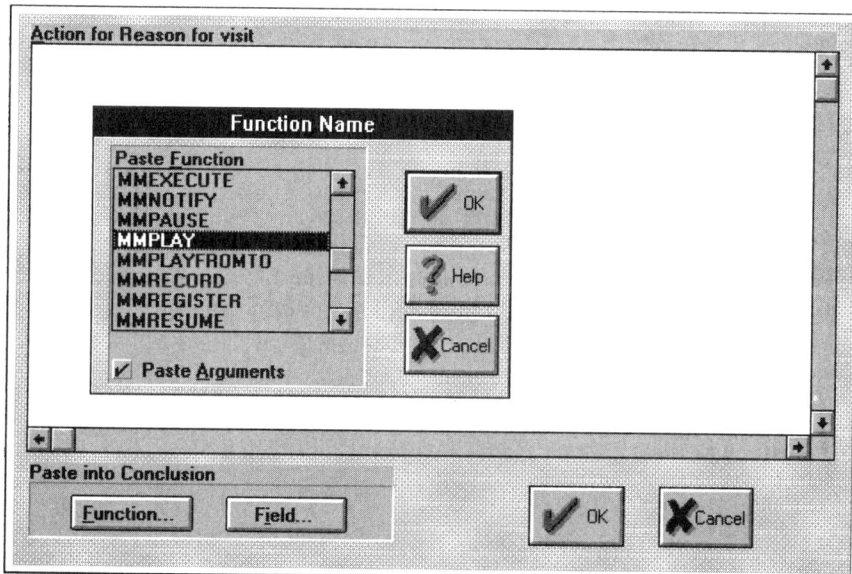

Action for Reason for visit

Function Name

Paste Function
MMEXECUTE
MMNOTIFY
MMPAUSE
MMPLAY
MMPLAYFROMTO
MMRECORD
MMREGISTER
MMRESUME

✔ OK ? Help ✗ Cancel

✔ Paste Arguments

Paste into Conclusion

[Function...] [Field...]

✔ OK ✗ Cancel

15-12
The Function Name window with MMPLAY highlighted.

Click on OK, and the MMPLAY function will be pasted into the Action for Reason for Visit window (these window adjectives are getting cumbersome!), waiting for you to supply the filename and driver name (see FIG. 15-13). The filename, with its path, is "C:\VISION\SAMPLE\HELLO.WAV", and the driver name is "SPEAKER.DRV". Don't forget to include the quotation marks! When you enter the function arguments correctly, the Action for Reason for Visit window should look like FIG. 15-14.

15-13
The MMPLAY @ function prompting for filename and driver name.

Action for Reason for visit
@MMPLAY("FileName","DriverName")

15-14
The Action for Reason for Visit window with filename and driver name entered.

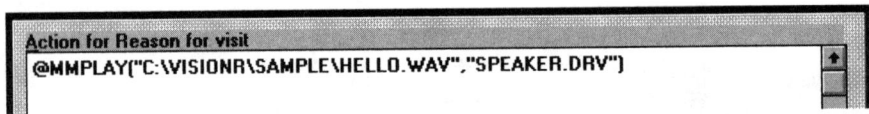

Action for Reason for visit
@MMPLAY("C:\VISIONR\SAMPLE\HELLO.WAV","SPEAKER.DRV")

Press Enter or click on OK, and your event tree will be complete, as shown in FIG. 15-15. Close the Event Tree window, press the close tool, and your job should be done. When you click on the Reason for Visit field, you should hear a voice saying "Hello. Welcome to ObjectVision." If you don't have a sound board and an external speaker, what you hear might sound like a voice on a very scratchy phonograph record saying something totally unintelligible.

Event tree for Reason for visit

15-15
The completed event tree for the Reason for Visit field.

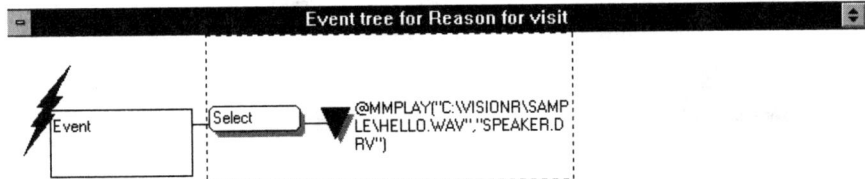

Event

Select

@MMPLAY("C:\VISIONR\SAMPLE\HELLO.WAV","SPEAKER.DRV")

Summary   Unintelligible mutterings are probably a less-than-satisfactory way to wind up this introduction to the Windows programming potential of ObjectVision PRO, but in fact they represent a triumph of technology and a portent of exciting things to come. You are now an intermediate-level programmer who has created a prototype program that includes a multimedia function. This achievement, however, is merely a brief prologue; great drama lies ahead as you perfect and polish your programming skills.

A Installing ObjectVision PRO

ObjectVision PRO comes in compressed files on three 5¼-inch disks. (ObjectVision 2.1 comes on two disks; the installation procedure for both ObjectVision PRO and ObjectVision 2.1 are, however, almost identical.) The fact that the files are compressed means you can't install ObjectVision PRO simply by copying files from the original disks onto your hard disk drive; you must use the Install program, which decompresses the files as it goes along.

To install the program, you should have loaded Windows (it will run on version 3.0, although if you want to use all features, including the multimedia functions, you should have version 3.1 or higher) and be at the Program Manager window. If you haven't loaded Windows, type WIN and Enter at the C:> prompt. The Windows logo will show on your monitor for a few seconds, and then the Program Manager window will open (see FIG. A-1).

1. Insert the Installation Disk, Disk 1, into either the A or B drive of your computer.
2. Open the File menu and click on Run (see FIG. A-2). The Run window will open in front of the Program Manager window.
3. On the command line, type A:INSTALL or B:INSTALL and click on OK (or press Enter), as shown in FIG. A-3.

The first thing that will appear on your screen is the Borland Install window telling you to wait (isn't it always the way?), then the ObjectVision PRO Installation window asking you to select the drive from which you're

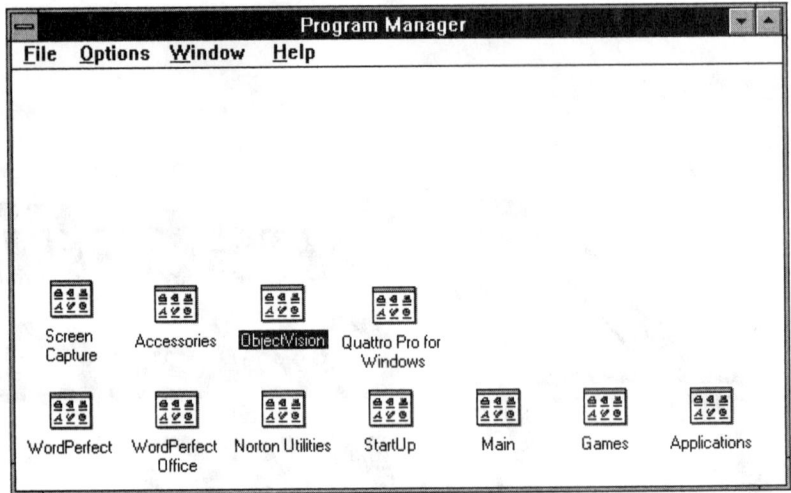

A-1
The Windows 3.1 Program Manager window.

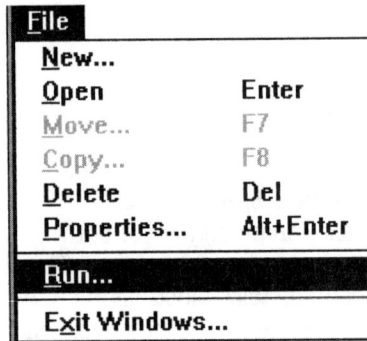

A-2
The File menu with Run highlighted.

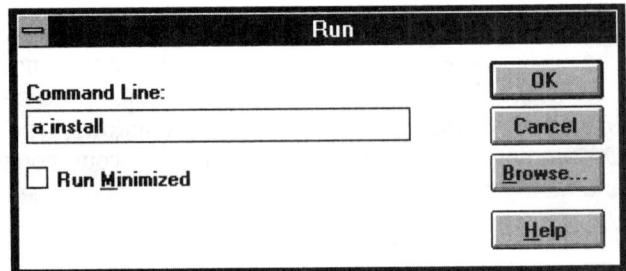

A-3
The Run window with B:INSTALL entered on the command line.

installing, and the hard drive and directories on which you're installing the program (see FIG. A-4). It also asks you to check some other options: you can elect to create an ObjectVision Windows group, enable Paradox 4.0 locking, and display the ObjectVision readme notes at the end of the installation process. If you don't want to change any of the default settings, simply click on Install and the process will begin.

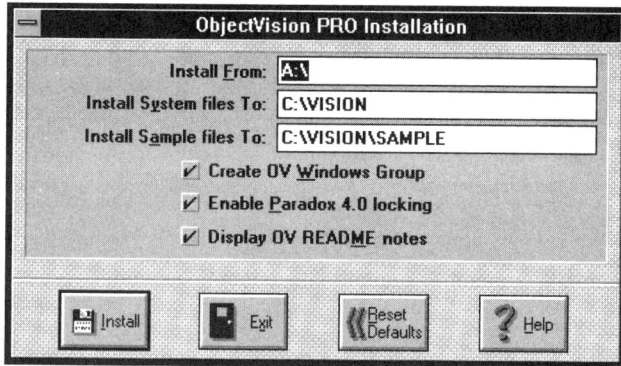

A-4
The ObjectVision PRO 2.1 Installation window.

As the program is installed, a cute graphic will appear on your screen with a driver's-eye view of a highway. You'll see a speedometer that registers the loading progress as a percent of the total, and an odometer that tells you how many kilobytes of data have been decompressed and copied to your hard disk. You'll also pass billboards on the highway that tell you to register your copy of the program, buy a training video, and other good stuff.

Eventually, you'll be prompted to insert the second disk, called the Runtime Disk (and, in due course, the third disk, called Runtime Disk 3). The unpacking and copying process will conclude, and at the end, if you don't have the Share command as part of your AUTOEXEC.BAT file, you might be prompted to add it (see FIG. A-5). The Install window will then remind you about some readme notes that are going to appear (see FIG. A-6). Click on OK and, sure enough, the notes will appear, shown in FIG. A-7.

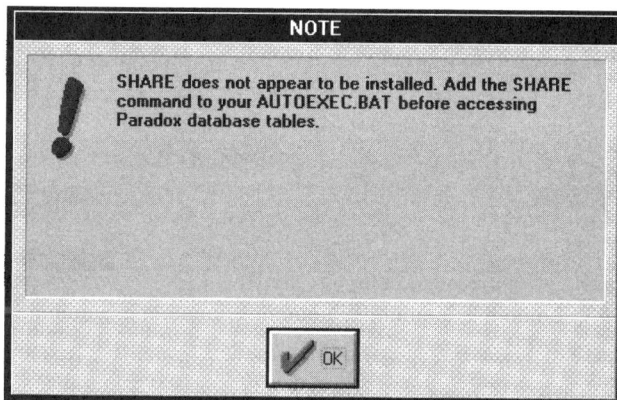

A-5
The Note window reminding you to add the Share command to your AUTOEXEC.BAT file in order to access Paradox database tables.

When you close the readme notes by clicking on the upper left-hand corner, you'll be rewarded with an Installation Successful window that reminds you once again to send in your registration card (see FIG. A-8). Click on OK, and you'll be returned to the Windows Program Manager, where you'll see a

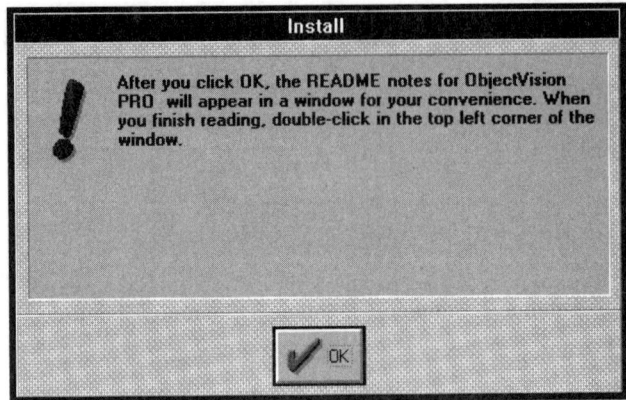

A-6
The Install window with a reminder about the README notes.

Install

After you click OK, the README notes for ObjectVision PRO will appear in a window for your convenience. When you finish reading, double-click in the top left corner of the window.

OK

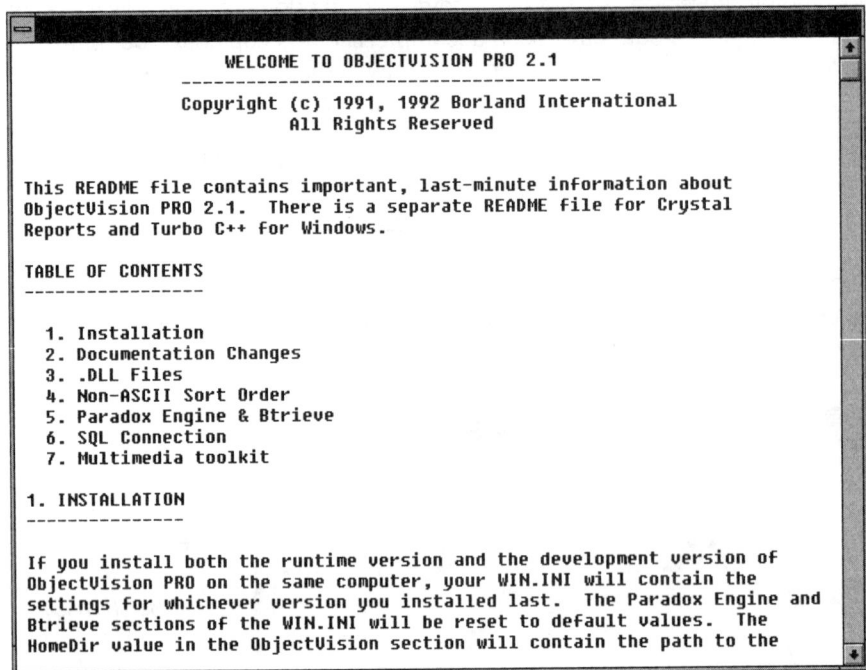

A-7
Screen 1 of the README notes.

```
                WELCOME TO OBJECTVISION PRO 2.1
        -------------------------------------------
          Copyright (c) 1991, 1992 Borland International
                      All Rights Reserved


This README file contains important, last-minute information about
ObjectVision PRO 2.1.  There is a separate README file for Crystal
Reports and Turbo C++ for Windows.

TABLE OF CONTENTS
-----------------


   1. Installation
   2. Documentation Changes
   3. .DLL Files
   4. Non-ASCII Sort Order
   5. Paradox Engine & Btrieve
   6. SQL Connection
   7. Multimedia toolkit


1. INSTALLATION
---------------


If you install both the runtime version and the development version of
ObjectVision PRO on the same computer, your WIN.INI will contain the
settings for whichever version you installed last.  The Paradox Engine and
Btrieve sections of the WIN.INI will be reset to default values.  The
HomeDir value in the ObjectVision section will contain the path to the
```

sparkling new ObjectVision group with three icons, labeled ObjectVision PRO, ObjectVision Demos, and Multimedia Demos, as shown in FIG. A-9. Another Install window will tell you that your installation of the first phase of

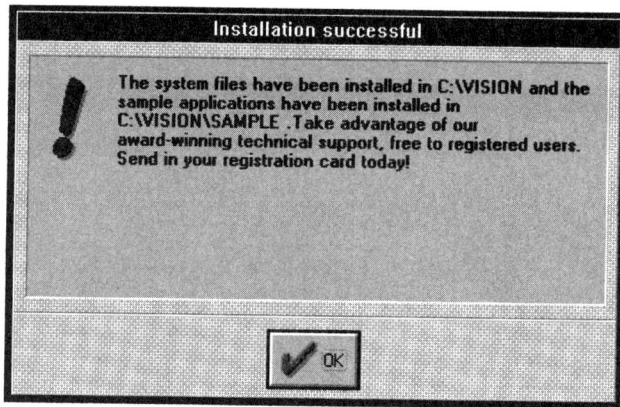

A-8
The Installation Successful window.

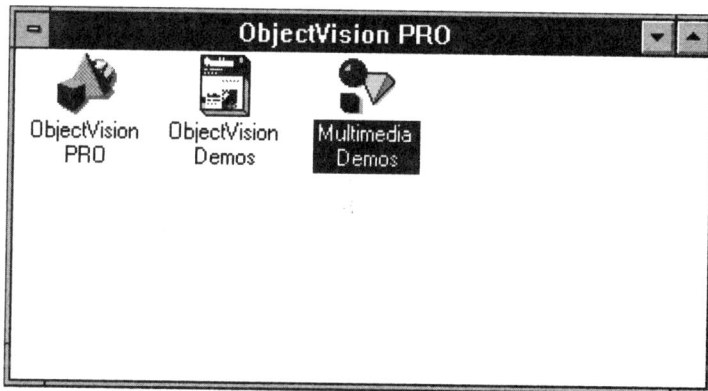

A-9
The new ObjectVision group with the program icon and the ObjectVision Demos icon.

ObjectVision PRO is complete, and that you can go ahead and install Turbo C++ and Crystal Reports. That's up to you; this is as far as we go in this book.

Check out your installation by double-clicking on the ObjectVision Demos icon. The ObjectVision logo will appear briefly, and then your monitor screen should fill with the Demo Application menu (see FIG. A-10). Click on any one of the 23 sample applications, and begin your exploration of the world of ObjectVision.

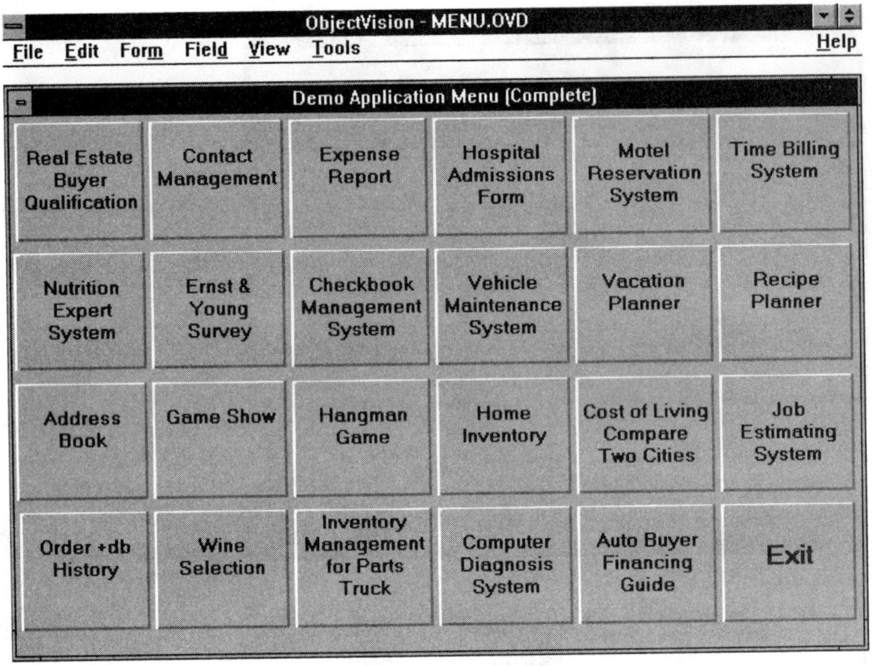

A-10
The Demo application Menu.

B Installing ObjectVision PRO in an OS/2 2.0 environment

ObjectVision PRO comes in compressed files on three 5¼-inch disks. The fact that the files are compressed means you can't install ObjectVision PRO simply by copying files from the original disks onto your hard disk drive; you must use the Install program, which decompresses the files as it goes along.

To install the program, you should have gone into a WIN-OS/2 session by clicking on the WIN-OS/2 Full Screen icon (see FIG. B-1) on the OS/2 2.0 desktop. The OS/2 2.0 version of the Windows 3.0 (or 3.1, by the time you read this) Program Manager window will eventually appear with a few toys strewn about the bottom of the screen, as shown in FIG. B-2. From here on, you go through a regular Windows installation process. See the installation process outlined in appendix A.

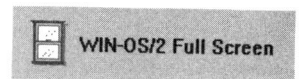

B-1 *The WIN-OS/2 Full Screen icon.*

After you close the readme notes and are rewarded with an Installation Successful window, reminding you once again to send in your registration card (see FIG. B-3), click on OK and you'll be greeted with yet another Install window telling you that, if you want to go all the way with ObjectVision PRO, you should next install Turbo C++ and then Crystal Reports (see FIG. B-4). We're going to stop right here, however, because Turbo C++ and Crystal Reports are beyond the scope of this book. Obviously, you can continue the installation process if you want to.

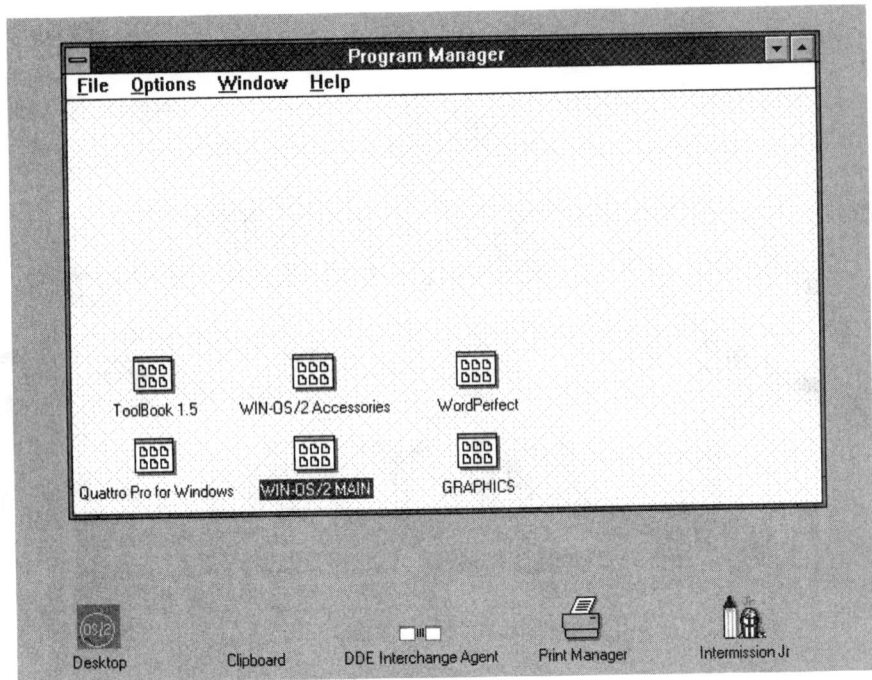

B-2

The WIN-OS/2 Program Manager window.

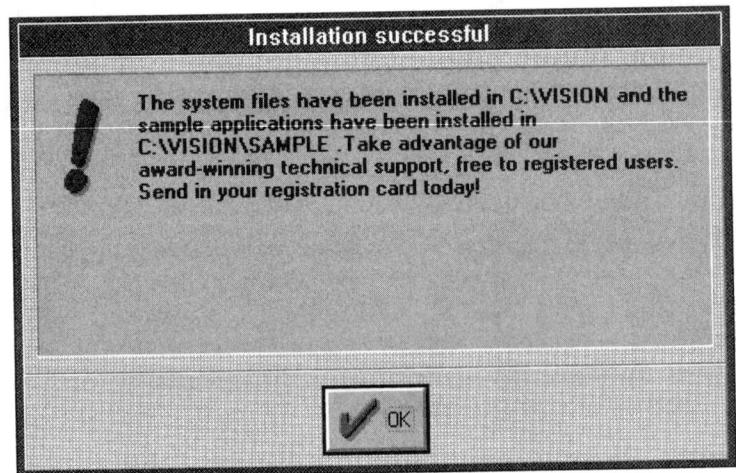

B-3

The Installation Successful window.

Click on OK, and you'll be returned to the Windows Program Manager and will see a sparkling new ObjectVision PRO group with three icons, labeled ObjectVision PRO, ObjectVision Demos, and Multimedia Demos (see FIG. B-5).

Check out your installation by double-clicking on the ObjectVision Demos icon. The ObjectVision logo will appear briefly, and then your monitor screen should fill with the Demo Application Menu (Complete), as shown in FIG. B-6.

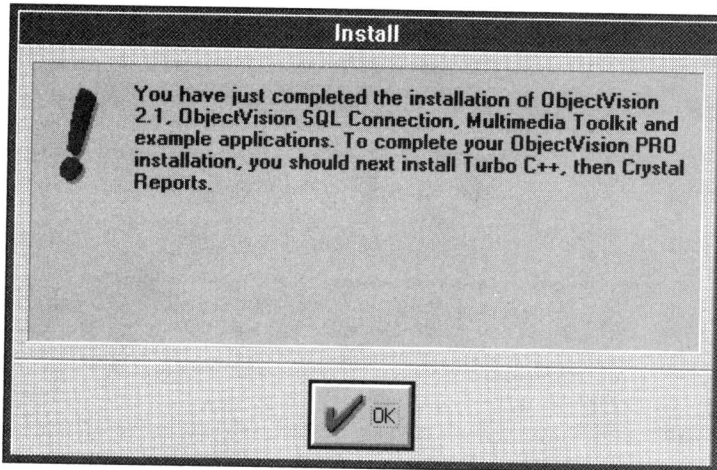

B-4
The Install window reminding you to complete the installation of ObjectVision PRO by installing Turbo C++ and Crystal Reports.

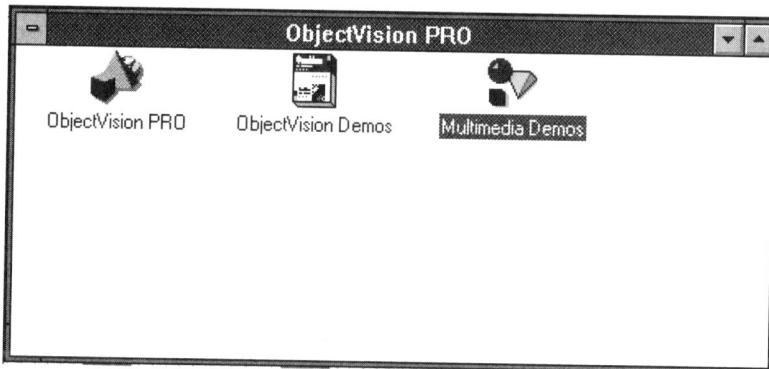

B-5
The new ObjectVision PRO group with the program icon, the ObjectVision Demos icon, and the Multimedia Demos icon.

Click on any one of the 23 sample applications, and begin your exploration of the world of ObjectVision PRO.

Because many Windows applications run better from the OS/2 2.0 desktop, you should migrate the application. Here's how:

1. Exit the Program Manager and end the WIN-OS/2 session by double-clicking on the Close box in the upper left-hand corner.
2. When you're returned to the desktop, double-click on the OS/2 System icon (see FIG. B-7).
3. Double-click on the System Setup folder (see FIG. B-8).
4. Open the Migrate Applications function by double-clicking on its icon. The Find Programs window will open, as shown in FIG. B-9.
5. ObjectVision is a Windows application, so click on DOS Programs and OS/2 Programs to leave only Windows Programs checked.
6. Click on Find. The Migrate Programs window will open, and the program will start listing the Windows programs it finds. When the process ends,

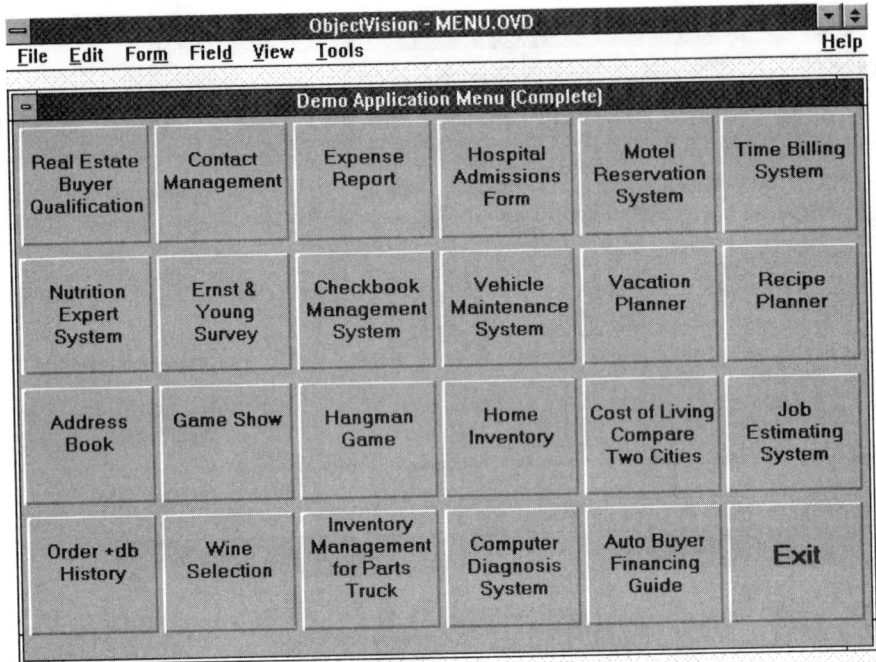

B-6
The Demo Application menu.

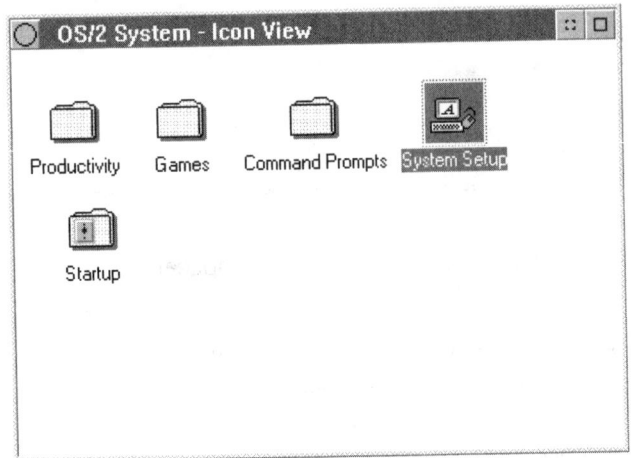

B-7
The OS/2 system Icon View window, with the System Setup folder highlighted.

click on any program you don't want to migrate in order to deselect it. In FIG. B-10, only ObjectVision is selected to be migrated.

7. Click on the Migrate button; when the migration process is finished, the Migrate Information window will tell you so, as shown in FIG. B-11.

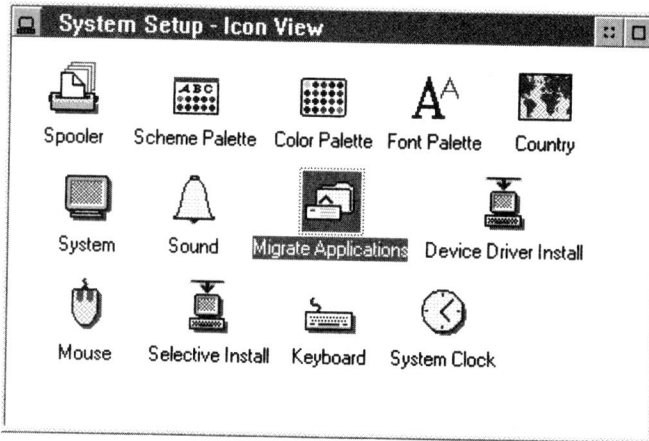

B-8
Contents of the System Setup folder, with Migrate Applications highlighted.

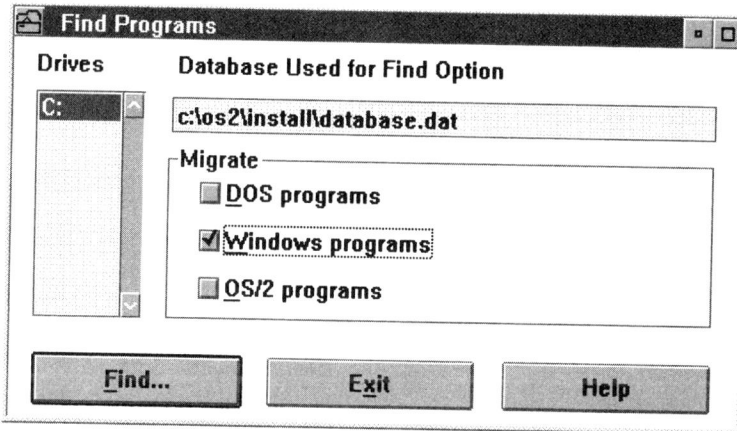

B-9
The Find Programs window, with Windows Programs checked.

8. Click on OK, then on Exit, and then answer Yes—you *do* really want to exit. Close the System Setup and OS/2 System windows, open the Windows Programs icon, and there—along with the other Windows you previously migrated to the OS/2 2.0 desktop—is your ObjectVision icon (see FIG. B-12).

Ready to test your results? Click twice on the ObjectVision icon; the characteristic cross-hatching will appear and in a few seconds the ObjectVision opening screen and logo will appear, shown in FIG. B-13. You're up and running under OS/2 2.0.

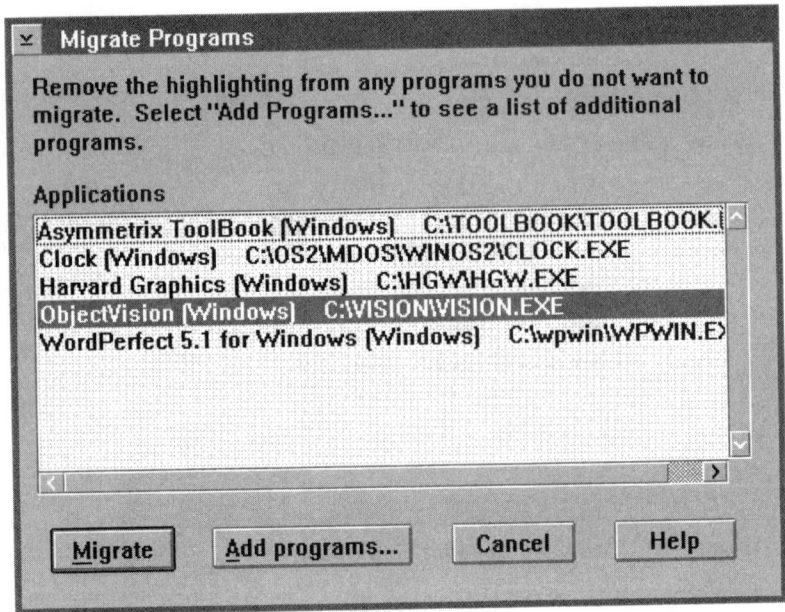

The Migrate Programs window, with ObjectVision selected for migration.

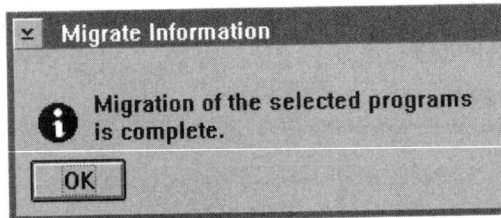

Migrate Programs

Remove the highlighting from any programs you do not want to migrate. Select "Add Programs..." to see a list of additional programs.

Applications

Asymmetrix ToolBook (Windows)	C:\TOOLBOOK\TOOLBOOK.
Clock (Windows)	C:\OS2\MDOS\WINOS2\CLOCK.EXE
Harvard Graphics (Windows)	C:\HGW\HGW.EXE
ObjectVision (Windows)	C:\VISION\VISION.EXE
WordPerfect 5.1 for Windows (Windows)	C:\wpwin\WPWIN.E>

Migrate   Add programs...   Cancel   Help

Migrate Information

Migration of the selected programs is complete.

OK

B-11

The Migrate Information window, announcing that the selected programs have been successfully migrated.

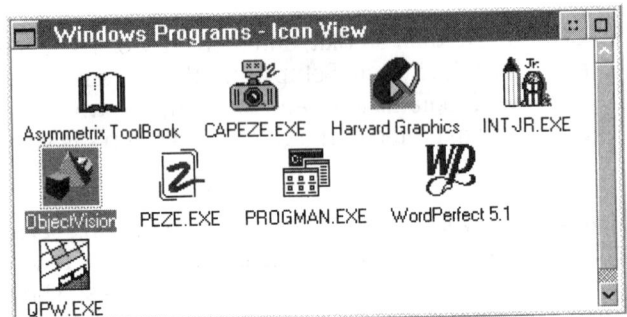

Windows Programs - Icon View

Asymmetrix ToolBook   CAPEZE.EXE   Harvard Graphics   INT-JR.EXE

ObjectVision   PEZE.EXE   PROGMAN.EXE   WordPerfect 5.1

QPW.EXE

B-12

The Windows Program window, with the ObjectVision icon selected.

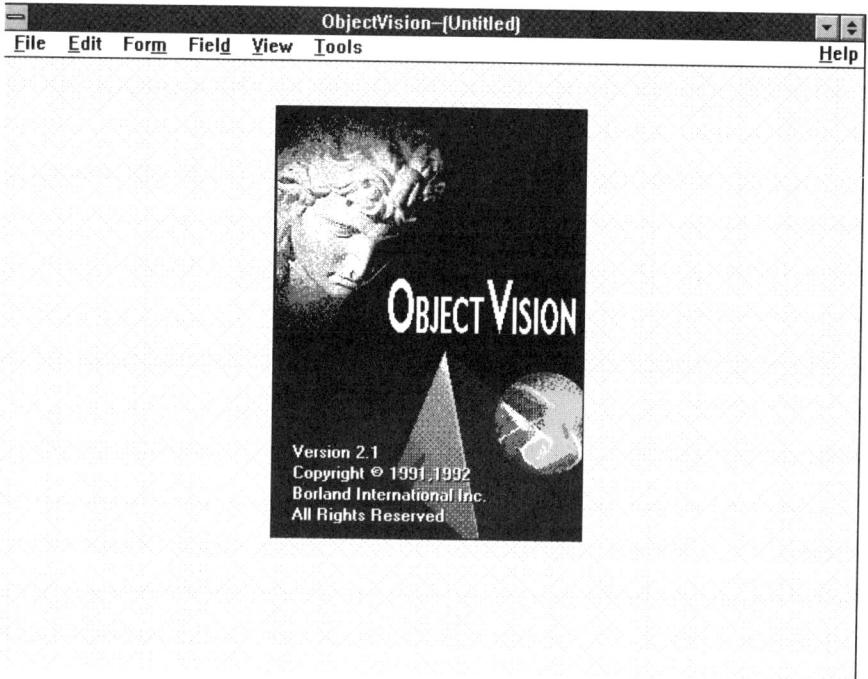

B-13
The ObjectVision opening screen and logo.

Order Form for Readers
Requiring Two 5.25" Disks

This Windcrest/McGraw-Hill software product is also available on a 5.25"/1.2Mb disk. If you need the software in 5.25" format, simply follow these instructions:

- Complete the order form below. Be sure to include the exact title of the Windcrest/McGraw-Hill book for which you are requesting a replacement disk.

- Make check or money order made payable to *Glossbrenner's Choice*. The cost is $5.00 ($8.00 for shipments outside the U.S.) to cover media, postage, and handling. Pennsylvania residents, please add 6% sales tax.

- Foreign orders: please send an international money order or a check drawn on a bank with a U.S. clearing branch. We cannot accept foreign checks.

- Mail order form and payment to:

  Glossbrenner's Choice
  Attn: Windcrest/McGraw-Hill Disk Replacement
  699 River Road
  Yardley, PA 19067-1965

Your disks will be shipped via First Class Mail. Please allow one to two weeks for delivery.

✂ . . . .

Windcrest/McGraw-Hill Disk Replacement

Please send me a replacement disks in 5.25"/1.2Mb format for the following Windcrest/McGraw-Hill book:

Book Title _____

Name _____

Address _____

City/State/ZIP _____

ObjectVision Programming for Windows
Donald Richard Read
Book #4258

The enclosed disk contains the forms and document files used in
ObjectVision Programming for Windows (Windcrest/McGraw-Hill book 4258),
© 1993 by Donald Richard Read. Use these files to follow along with the
examples in the book.

You can access these files with the ObjectVision for Windows program. They
are in a ready-to-use format.